POLICING AND PRESCRIBING

Policing and Prescribing

The British System of Drug Control

Edited by
David K. Whynes

Senior Lecturer in Economics
University of Nottingham

and

Philip T. Bean

Reader in Criminology
University of Loughborough

M

First published 1991

Published by
MACMILLAN ACADEMIC AND PROFESSIONAL LTD
Houndmills, Basingstoke, Hampshire RG21 2XS
and London
Companies and representatives
throughout the world

Printed in Hong Kong

British Library Cataloguing in Publication Data
Policing and prescribing: The British
System of drug control
1. Great Britain. Drug abuse
I. Whynes, David K.   II. Bean,
Philip T.
362.2930941

ISBN 0–333–52229–X

Contents

Contents

List of Figures

Foreword

Occasionally one meets someone whose sheer professionalism shines through. That someone in this case is H. B. (Bing) Spear, to whom we are dedicating this book. Bing has worked tirelessly in the drug field for many years. I doubt if there is anyone else in Britain who has seen more of the drug scene, read more of it, talked more of, and about it, and yet retained the same commitment throughout as Bing. In retirement and lacking good health he is what he always was; a professional dedicated to understanding the drug problems in the UK, improving the lot of those who take drugs, yet preventing its spread to others.

Henry Bryan Spear was born on 6 July 1928 in Wadebridge, North Cornwall. He was an only child of parents deeply involved in local community affairs: his father was a regular contributor to the local paper, the *Cornish Guardian*. Bing has retained that interest in things Cornish and in his family, and its origins. Bing – the nearest he could get to Bryan and the name stuck (thus he was not named after a famous crooner as he sometimes would have us believe) – was educated at Bodmin Grammar School. From there he attended Exeter University where he took an Honours degree in Chemistry. This was followed by National Service in the RAF as an Instructor. In 1952, at the age of 24, he entered the Home Office in the Drugs Branch where he remained the whole of his working life until he took early retirement in 1986, at the age of 58. He became Deputy Chief Inspector and later Chief Inspector when Charles Jeffrey retired in 1977. In 1985 he was awarded the Imperial Service Order in the New Year's Honour list, one of many honours given to him throughout his long career. He married Ella in 1959 and there are three children of the marriage – Christopher, Giles and Jonathan. When he first became ill in 1972 and received haemo-dialysis, and later a kidney transplant in 1986, he found as always comfort from his family, and the necessary security.

Bing is not what he would have us believe. He disclaimed academic prowess yet he writes well, has published much and of high quality. He claims a hard line on all matters, political, social and personal, yet is kind and generous in his personal life and a soft liberal in his professional one. His influence on public affairs is immeasurable: whether giving formal evidence to Parliamentary Committees or informal advice to Ministers or when advising the Chairmen of Committees, senior civil servants or academics. Always the argument would be put persuasively, yet within that liberal tradition in which the British system of drug control has remained. As the work of the Drugs Branch expanded Bing found it necessary to decentralise: branches were opened in Leeds, Bradford and Bristol. Gone then were the heady days of the 1960s when he knew personally almost every addict – and they knew him.

The award given to him in Washington in November 1989 for Achievement in the field of Drug Control and Enforcement says it all: it reflects Bing's professional working life. In this book we have tried to remain faithful to Bing's ideas without being too fixed in the choice of authors, or of the content. Some contributors know him well, others less so and one or two not at all. We have tried to make the book contemporary, believing that policing and prescribing have and probably always will remain central to the British system of drug control. We have tried to encompass those themes. Although dedicated to Bing, *Policing and Prescribing* is also concerned with matters of general and contemporary importance. We know Bing would want it that way.

Philip Bean
May 1990

Notes on the Contributors

Philip T. Bean is Reader in Criminology and Director of the Midlands Centre for Criminology and Criminal Justice, University of Loughborough.

Virginia Berridge is Senior Lecturer in Public Health and Policy, and Deputy Director of the AIDS Social History Unit, London School of Hygiene and Tropical Medicine.

Nicholas Dorn is Research and Development Director, Institute for the Study of Drug Dependence, London.

Jane Falk-Whynes, formerly Health Education Authority Academic Lecturer, University of Nottingham, is Quality Assurance Manager, Derbyshire Family Health Services Authority.

Cindy Fazey is Honorary Research Fellow at the Centre for Urban Studies, University of Liverpool.

John Giggs is Reader in Geography at the University of Nottingham.

Mark Gilman is Prevention Development Officer at the North West Regional Drug Training Unit, Prestwich Hospital, Manchester.

Gordon Graham is Reader in Moral Philosophy at the University of St Andrews.

Kenneth Leech is Director of the Runnymede Trust.

Joy Mott is Principal Officer at the Research and Planning Unit, Home Office, London.

Geoffrey Pearson is Wates Professor of Social Work at the University of London, Goldsmiths' College.

Notes on Contributors

Nigel South is Research Officer, Institute for the Study of Drug Dependence, London.

Richard Stevenson is Lecturer in Economics at the University of Liverpool.

Arnold Trebach is Professor in the Department of Justice, Law and Society, The American University, and President of the Drug Policy Foundation, Washington DC, USA.

David Whynes is Senior Lecturer in Economics at the University of Nottingham.

Jane Falk-Whynes, formerly Health Education Authority Academic Lecturer, University of Nottingham, is Quality Assurance Manager, Derbyshire Family Health Services Authority.

James Willis is a retired consultant psychiatrist, formerly practising at Guy's and King's College Hospitals, London.

1 Drug Problems, Drug Policies

David Whynes

This book is written at a time when drug use occupies a particularly prominent position on the UK political agenda, a time also when an indigenous approach to drug control known as the 'British system' appears finally to have fallen from grace. The debate over the appropriate direction and content of drugs policy is more heated now than at any time in the past, a reflection of changing perceptions of the magnitude and nature of the British drug problem. That such a debate is taking place is, of course, both right and proper, and the papers in this collection are offered as further contributions in the search for the appropriate policy response. This introductory essay outlines a background for the ensuing discussions.

THE EVOLUTION OF BRITISH DRUG POLICY

Berridge and Edwards (1981) have shown that the use of psychoactive drugs, specifically opium, began to be considered a medical problem in Britain in the latter part of the nineteenth century, although statutory limitations on availabililty were minimal until well into the twentieth. Up until the time of the First World War and even beyond, opiates and cocaine could be purchases from pharmacies with the minimum of formalities. The first piece of stringent legislation in Britain was the 1920 Dangerous Drugs Act, inspired directly by Britain's participation in the 1912 International Opium Convention. This treaty had required signatories to implement their own domestic control policies with respect to dangerous drugs and, whilst acknowledging that the use of such drugs in Britain was uncommon, the 1920 Act took steps to control supply. Availability was confined to medical prescription and possession was otherwise made illegal. Importation and manufacture became the subjects of regulation. Within the next few years a system of recording was initiated, penalties against offenders were increased, police powers of search were enhanced and, in 1925, cannabis was added to the list of proscribed substances (Bean, 1974).

In 1926, a report from a Ministry of Health Departmental Committee chaired by Sir Humphrey Rolleston both institutionalised a new attitude towards drug use and established the framework of public policy for the next five decades. Prior to this time, the principal medical concern over drug use had been the risk of poisoning as an unintended consequence of the private pursuit of pleasure from drug-taking. Based upon newly-emerging medical and social theories. Rolleston redefined persistent drug use as disease, rooted in addiction. Accordingly, the medical prescription of dangerous drugs was deemed legitimate in cases where (a) addicts were undergoing treatment by the method of gradual withdrawal, (b) complete withdrawal would produce serious and otherwise untreatable symptoms, (c) a 'normal' life could be led with the taking of a non-progressive maintenance dosage. In other cases, possession by non-addicts was to remain the subject of the criminal law. The Rolleston report also put on a firmer footing the system of medical tribunals initiated some years earlier to regulate prescribing practices amongst members of the medical profession.

The Rolleston Committee considered the drug user in Britain to be a member of a rare (and, in a very real sense, an endangered) species, and from the Committee's recommendations there emerged what came to be known as the 'British system' of drug control. This consisted of a combination of punitive measures against a class of illegal users and the treatment of, including the supervised administration of drugs to, legitimate users, a policy of 'policing and prescribing'. Thirty-five years later, in 1961, a Ministry of Health Committee chaired by Sir Russell Brain reaffirmed that addiction was a medical rather than a criminal matter and that the prevalence of dangerous drug use in Britain remained minimal. No major departures from the Rolleston recommendations were deemed necessary.

Within a very few years, however, the media appeared to be painting a picture of a new epidemic of recreational drug use, particularly cannabis and amphetamines, amongst the young people of Britain. Whilst the incidence of drug use was undoubtedly on the increase at this time the public response was essentially one of moral panic; as Plant (1987) notes: 'The vast media coverage of illegal drug-taking by young people is due to the fact that such behaviour has been combined with new lifestyles which, to the older generation at least, appear alien and possibly menacing. Rampant hedonism is both fascinating and sinister' (p. 5). With a rising drug demand, however, the authorities also became fearful that the licit opiate supply system was acting as a source for the illicit market. Limitations on the availability of amphetamines and LSD were hastily enacted and the Brain Committee was reconvened. The second Brain report of 1965 was significant in that it now acknowledged drug use to be a social as well as an individual problem. It recommended substantial limitations to the medical profession's powers of prescription, arguing that drug administration should be restricted to established and regulated clinics or 'drug dependency units', in which users could receive specialist treatment. These and other recommendations were subsequently embodied into the 1967 Dangerous Drugs Act. The 1971 Mususe of Drugs Act, which consolidated the legislation of the 1960s and earlier, remains, in effect, the statutory framework of drug policy in the United Kingdom today.

Throughout the 1970s the clinic remained the flagship of the 'prescribing' side of drug control, although its efficacy increasingly became called into question. *De facto*, clinics defined drug use as a medical problem with medical solutions, whereas a growing body of opinion saw such an emphasis as being unrealistically narrow. The 1982 report of the Advisory Committee on the Misuse of Drugs (a body established under the 1971 Act) firmly supported a wider interpretation of appropriate treatment. It asserted that the provision of care should no longer be centred on medical diagnosis or nature of the drug taken but should instead devolve from a range of available services, over and above those provided by medicine, for example, social work, and housing and employment agencies. Multi-disciplinary drug teams were to be established at the local level, with the provision for the training of personnel (MacGregor and Ettore, 1987).

The 1982 report coincided with evidence of a new heroin epidemic in urban centres such as London, Liverpool and

Glasgow. Moreover, two additional factors were emerging to complicate the matter of policy design, first, the now-established link between injecting drugs and the transmission of the human immunodeficiency virus (AIDS) and, second, the presence in the world drug economy of very powerful criminal syndicates controlling illicit supply. The official policy response was first elaborated in 1985 in the Home Office's *Tackling Drug Misuse* and this document, with its subsequent revisions, represents the current statement of UK drug control policy. The major part is devoted to attempts to control supply, for example, international efforts to curtail production, the strengthening of enforcement agencies, the tightening of control over licit availability and the deterrence of traffickers by means of harsher penalties. Attention is also drawn, however, to the importance of the prevention of drug use, by a combination of policing and education/information strategies, and to the necessity of effective treatment and rehabilitation of users (Stimson, 1987). Practical manifestations of this policy have included a high-profile media campaign, the 1986 Drug Trafficking Offences Act and the disbursement of funds to statutory and voluntary organisations at the local level, to assist in the development of new services to drug users.

WHAT IS THE DRUG PROBLEM?

The definition of the drug problem predetermines the outcome of the search for the drug solution, and the former has become ever more complicated. Prior to Rolleston, drugs hardly figured on the collective political agenda, that Committee being of the opinion that their use was confined to members of the medical and pharmaceutical professions and those 'specially liable to nervous and mental strain' (quoted in Edwards, 1981, p. 8). Excessive use, therefore, could be interpreted as individual vice or plain bad habit, much as an individual's excessive intake of alcohol is interpreted today. Although sporadic outbreaks of cocaine and heroin use came to the attention of the authorities in the early 1920s, the commissioning of the Rolleston report was primarily a response to uncertainties relating to the legality of certain prescribing practices under the terms of the 1920 Act (Bean,

1974). Irrespective of the initial intentions on the part of the authorities, it was this report which compartmentalised drug users into deviants, to be the subject of the full weight of the criminal law, and sufferers from the disease, for whom medical treatment (including drug prescription) was the appropriate remedy. Drug users were thus classified into the bad and the sick, and this clearly distinguished British policy from that prevailing in the USA. There, drug users were simply bad, the 1914 Harrison Act having outlawed the medical prescription of opiates (Berridge, 1989). This dual classification of the drug user in Britain continued well into the modern period although, in the popular image of deviancy, the Chinese opium den was soon replaced by long-haired youths in flared trousers.

It is only in the recent past that a more holistic perception of the drug problem seems to have emerged. First, following the 1982 Advisory Committee report, the 'disease of addiction' is now seen as an over-simplistic interpretation of a more complex phenomenon and 'dependence' is the preferred terminology. Far more factors are seen as contributing to drug-taking than the straightforward medical model allows, including socio-economic opportunities and lifestyles: 'there are no drug poblems, there are only people problems' (Aitken, 1978, p. 137). In consequence, the clinics are now obliged to share the spotlight. Resources have been channelled into a wide variety of alternative policy areas, including drug education and social support services and, starved of resources even at their inception, a number of clinics have closed down in recent years. Second, it is evident that the contemporary notion of the 'dangerousness' of dangerous drugs differs from that of ealier times. In the Rolleston world, the harm done by drugs was essentially that self-inflicted by the individual user, for prevalence was very low. To complement this, an element of social harm emerged in the 1960s, manifested largely as an apparent confrontation of lifestyles. By the 1980s, however, social harm had become much more tangible for, with the escalation in drug usage, distinct and identifiable social costs were emerging — policing the drug laws was absorbing increasing quantities of public resources, drug-related crime (especially violence- and property-related) was impacting upon entire communities, and the risk to public health (AIDS) was growing. Third, a changing attitude to the drug problem is evidenced by the changing language of policy. Modern statements, constructed in terms of drug 'abuse' or 'misuse', convey a distinctly different moral message from the earlier drug 'use' (Dally, 1989). In both Britain and America, the 'war on drugs' is a popular rallying-cry, creating the impression of battle between good and evil forces, society versus the syndicates. By implication, the contending forces are not unevenly matched and the war will take the form of a protracted crusade. As a consequence of the new vocabulary, drug use (or rather 'abuse') appears axiomatically to have criminal connotations and the social control element of drug policy using penal methods (the 'American system') thus tends to insinuate its way onto the British policy agenda.

As is invariably the case with any official policy, the British governments' approaches to drug control have never been without their critics. Temperance societies of the 1920s, for example, were at a loss to understand why alcohol was not included amongst the 'dangerous drugs', given its evident contribution to personal health and social problems. Even nowadays there are those who, whilst accepting the broad direction of current government policy, feel that it does not go far enough. The devolution of responsibility and resources to a wide range of local agencies is interpreted as disorganisation and a lack of coordination. Drug policy, furthermore, would need to be integrated into a far more generous social and economic assistance package, given the evident coincidence of drug use and relative deprivation (MacGregor, 1989).

Such specific criticisms notwithstanding, there have always been, as there continue to be, two central lines of questioning directed firmly at each of the foundations of the 'policing and prescribing' approach. These are, first, whether the enforcement of legal prohibitions against drug use is either desirable or even, in the long run, feasible and, second, whether the treatment given to drug users is actually effective. Let us first consider the treatment issue.

We noted earlier that the later 1960s witnessed the establishment of specialist clinics designed to address the needs of problem drug users specifically. This establishment coincided with an innovation in treatment method, introduced from the USA, where clinicians were reporting the successful use of methadone in long-term narcotic substitution therapy. A large proportion of patients so treated appeared to be limiting or abandoning their drug use, ceasing criminal activities and obtaining employment (Senay, 1983). Methadone maintenance quickly became the primary treatment option in Britain; during the 1970s, opiate prescription fell by approximately 66 per cent whilst methadone prescription increased by over 200 per cent (Spear, 1982). Since that time it is evident that the temporal dimension of treatment has been shortened. The Department of Health guide to clinical practice (DHSS, 1984) advises practitioners to stress to patients that long-term maintenance is no longer on offer and that even short-term prescription will entail additional therapies intended, in total, to wean the user off drugs in a relatively brief period of time (months rather than years).

Having been apparently eclipsed by the specialist clinics, it is interesting to note that the treatment role of the general practitioner (GP) has reasserted itself in recent years; the number of new opiate addicts notified by GPs has risen from less than 20 per cent of the total in the early 1970s to more than 50 per cent by the mid-1980s (Banks and Waller, 1988). In many respects this trend could be interpreted as progressive in view of the advantages conferred by a GP-based treatment system. GPs are generally considered to be more accessible than clinics based in psychiatric hospitals and they do not impart the stigma of mental disorder. Being placed within the community network they are perhaps more capable of offering support, both to the patients and their families. On a more cautious note, however, surveys do reveal that GPs are concerned about their role as drug therapists and are uncertain of their competence to deal with such matters (Glanz and Taylor, 1987).

As regards the efficiency of treatment it is fair to say that recent British research has failed to replicate the results from the USA in the 1960s. Thorley (1981) summarises British longitudinal studies and concludes that, as a result of treatment and rehabilitation, around one third of users are likely to be abstinent after five years. Stimson and Oppenheimer (1982) report a similar proportion for their London study although Strang (1989) claims somewhat more success for the Manchester area following the introduction of an integrated treatment network including clinics, community drug teams, rehabilitation houses and self-help groups. Whatever the degree of success such data are taken to imply they need to be interpreted in the light of further considerations. To begin with, individuals principally enter the treatment system via one of three routes, as a consequence of apprehension by the authorities, as a result of perceived ill health (drug-related or otherwise), or on a voluntary rehabilitation basis. The numbers undergoing treatment thus depend *pari passu* on the strategies and efficiency of the enforcement agencies, the health consequences of the drugs in question and the quality of the treatment provided, as perceived from the user's point of view. For the committed user, quality of treatment provided will depend on whether or not supplies of acceptable drugs are going to be available and, as Spear (1982) notes, methadone is not always regarded as an acceptable substitute for heroin. Undetected users who see the treatment system as offering no benefit will clearly elect to remain outside it. Thus Parker *et al.* (1988) estimated the heroin-using population of Merseyside at three times the number known to the official agencies, that is, at least two-thirds of users were not in receipt of treatment. Such a proportion would be very much higher for the most widely used illicit drug, cannabis, for which the risks of physical dependence and withdrawal symptoms are minimal (Wells, 1982); similar remarks might be made with respect to another currently-popular drug, amphetamines.

Treatment, therefore, is likely to be received only by a very small sub-set of the drug-using population although evidence further suggests that the simple provision of therapy does not necessarily reduce the social damage of drug use. Bennett and Wright (1986) have shown that most opiate users continue to engage in 'black market' activities in order to obtain supplies over and above the amount and type prescribed to them, implying that, at the present rate of prescription, treatment does not substitute for drug-related crime. Finally, it is evident that the efficacy of drug therapy is intimately linked to the user's economic and social environment, along the lines of 'getting off is easy, staying off is hard'. This proposition has been most graphically demonstrated in reverse by the 'Vietnam experience', wherein in excess of 90 per cent of the

American soldiers who had become habitual heroin users during their military service in South-East Asia in the 1960s and 1970s abruptly abandoned the practice on their repatriation and reintegration into a more normal civilian life in the USA (Robins, 1978). As noted above, no clinic-based studies have produced such impressive results although it is hard to imagine a transition in social environment more profound than that of the Vietnam case.

On the basis of this discussion it is not difficult to see how the battle-lines in the treatment debate are drawn. On the one hand, it can be argued that drug treatment is relevant for only a minority of users and, even then, will produce low remission rates in the absence of substantial improvements in the socio-economic environment of former users. Treatment, moreover, does not seem to reduce significantly users' involvement in criminal activities, that is, social harm is not necessarily thereby reduced. The conclusion might be reached that the treatment avenue is unlikely to lead to the solution of the drug problem in the vast majority of cases and that a disproportionate allocation of public resources in such a direction cannot therefore be legitimated. On the other hand, the same observations might be employed to justify the opposite deduction, namely, that treatment could be much more successful if it were to be better resourced than at present, especially if it were to be supported by economic policies favouring those communities with endemic drug use. Users will cease drug taking, it could be argued, if such a course of action is seen to be in their own interests and if the widest possible variety of assistance is provided to them.

The second central line of questioning referred to the virtues of legal prohibition. Running directly counter to the flow of contemporary government ideas about drug control, there appears to be emerging support for, if not the outright legalisation of dangerous drugs, then at least a degree of decriminalisation. Such a position has been reached from a variety of directions. First, there are, as there always have been, libertarians who feel that the state has no right to interfere in the individual's choice of consumption opportunities, irrespective of the nature of the commodity in question. Second, there are those who fail to see why illegal drugs such as cannabis and cocaine should be considered any more 'dangerous', either to the user or to the rest of society, than legal drugs such as tobacco. In support of their case, such critics of government policy cite the abundant medical data which grimly support the notion of the cigarette as a principal instrument of death in modern Britain. Thus, if society is content to see such dangerous drugs as tobacco freely used why should the same not be true for others? Third, legalisation is advocated by some on the grounds of cost-effectiveness. On the one hand, it is argued, any substantial constriction on drug imports would require an enormous increase in the allocation of resources to enforcement, over and above present levels. Even if the increase in effort were to be in some degree rewarded this makes the war on drugs a very expensive one to fight. On the other hand, legalisation via a regulated drug market would not only permit such policing resources to be saved, but a structure of taxation could then be applied (as for alcohol) to yield government revenue. Fourth, there are those who argue that the government of Britain has failed to learn the lessons of the Prohibition Era in the USA. The illegalisation of a commodity (in that case, alcohol) for which a demand existed simply facilitated the earning of monopoly profits on the part of those who were willing to continue supplying the 'black' market. The criminalisation of alcohol in the USA caused prices to soar and contributed directly to the enhancement of the economic and political power of the mobs who ran the rackets. By analogy, the continued illegal status of heroin, cocaine and other dangerous drugs in Britain can be said to act as a price-support system to benefit the criminal supply organisations, paid for ultimately by the British drug consumer. Finally, the illegal status of drugs must discourage a proportion of users from having recourse to treatment. Decriminalisation might therefore be expected to increase the flow of those seeking help via therapy, thereby both ameliorating the drug problem and improving the perceived effectiveness of the treatment system.

At the time of writing, no British politician has openly embraced a legalisation policy for drugs. The furthest any form of legislation has permeated into official thinking has been the Wootton Committee report on cannabis (Home Office, 1968), which concluded that the dangers of this substance were over-rated and that continued illegality was both unworkable and damaging. Needless to say, most of its recommendations were not accepted, yet the report does serve to point out a specific bias in the British approach to drug problems. The binary distinction in law between licit and illicit drugs does seem to imply that the former are all equally safe and the latter equally dangerous. Clinically, sociologically and criminologically, this categorisation is not immediately self-evident.

Looking to the future, it remains to be seen how far the British system of drug control will have to be restructured, following the continued integration of UK social policy into that of the European Community. The establishment of the 'single market' after 1992 has clear long-term implications for the formation of some type of trans-European drugs policy, if only because the structural changes facilitating trade in licit items might also be expected to facilitate trade in illegal drugs. Particular attention will surely be focused on the new 'Dutch system', which has attemped to break down that country's binary drug distinction. Since 1976, cannabis has been effectively decriminalised in Holland and 'harm reduction' policies towards addicts have been introduced (involving methadone-maintenance and needle exchanges), whilst traffickers in 'hard' drugs have been pursued with more vigour (van Vliet, 1989).

POLICING AND PRESCRIBING: ABOUT THIS BOOK

The contributions to this collection have been edited into two sections. The first, 'Drug Use and the British System', takes as its theme the approach to drug control which has been employed since the days of Rolleston. It examines the rationale of the approach and appraises the ingredients. Opening the section, Cindy Fazey addresses an issue fundamental to any control policy, namely, the actual consequences of illicit drug use. These are examined both at the level of the individual user — health effects, crime and punishment — and at the social level — from consequences for users' families to effects in drug-producing countries. Fazey concludes that the British model of drug control proves itself more than adequate in coming to terms with the adverse consequences of drug use.

The next three papers all focus specifically on the drug prescription issue, a defining characteristic of the British system. Kenneth Leech draws on his first-hand experience to comment on the prescribing practices of London practitioners in the 1960s which gave rise to public fears of overprescribing. He locates in this period the origins of significant changes in the pattern of drug taking which have contributed to that which prevails at the present time. Philip Bean then reviews the system of medical tribunals which has long operated as a means of policing the prescribing practices of the medical profession. He argues that, in the past, tribunals have evidenced both weakness and strength in controlling drug availability although, on balance, the retention of the present system is justified. Finally, James Willis provides a more personal and clinical perspective on the wisdom of prescribing to users, arguing that prescription is an important ingredient in the range of treatment techniques open to practitioners.

The final three papers in this section address the policing side of British drug control. First, Joy Mott links prescribing and policing by examining the relationship between opiate availability and drug-related crime. Based upon her own researches in the field, and drawing on the findings of others, she concludes that more generous prescription and improved treatment facilities are unlikely to eradicate criminal activities on the part of users, although they would tend to operate in that direction. Mark Gilman and Geoffrey Pearson delve into the sociology of drug using cultures, both in the USA and in Britain, in order to understand the British 'heroin epidemic' of the 1980s. Central to their discussion is the attitude of users to the enforcement agencies and, most importantly, the evolving attitudes of such agencies to ways of dealing with illegal drug use. They argue that flexibility in response is an essential element of successful drug control and that the traditional British system is indeed capable of accommodating such flexibility. Finally, Nick Dorn and Nigel South examine the most recent British legislation relating to drug control — the 1986 Drug Trafficking Offenses Act and the subsequent Criminal Justice Acts — with a view to identifying likely implications for enforcement strategies and civil liberties.

The second section of the book includes a diversity of essays under the collective heading of 'Contemporary Policy Themes'. These papers address particular aspects of drug control of relevance to debates over the direction of drug policy in the 1990s. In order to discover where one is going in the future one must first understand where one is, and the opening paper by John Giggs collates and appraises contemporary epidemiological data to provide a detailed picture of illicit drug use at the present time. Virginia Berridge then considers drug policy in relation to the growing incidence of AIDS, control of drug use and the control of AIDS having become almost inseparable policy targets during the 1980s. She enquires whether the post-AIDS drug programmes really do constitute a novel approach to a growing problem.

In common with all public policies, drug control has an economic dimension. Richard Stevenson lays out the basic economics of drug policy and concludes that it is only with respect to demand limitation that a cost-effective management regime is likely to result. Jane Falk-Whynes then considers demand reduction specifically from the point of view of health education, which is currently accorded a high profile in official policy. After appraising the initiatives of recent years she enquires into the conditions which make such an approach viable. The next paper, by Gordon Graham, is perhaps the most radical in the entire book, because it questions the very foundations of the contemporary British approach to drug control. Graham approaches the criminalisation of drug users from the philosophical standpoint and finds many of the conventional control arguments wanting.

Although essentially concerned with the British system of drug control, the book concludes with an American contribution. Arnold Trebach debates lessons from the US experience of drug control which might fruitfully be learned by British policy makers.

REFERENCES

Aitken, D. (1978) 'What is a Drug Problem?', in D. J. West (ed.) *Problems of Drug Abuse in Britain* (Cambridge: Insititute of Criminology).

Banks, A. and T. A. N. Waller (1988) *Drug Misuse: A Practical Handbook for GPs* (Oxford: Blackwell Scientific).

Bean, P. T. (1974) *The Social Control of Drugs* (London: Martin Robertson).

Bennett, T. and R. Wright (1986) 'The Impact of Prescribing on the Crimes of Opiate Users', *British Journal of Addiction*, 81, pp. 265–73.

Berridge, V. (1989) 'Historical issues', in MacGregor (1989).

Berridge, V. and G. Edwards (1981) *Opium and the People* (Harmondsworth: Penguin).

Dally, A. (1989) 'The Scandal of Cold Turkey', *Weekend Guardian*, October 7–8, pp. 2–6.

DHSS (1984) *Guidelines on Good Clinical Practice in the Treatment of Drug Misuse* (London: DHSS).

Dorn, N. and N. South (eds) (1987) *A Land Fit for Heroin?* (Basingstoke: Macmillan Education).

Edwards G. (1981) 'The Background', in Edwards and Busch (1981).

Edwards, G. and C. Busch (eds) (1981) *Drug Problems in Britain: A Review of Ten Years* (London: Academic Press).

Glanz, A. and C. Taylor (1987) 'Findings of a National Survey of the Role of General Practitioners in the Treatment of Opiate Misuse', in T. Heller, M. Gott and C. Jeffrey (eds), *Drug Use and Misuse* (Chichester: John Wiley and Sons).

Glatt, M. M. and J. Marks (eds) (1982) *The Dependence Phenomenon* (Lancaster: MTP Press).

Home Office (1986) *Report of the Advisory Committee on Drug Dependence: Cannabis* (London: HMSO).

MacGregor, S. (ed.) (1989) *Drugs and British Society* (London: Routledge).

MacGregor, S. and B. Ettore (1987) 'From Treatment to Rehabilitation — Aspects of the Evolution of British Policy on the Care of Drug-takers', in Dorn and South (1987)

Parker, H., K. Bakx and R. Newcombe (1988) *Living with Heroin* (Milton Keynes: Open University Press).

Plant, M. A. (1987) *Drugs in Perspective* (London: Hodder and Stoughton).

Robins, L. M. (1978) 'The Interaction of Setting and Pre-dispositions in explaining Novel Behaviour: Drug Initiations Before, In and After Vietnam', in D. B. Kandal (ed.), *Longitudinal Research on Drug Use* (New York: Halstead).

Senay, E. C. (1983) *Substance Abuse Disorders in Clinical Practise* (Bristol: John Wright).

Spear, H. B. (1982) 'Management of Opiate Dependence in Britain', in Glatt and Marks (1982).

Stimson, G. (1987) 'The War on Heroin: British Policy and the International Trade in Illicit Drugs', in Dorn and South (1987).

Stimson, G. and E. Oppenheimer (1982) *Heroin Addiction* (London: Tavistock).

Strang, A. (1981) 'A Model Service: Turning the Generalist on to Drugs', in MacGregor (1989).

Thorley, A. (1981) 'Longitudinal Studies of Drug Dependence', in Edwards and Busch (1981).

van Vilet, H. J. (1989) 'Drug Policy as a Management Strategy: Som Experiences from the Netherlands', *International Journal on Drug Policy*, 1(1), pp. 27–9.

Wells, F. (1982) 'Cannabis and Dependency', in Glatt and Marks (1982).

Part I
Drug Use and the British System

2 The Consequences of Illegal Drug Use

Cindy Fazey

The consequences of drug use can be analysed at individual, group, community, societal and international levels, for the consequences may range from individual health problems such as abscesses and gangrene to the development of a very rich cartel of drug dealers which challenges the power and authority of the state, as at present in Colombia. Consequences are also dependent upon the society, upon the norms and values in a society, and the normative and legal framework which develops to control the use of drugs. Thus the consequences of say, being addicted to heroin, vary considerably according to whether that person is in the USA or in the UK. In the USA the consequences of heroin addiction for Vietnam veterans in terms of ability to stop using (Robins, 1973) was very different from that of the urban poor black. In the UK consequences can vary again according to where that person lives. Whereas the legal status of the drugs is the same throughout the UK, how that status is translated into policy and how that policy is implemented can vary from police force to police force, and not only from one health district to another, but within health districts.

Nicotine and alcohol are the only two powerful psycho-active and addictive drugs not controlled by the medical profession. All others come under their control, and this control is backed by legislation, which is enforced by the police. It is therefore to the police and medical professions that attention must be paid, as well as to the legislators, if we are to understand the reasons for the consequences of drug use, for most of the present consequences are far from inevitable. There are legal restrictions on the use of both nicotine and alcohol, but the most powerful restrictions are normative ones. When and where it is appropriate to smoke and drink are mostly determined by social norms. The increase in non-smoking areas is led not by legislative

17

intervention, but by safety concerns (fire hazards) and health concerns of those who are 'passive' smokers. Legal restrictions on the opening times of public houses have been eased, as the arbitrary nature and often self-confounding nature of these restrictions was recognised. The notorious Australian 'six o'clock swill' was, perhaps, an extreme example of the results of imposing restrictions against the wishes of considerable numbers of citizens. When the bars closed at six in the evening, drunks were littering the street by 6.15, having consumed as much alcohol as they could between leaving work and the bars closing. Prohibition does not encourage responsible behaviour — that is, behaviour which minimises harm, does not incapacitate and which does not affect a neighbour. Tobacco is likely to cause lung cancer and its consequences can be graphically pointed out, but to make it an illegal substance would be to create a black market, turn people into criminals, and provide a certain income for a whole criminal subculture. We have seen the consequences of the prohibition of alcohol in the USA — both more alcohol consumed and more crime (Kefauver, 1952; Allsop, 1961).

In the UK all the main psychoactive drugs, including heroin, are legal in so far as a person can be in legal possession. For most psychoactive drugs, they can also be in illegal possession. The difference between the status of nicotine and alcohol and the other drugs lies in the distribution system. Both systems require the distributor to be licensed, but in the former case it is a retailer, in the latter a member of the medical profession. It is the distribution system, or rather the lack of an adequate one, which causes most of the consequences of drug use, together with attitudes of non-illegal drug users towards the problem.

CONSEQUENCES FOR THE INDIVIDUAL

Perhaps the most obvious consequence of drug use is the risk to health. Consequences from taking psychoactive drugs vary according to the drugs. Many would argue that the health consequences of taking tranquillisers, which include symptoms such as agoraphobia, are far more serious than taking heroin. This is particularly true if heroin is smoked. Since heroin sublimes (that is, goes from a solid to gaseous state without becoming liquid first) even if the person smoking it (chasing the dragon) is buying street drugs which have been adulterated (cut) with other substances, such as powdered milk, talcum powder, brick dust or violin rosin, these impurities are left behind. If they continue to smoke they get drowsy and pass out before taking a fatal overdose. Overdoses and deaths from intravenous use of drugs are usually the result of varying strengths of drugs sold on the street. The relatively high street purity of heroin in the UK (60 per cent) can lead to many deaths of visiting heroin users coming from the USA where purity can be down to 3 per cent. The deaths for 1987 from drug addiction were 165, plus 65 recorded deaths due to non-dependent abuse of drugs, for alcohol 1589 deaths, with a further 1556 due to chronic liver disease and cirrhosis where alcohol was not specifically reported as a cause (making a total of 3145) and from tobacco 42 463 (cancer), 8524 (diseases of the circulatory system) and 42 996 (diseases of the respiratory system). This makes a grand total of 79 128 deaths which can be directly or indirectly attributed to the effects of alcohol and tobacco, and 230 to drug dependence and 'abuse' (Parliamentary Debates, Hansard, 1987–88).

One consequence of intravenous heroin use is abscesses, but then milk powder and brick dust are not the best things to put into people's veins. Pure heroin, however, presents no problems, as long as the person does not overdose. There are no long-term adverse physical effects from heroin which are recorded in the standard textbook on pharmacology (see Goodman and Gillman, 1980). The Canadian Le Dain Commission concluded in its final report in 1973 that:

> Morphine has little effect on other senses, and . . . it can often control severe pain at doses which do not necessarily produce marked sedation, gross intoxication or major impairment of motor coordination, intellectual functions, emotional control or judgement . . . opiate narcotics typically do not disrupt physchomotor performance to any significant degree. . . . There is no evidence of permanent changes in cognitive or intellectual functioning due to chronic opiate narcotic use. Nor is there any indication of psychosis or any other major psychiatric complications

caused by these drugs. . . . There appears to be little direct permanent physiological damage from chronic use of pure opiate narcotics [pp. 308–9].

Studies on the effects of long-term methadone maintenance have yielded similar results (Kleber *et al.* 1980).

The health consequences of drug addiction relate almost entirely to the effects of buying and injecting 'street' drugs. The techniques of injecting of many addicts leave a lot to be desired. All too often, practice does not make perfect, merely more of a mess.

Whether access is given to these drugs by any members of the medical profession is largely a matter of 'professional judgement'. This clinical judgement is rarely illuminated by any scientific study, but is usually based on individual, idiosyncratic experience. Evaluations of clinical practice have only been done twice in this country (Hartnoll *et al.* 1980; Fazey, 1987, 1988). Most of the literature is mainly anecdotal, which masquerades as case studies. With no agreement as to the goals of treatment let alone what is being treated, it is not surprising that a rag-bag of treatment regimes should develop.

The goal of treatment is obviously for the addict to be drug free, but some doctors doubt if this is a reasonable short- or even medium-term realistic goal for some people. Also, the prevention of the spread of HIV infection is seen by many as a higher priority, and these two goals might not necessarily coincide. When being a junkie is part of a lifestyle, a social and economic enterprise (see Prebble and Casey, 1969; Agar, 1973; Johnson *et al.* 1985) then what is being treated could be an addiction, a passport to a lifestyle and friendship network, criminal activity, a means of supplementing income, lack of finances, pleasure, or some combination of all of these. The fact that many pop stars who are addicted to heroin do not seek treatment nor come before the courts, but continue to work as musicians could be advanced as an argument that for many heroin users and addicts, their problem is not the drug but lack of money to buy it. Lack of money usually leads to three serious consequences of drug abuse — namely treatment, crime and punishment.

Many tales of the hoops drug addicts have been made to jump through may sound apocryphal but are not (see, for example, the patients' perception of treatment in Stimson and Oppenheimer, 1982). Tests, retests and more tests of everything from urine to motivation have been put between the would-be patient and any serious consideration of their condition. The tests themselves are often justified on the basis of a needed assessment, but too often they have operated as a way of sifting out the 'non-compliant' patient, that is, only people who are likely to follow the prescribed course of treatment are accepted as 'suitable', that is, those who will do exactly as the doctor says. This is often covered up by more semantic pyrotechnics under the guise of the word 'contract'. A doctor and a patient will negotiate a contract, whereby the doctor agrees to give the patient what they want (or at least almost so) in return for the patient agreeing to give the doctor what he wants (that they give up drugs). The patient will therefore agree to reduce and come off drugs within a specified time period in return for the satisfying of immediate needs — they will be prescribed drugs. The nature of a contract, however, is that to be valid there has to be a genuineness of consent by the parties to the terms of the contract. Again, in law, the concept of undue influence enters — particularly where there is inequality of bargaining power between the parties to a contract. An addict is addicted to heroin. That person needs the drugs immediately. Is it any wonder that they will agree to a reduction or cessation at some future date in return for drugs now? No matter how the 'caring' professions, as many wish to be known, may try to sugar the bitter pill that they deliver, the more usual word for such behaviour is blackmail.

The other two consequences for the individual are crime and punishment. To buy or be given drugs which were not prescribed for that individual usually means that they are in illegal possession and are therefore committing a crime. However, it is the crimes that people commit in order to pay for their drugs that cause the most problems. If the drugs to which someone has become addicted are not made available through legal (medical) means the consequences are three-fold: firstly, the addicts will probably start dealing in drugs in order to secure their own supply, thus adding to the increased availability of the drugs; secondly, they are likely to commit crime to pay for their drugs; and thirdly, a new way of making money will become part of the criminal infrastructure.

According to how much money is to be made, so the strength of this infrastructure will be determined. Many people who take drugs have committed crimes and have convictions before they become problem users, but illegal drug use escalates their criminal activity (Ball *et al.*, 1981; Johnson *et al.*, 1985; Parker and Newcombe, 1987; Jarvis and Parker, 1989; Fazey, 1987) and treatment decreases it (Fazey, 1988; McGlothlin and Anglin, 1977). About one quarter, however, only began committing crime after they became addicted, and as a direct result of their drug use. However, as the Shafer Report (1973) concluded, 'The only crimes which can be directly attributed to marijuana-using behaviour are those resulting from the use, possession or transfer of an illegal substance' (p. 159) (see also Wootton Report, 1968).

The sort of crime committed by drug users in the UK is typically acquisitive crime, rather than the violent crime of the USA which mainly arises through fights between drug gangs for the lucrative drug market. Nevertheless, where there is an increase in illegal drug use, there is an increase in the amount of crime. For female drug users, shoplifting is a common way of getting money but many are forced into prostitution to pay for their drugs. This then induces a vicious circle whereby they cannot get out of prostitution because they need the money for drugs, and can't stop using drugs because of the life that they lead. Many female addicts admit to months or years as a prostitute before getting the medical treatment which either stabilised their drug taking or weaned them off drugs, thus removing the necessity of prostitution. Unhappily there are still cases where ex-prostitutes have been forced back to prostitution because of a change in medical regimes where it has been decided, for example, not to prescribe intravenous drugs to anyone, and to bring off all those on such a prescription. Such changes in the treatment regime always benefit a very few, but wreak havoc in the lives of the many (see, for example, McGlothlin and Anglin, 1981).

Whereas punishment is not an inevitable consequence of crime, the liklihood that offenders will be detected increases as the number of offences which they commit increases. For the drug user this means not only the stigma of a conviction, but also an increased risk of becoming HIV infected. The risk is greater for a drug user because of the availability of drugs in most prisons, and the relative unavailability of needles. It was publicly admitted by one prison governor that if all drugs were successfully stopped from entering some prisons there would be riots and the prison staff would not be able to control the inmates. Inevitably needles are shared, not just with a few but in some cases hundreds of people. As long as magistrates and judges keep sending drug users to prison the risks will increase.

Another aspect of punishment is the informal punishment that many known drug users suffer, particularly women, simply because they are drug users. This takes many forms, from discrimination in the job market to having children taken into care. Whereas being a notified drug addict in many Social Services departments no longer means that the children are automatically taken into care, in some departments it still does automatically mean that a case conference will be called. Taking children of heroin-addicted mothers into care, and the belief (even if wrongly held) that this is the case, means that pregnant drug-users avoid ante-natal services, and are reluctant to approach drug services for help because they fear that they will become known to the Social Services.

Many services set up to provide for drug users have not been 'user friendly'. The attitudes to drug users often mean that they are treated as inveterate and incurable liars whose lives are a complete shambles and do not deserve even elementary courtesy. There are indeed individuals who would neatly fit this stereotype, but there are many more who have to suffer an additional burden as a result of their drug-taking, and that is being treated as though they too fitted this image (Dole and Nyswander, 1976; Lidz and Walker, 1980).

Backgrounds of severe social deprivation and high unemployment characterise a disproportionate number of those with severe enough problems to attend drug treatment clinics, and whereas addiction to, say, heroin, does not actually help to improve any of these factors, they cannot be said to be consequences of drug use. They are rather important variables when trying to understand the cause.

SOCIAL CONSEQUENCES

All the above consequences are related to how drug use and drug addiction can affect the individual drug users, but inevitably their actions have consequences for other people.

The people most immediately affected by someone becoming a problem drug user are members of their own family. The families of illegal drug users often suffer in many ways from having cash stolen, having goods taken and sold for cash, to introducing brothers and sisters to drug use. The growth of Family Support Groups testifies to the misery and sense of powerlessness and inability to stop what is happening to their children that many parents feel. But extensive drug use and drug dealing also makes communities feel that they have almost been taken over by 'outside pushers' and they feel afraid and unable to effect change. Even if the reality is that the users are local people there is often the sense of invasion and threat.

Communities are also affected because drug dealing adds a new income to the criminal black economy which is perhaps thriving. Dealing in drugs can become like fencing goods from a warehouse robbery. Since the drug trade is so lucrative whole local economies can become dependent upon it. This is certainly true of many deprived areas in the larger cities of the US. The communities themselves are also one of the main victims of the increase in crime. Whereas at first the large city centre stores might feel the brunt in the increase in shoplifting, car radios will be taken and houses burgled locally.

The costs to society can be seen in both social and economic terms. Costs are in terms of health care for addicts and the provision of services for those with drug problems, but there are even greater costs if the addicts and users are not treated. These costs include those of treating and looking after HIV infected people and AIDS patients, the costs of processing criminals through the courts and the costs of incarceration. Added to this is the cost of crime that they commit, the cost of increased insurance rates, as well as the toll that all this takes upon the quality of life.

The consequences of illegal drug use have a ripple effect right through society, and affect other societies, particularly the producers of these drugs. It should be remembered however, that the international treaties defining what is or is not an illegal drug bear very little relation to the seriousness of the consequences of consumption (Brunn *et al.* 1975).

The sources of supply of illicit drugs are well known (INCB, 1988, RCMP, 1988), but because of the difficulty of the terrain and lack of resources and/or because of, often government, vested interests, production continues apace, and in the case of cocaine, has increased dramatically. (Various governments' involvement in the drug trade is well documented from the earliest days of the trade to the present day — Chang, 1964; McCoy, 1973; Lamour and Lamberti, 1974.) East and South East Asia continues to be one of the main opium suppliers to the world, specifically Burma, Laos and Thailand, distributing the drugs mainly through Hong Kong for trans-shipment to Australia, Europe and North America. The development of this trade has been helped not a little by the American Government (McCoy, 1973) and Australian Unions and organised crime (McCoy, 1980). Cannabis is also produced by these countries, although most North American supply is from home production, Central and South America. In the Caribbean cannabis is endemic (Rubin, 1975a) as it is in other parts of the world (Rubin, 1975b). Malaysia continues to occupy a central role in the trafficking route, but attempts to use China and Russia have not met with much success. Pakistan, India and Bangladesh are producing large amounts of opium mainly destined for the European market. A previously large exporter, Afghanistan, presently has an unknown production, but Pakistan has increased its production by at least an equivalent to the Afghan shortfall. Iran is still a producer as well as trans-shipper of heroin, as is the Lebanon, despite — or because of — the wars in this area. Although Egypt is a producer of both opium and cannabis, most opium is trans-shipped from Pakistan.

Virtually every country in Central and South America is engaged in a growing cocaine trade, and to a lesser extent, the cannabis trade. Peru, Bolivia, Ecuador and Colombia are the main producers and processors, but processing is now also taking place in Brazil and Argentina, and now encompasses virtually every country on the sub-continent. The smuggling routes through the Caribbean and central America are legion, the latter also producing cannabis and opium — in Belize, Guatemala, Panama and Mexico.

Smuggling routes into Europe exist directly from Pakistan, but increasingly through African states, particularly Nigeria.

Morocco used to be a main producer of cannabis but has also become a transit country for cocaine, with Spain the main country of entry for the drug into Europe.

At an international level the trade in drugs has produced hitherto unknown degrees of cooperation with different national groups and the criminalisation of fellow nationals who are immigrants in other cities and countries. The drug trade, like no other criminal enterprise before, including the gold and slave trades, has developed multiple international connections. The profits from the trade are so great that, when put into legitimate business to provide a legitimate 'front' for more drug dealing, detection and apprehension of the criminals is made even more difficult. When the money from drugs is 'repatriated' to the country which provided the drugs, as in Peru where coca is said to earn $650 million per year, the money can be used to challenge the legal government of a country. The extent of the value of the cocaine trade can be gauged from the fact that General Noriega in Panama was said to earn some $10 million per month.

At a national level, many guerrilla organisations, both on the left and right of the political spectrum, have financed at least some of their activities through drug production and/or distribution, which include the Maoist guerrillas of Peru, the Red Brigades, the IRA, the FARC, Kurds, highland Burmese, and many other groups. In many South American states these drug barons and/or guerrilla groups form a parallel power to that of government which challenges the rule of law and the government itself. They become a state within a state which cannot be controlled by police, military or government. Sometimes, however, it is the government itself which is implicated in the trade.

All this can be brought about because of the vast sums of money that the drug trade produces, which arises because of the price that people are willing to pay to get hold of these drugs. By far the most lucrative trade internationally is in cocaine, said to account for $20 billion annually, with a 12 000 per cent mark up between production costs and street sales; heroin is now second to it, and cannabis in third place. Another effect of the vast sums of money available is the criminalisation of government officials, civil servants, customs and police services, the very people who are appointed or elected to serve the society as a whole. Recent prosecutions of cabinet ministers and accusations of the involvement of at least one Caribbean prime minister, testify to the power of the money from the drug trade, particularly in smaller and poorer nations, although they are by no means the only officials subject to corruption.

At a national level also, the drug trade is beginning to draw in whole categories of people not traditionally associated with criminal activity, or at least not criminal activity which results in direct harm to people, such as lawyers, accountants, bankers, stockbrokers and investment houses. By financing drug deals, laundering drug money, arranging for trans-shipments and providing transport, whole sections of the middle classes have been criminalised by the temptation to make easy money at perceived low risk. This is certainly true of Florida, and particularly Miami, but a respected Wall Street stockbroking firm was recently found guilty of laundering drug money, and a London bank stands accused, as does a Luxembourg-based international bank. It is interesting that this very same phenomenon was noted by Kefauver in looking at the effects of the years of prohibition of alcohol in the US (Kefauver, 1952; Allsop, 1961).

The lucrative nature of the drug trade has also meant a cross-fertilisation with other criminals — the transfer of 'regular' criminal skills into the drug world. The processing and distribution of illegal drugs becomes part of the criminal underworld, and many criminals switch from their previous criminal activity and turn to drugs. For example, the ampheta-mine for much of the UK and European market came for several years from London convicted criminals from the pornography trade, operating out of Eire (Raymond and Rusty Humphreys who are now in 'retirement' in Mexico).

The drug trade is now so lucrative and the criminal networks (particularly the Colombians and the Mafia) making so much money out of it that it is difficult to see why the policy of war on drugs is being pursued when it is obviously impossible to win. When governments are suborned and challenged by drug barons, the police and army undermined by corruption, the war has been lost. Only the rhetoric is left, and it is the rhetoric of a moral crusade of the righteous against the forces of evil. What it is not is a pragmatic approach to containing a form of behaviour which many regard as harmful to the individuals who wish to pursue it and therefore a danger to the young who may wish to try drugs through curiosity or from example.

THE WAY FORWARD

If the more serious consequences of our present policy to illegal drug use are to be ameliorated then we must re-examine some of the fundamental propositions upon which it is based.

One first step is to stop treating all illegal drugs as though they were the same. Alcohol and tobacco are not treated alike even though they are both legal, powerful, addicting and harmful drugs. Some new policies should be tried and a few old ones restored. There is a dangerous re-writing of history, particularly of the 1960s and early 1970s drug scene in the UK either by those who were not around at the time and take their versions of events from those who had a vested interest in justifying their policy, or from the very people who brought about a change in policy. History indeed may be the propaganda of the victor. The distortions which are occurring revolve particularly around whether there was a 'British System', and whether it worked. The answer to both is quite simply 'yes'. Those who argue that there was no 'British System' because there was no single system are themselves right in one sense — that there was no unified formal treatment procedure for dealing with drug addicts. There was, however, as laid out in the Rolleston Report (1926), a broad philosophy that should be followed — and there was, of course, variation in how this was done. It recommended a general approach to people who were addicted to heroin and cocaine, not detailed specific regimes to follow.

Similarly, there are many illnesses which will be handled differently by different doctors — some might recommend surgery while others drug therapy. The system was really a method of delivery of drugs to drug addicts by those prepared to undertake it in the medical profession. As such it was patchy in its delivery rather than uniform, but was a way, a means, a system in that sense, for dealing with addicts (Spear,

1975). The danger of these semantic arguments lies in the fact that if no system existed, then the assumption lies in the fact that there is no system to study, and so the British experience can be ignored or at the most consigned to the category of 'interesting historical experiment'. What made the British System different from the American System was that in Britain addicts could be maintained or weaned off heroin by doctors; in the States no doctor could prescribe heroin under any circumstances — it became a completely prohibited drug. Just because the United States has decided that it will not have recourse to the full range of treatment options that are available elsewhere, and that it will deny any possibility of net beneficial effects of prescribing heroin, why should we deny that we did, that we do, and that it is successful? It seems to be the ultimate in subservience to another country to deny our own history and to re-write it in a form which fits in with their prejudices. As long as heroin and morphine are banned options in the United States, orally or intravenously, and intravenous methadone is not countenanced, then they have a vested interest in saying that our system did not work. They are colluded in this by one or two people who brought about the decline if not the death of the system, partly because it would entail admitting that they were wrong and partly because they would rightly be blamed for at least some of the present size of the problem. It is very sad that the pioneering work done by Dr John Owens at All Saints Hospital in Birmingham in setting up one of the first modern drug dependency clinics which effectively contained the growth of heroin in the West Midlands is overlooked because of subsequent problems. As Judson (1973) noted, the 'procedures that Owens and Hill devised have become standard clinic practice' (p. 90). The achievement nevertheless remains and hopefully ultimately will be recognised.

Change in the system was brought about by the need to control the very few over-prescribing doctors, and in fact really one in particular, Lady Frankau. In 1965, the second Brain report (the Interdepartmental Committee on Drug Addiction which was chaired by Lord Brain) discovered that:

One doctor alone prescribed almost 600 000 tablets of heroin (i.e. 6 kilogrammes) for addicts. The same doctor, on one occasion, prescribed 900 tablets of heroin (9 grammes) to one addict and, three days later, prescribed for the same patient another 600 tablets (i.e. 6 grammes) 'to replace pills lost in an accident'. Further prescriptions of 720 (7.2 grammes) and 840 (8.4 grammes) tablets followed later to the same patient. Two doctors each issued a single prescription for 1000 tablets (i.e. 10 grammes).

In fact there were only a handful of over-prescribing doctors, and to have only that number of mad, bad, incompetent or just plain greedy doctors is a tribute to, and not a slur on, the medical profession. The mad one ended up in Broadmoor, the bad in prison, the incompetent died and the greedy either died or were warned to desist. As a researcher in the field it was an enlightening experience to be taken by a certain Mr Bing Spear to watch the notorious Dr Petro at work. It was at a time after he had been struck off the medical register, but before his appeal had been heard (rules regarding prescribing at this time have now been changed), and before he went to prison. He was in Picadilly underground station opposite the ticket desk, sitting with his back against the wall and legs stretched out in front of him writing prescriptions for a queue of addicts which stretched almost the whole way around the station. The most impressive parts of this whole operation were the speed at which he could write prescriptions and the orderliness of the queue. Any pretence that clinical judgement was being exercised had long been abandoned. The problem, however, was that the GMC and BMA could not agree to there being any 'interference' between the doctor and patient, and so would not accept any mechanism for curbing the activities of the very few. The system changed, and in doing so for the first time the means of limiting the prescribing of certain drugs was introduced.

In recommending the setting up of treatment centres the second Brain report saw them as preventing 'this abuse' (that is, the overprescribing by some doctors) 'without sacrificing the basic advantages of the present arrangements'. It was not the system which was at fault, but a few doctors.

The consequences of returning to a system supported by the Brain committee are likely to be a short-term increase in the numbers of notified addicts, and a longer-term decrease. The increase would be caused by those already addicted coming in from the cold, but also the numbers swelled by some who are not really addicted but availability might tip them into that category. That is why availability of any drug which can harm people should be controlled, but controlled availability does not equate with prohibition. The advantages will accrue to the individual in terms of better health and the removal of the necessity to commit crime, to the families of addicts, to the neighbourhood where dealing is rife, to the victims of crime, and to all those who have to pay higher rates of insurance because of living in criminal areas. Society as a whole will benefit because police resources can be redirected, and those countries which supply and distribute the drugs will not be challenged by a parallel power which can corrupt the national army and police forces, and it would lessen the incomes of those government officials who are directly and indirectly involved in the drug trade and who keep their power through its finances and not the ballot box.

Most of the above discussion refers to heroin and methadone use because it was argued at the start that different drugs might need different approaches. It perhaps would not be appropriate to make crack readily available, but some form of cocaine could be provided, and the same for amphetamines, as was the case up to the early 1970s. Experiments along these lines are beginning on a very small scale, but if different methods of dealing with those who have problems because of their drug use are not tried it will not be long before their problems become our problems, whether we like it or not.

The American approach of only tackling the supply side with the 'War on Drugs' clearly is failing as many American academics (Trebach, 1987) and people in the media in this country are now at last recognising, if not the politicians (*Economist*, 1989). Earlier attempts to tackle the demand side did not bring the desired degree of success. At the instigation of the United States and Canada, the United Nations Commission of Narcotic Drugs requested the Division of Narcotic Drugs in 1976 to undertake a study on measures to reduce illicit demand for drugs. This was done (1979) but governments chose to ignore this approach perhaps because there was not a simple single answer. Treatment provisions would not only have to be expanded but changed and made more flexible to needs of the patients. One paper also concluded that we may need to change what the establishment thinks about drugs and we should, in effect, educate our masters. It was also clear that in tackling the drug problem it might entail tackling the housing problem, the unemployment problem, the education problem and the poverty problem as well. Little wonder perhaps that the response was to opt for the definition of the problem for which a single solution could be put forward.

To suggest that the worst consequences of the present policy can be eased by increasing legal availability is not to advocate selling drugs with the same availability as tobacco; nor advertising or in any way encouraging the consumption of heroin. It is merely a plea to treat heroin addicts in particular in a more humane fashion, not only for their sakes but for the sake of the rest of society, so that the damage and havoc that they can directly and indirectly cause can be minimised. Relaxing the controls, not abandoning them, is likely to yield a considerable net gain for the whole of society.

REFERENCES

'Mission Impossible', *The Economist*, 2 Sept. 1989.

'Drugs. It doesn't have to be like this', *The Economist*, 2 Sept. 1989.

Agar, Michael (1973) *Ripping and Running: A Formal Ethnograpy of Urban Heroin Addicts* (New York: Seminar Press).

Allsop, Kenneth (1961) *The Bootleggers: The Story of Chicagos's Prohibition Era* (London: Hutchinson).

Ball, J. *et al.* (1981) 'The Criminality of Heroin Addicts: When Addicted and when off Opiates', in J. A. Inciardi (ed.), *The Drugs-Crime Connection* (London: Sage).

Brain (Lord) (Chairman) (1965) *Drug Addiction. The Second Report of the Interdepartmental Committee*, Ministry of Health, Scottish Home and Health Department (London: HMSO).

Bruun, K. *et al.* (1975) *The Gentleman's Club (University of Chicago Press)*.

Chang, Hsin-Pao (1964) *Commissioner Lin and the Opium War* (Cambridge, Mass.: Harvard University Press).

Division of Narcotic Drugs (1979) *Study on Measures to Reduce Illicit Demand for Drugs*, preliminary report of a working group of experts (United Nations).

Dole, V. and M. Nyswander (1976) 'Methadone Maintenance Treatment: a Ten Year Perspective', *Journal of the American Medical Association*, Vol. 235, pp. 2117–19.

Economist, 'Does this war make sense?, 21 January, 1989, 41–3.

Fazey, C. S. J. (1988) *Heroin Addiction, Crime and the Effect of Medical Treatment*, a report to the Home Office Research and Planning Unit.

Goodman, L. S. and A. G. Gilman, *The Pharmacological Basis of Therapeutics*, 6th edn. (London: Macmillan, 1981).

Hartnoll, R. L., M. C. Mitchelson, A. Battersby, G. Brown, M. Ellis, P. Fleming, N. Hedley (1980) 'Evaluation of Heroin Maintenance in Controlled Trial', *Archives of General Psychiatry*, vol. 37, pp. 877–84.

Home Office (1968) *Cannabis*, report by the Advisory Committee on Drug Dependence (The Wootton Report) (London: HMSO).

INCB (1988) The International Narcotics Control Board, *Report for 1988*, E/INCB/1988/1 (New York: united Nations).

Jarvis, G. and H. Parker (1989) 'Young Heroin Users and Crime. How Do the "New Users" Finance their Habits?' *British Journal of Criminology*, vol. 29, p. 175–85.

Johnson, Bruce D. *et al.* (1985) *Taking Care of Business: The Economics of Crime by Heroin Abusers* (Lexington, Mass.: D. C. Heath).

Judson, Horace F. (1973) *Heroin Addiction in Britain* (New York: Harcourt Brace Jovanovich).

Kefauver, Estes (1952) *Crime in America* (London: Gollancz).

Kleber, Herbert D., Frank Slobetz and Marjorie Maeritz (eds) (1980) *Medical Evaluation of Long-Term Methadone Maintained Clients* (Rockville, MD: National Institute of Drug Abuse).

Lamour Catherine and Michael, R. Lamberti (1974) *The Second Opium War* (London: Allen Lane).

Le Dain, G. (Chairman) (1973) *Final Report of the Commission of Inquiry into the Non-Medical Use of drugs* Ottawa: Information Canada.

Lidz, C. Q, and A. L. Walker (1980) *Heroin, Deviance and Morality* (London: Sage).

McCoy, Alfred W. (1973) *The Politics of Heroin in Southeast Asia* (New York: Harper & Row).

McCoy, Alfred W. (1980) *Drug Traffic* (Melbourne: Harper & Row).

McGlothlin, W. H. and M. D. Anglin (1981) 'Shutting off Methadone: Cost and Benefits', *Archives of General Psychiatry*, vol. 38, pp. 885–92.

McGlothlin, W. H. and M. D. Anglin (1977) *An Evaluation of the California Civil Addict Program*, NIDA Research Monograph, pp. 75–558.

Parker, H. and R. Newcombe (1987) 'Heroin Use and Acquisitive Crime in an English Community', *British Journal of Sociology*, vol. 38, pp. 331–41.

Parliamentary Debates, Hansard (1988) *House of Commons Official Report. Session 1987–88*, sixth series, vol. 137, col. 878.

Prebble, Edward and John J. Casey (1969) 'Taking Care of the Business: The Heroin User's Life on the Street', *International Journal of the Addictions*, vol. 4, pp. 1–24.

Robins, Lee N. (1973) *The Vietnam Drug User Returns*, Special Action Office Monograph, series A, no. 2.

Rolleston, Humphrey (Chairman) (1926) *Report on the Departmental Committee on Morphine and Heroin Addiction* (London: HMSO).

Royal Canadian Mounted Police (RCMP) (1988) *National Drug Intelligence Estimate*, Annual Report.

Rubin, Vera (1975) *Cannabis and Culture* (The Hague: Mouton).

Rubin, Vera and Lambros Comitas (1975) *Ganja in Jamaica. A Medical Anthropological Study of Chronic Marijuana Use* (The Hague: Mouton).

Shafer, Raymond P. (Chairman) (1973) *Drug Use in America: Problem in Perspective*, Second Report of the National Commission on Marijuana and Drug Abuse.

Spear, H. B. (1975), 'The British Experience', *John Marshall Journal of Practice and Procedure*, 9, 67–98.

Stimson, Gerry and Edna Oppenheimer (1982) *Heroin Addiction. Treatment and Control in Britain* (London: Tavistock).

Trebach, A. S. *The Great Drug War* (New York: Macmillan, 1987).

Wootton Report – Home Office (1968), Report of the Advisory Committee on Drug Dependence: Cannabis (London: HMSO, 1968).

3 The Junkies' Doctors and the London Drug Scene in the 1960s: Some Remembered Fragments

Kenneth Leech

When doctors lose their privilege to prescribe for addicts, they also lose their opportunity to treat addicts, whether with drugs or without. Although hospital treatment was permitted, there were virtually no hospital facilities. A breach was made between the addict and the physician that has only recently been narrowed.

(John C. Kramer (USA), 1971)[1]

They [the junkies' doctors] have been filling for some time an essential gap while we have been deciding rather slowly what to do.

(William Deedes, MP, 1968)[2]

BRAIN: SOLUTION OR SYMPTOM?

The Second Report of the Interdepartmental Committee on Drug Addiction, the Brain Report, was published at the end of November 1965. Its curiously limited feel was partly due to its narrow terms of reference. While it was entitled *Drug Addiction*, its concern was almost exclusively with the regulations controlling prescribing of heroin and cocaine for addicts. It is true that it did make one passing reference to the wider social context in the memorable words of paragraph 40:

Witnesses have told us that there are numerous clubs, many in the West End of London, enjoying a vogue among young people who can find in them such diversions as modern music and all night dancing. In such places it is known that some young people have indulged in stimulant drugs of the amphetamine type.[3]

However, its central claim was contained in paragraphs 11 and 12. Here we were told that 'the major source of supply has been the activity of a very few doctors who have prescribed excessively for addicts' (para. 11). The report went on to claim that 'not more than six doctors have prescribed these very large amounts of dangerous drugs for individual patients and these doctors have acted within the law and according to their professional judgment' (para. 12). These two crucial paragraphs were descriptive and avoided explicit condemnation of the doctors. The existence of this small group—Schur in a study three years earlier had referred to 13 doctors[4]—was well known. They were the 'junkies' doctors'. Yet readers were left to draw their own conclusions from the fact that one doctor had prescribed six kilogrammes of heroin (600 000 tablets) in 1962 (para. 12). When this is mentioned today, even in audiences of well-informed people, there are always gasps of horror. Why?

Because it provided no context for its observations, such implicit condemnation, and the sense of instinctive horror that still follows it, occurred in a vacuum. It lacked the necessary background which was needed to interpret the situation in the formative years of the early 1960s. The writers of Brain did not provide that background, or help towards that interpretation. The truth is that, even allowing for its limited terms of reference, this was an odd and unhelpful document. So in paragraph 8 it is pointed out that the UK produced 36 kilogrammes of heroin in 1962 and consumed 40 kilogrammes, while in 1964 it produced 55 and consumed 50. 'These figures', says the report, 'far exceed those of any other country'. But of course they did since most countries had banned heroin. There had in fact been an attempt to ban heroin in Britain in 1955 which had been defeated by overwhelming opposition from the medical profession. In countries where heroin was not legal, the figures of addicts were often far higher: over 18 000 in Hong Kong, 150 000 in Canada, and 350 000 in the USA. To claim that figures for manufacture and consumption of legal heroin are greater in a country where heroin is legal than in countries where it is not is little short of tautology. Yet if readers were to consult Appendix II of the report, they would find that production of heroin actually declined from 68 kilogrammes in 1959 to 66 in 1960, rising to 69 in 1961, while consumption increased from 45 in 1959 to 50 in 1964. Yet addicts of heroin increased from 68 in 1959 to 342 in 1964. So on the basis of these figures 342 addicts in 1964 consumed only 5 kilogrammes more than did the 68 addicts some years earlier! (It should be pointed out also that the figures include heroin used medically in linctuses, ampoules and in terminal analgesics.) Brain did not analyse its data very well. In fact what was happening was not a sudden massive increase but the fact that addicts who had been around for some time were surfacing during these years.

So what do we make of the doctor mentioned in paragraph 12? If she—and it was a she!—prescribed six kilogrammes out of 40, and if there were only around six doctors prescribing for addicts to any significant degree at the time, one-seventh of the total seems fairly reasonable, in fact the kind of figure one would expect.

A PERSONAL NOTE

I had been ordained priest on 13 June 1965, five months before Brain. As a curate in Hoxton, a district between London's East End and Islington, my first encounters with the London drug scene were from two directions. The first came through involvement in one of the early unattached youth work projects, the Hoxton Café Project, set up with the help of the probation service at Old Street. Many of the young people who frequented the café at 113 Hoxton Street were using drugs, mainly cannabis and amphetamines, their principal sources of supply being the cafés of Old Montague Street in the East End and the big Soho clubs such as 'The Scene' in Ham Yard, the 'Flamingo' and 'Discotheque' in Wardour Street, and the 'Roaring Twenties' in Carnaby Street. It was through these kids that I made my first contacts with Soho. The second direction from which a deep involvement grew was through the son of my churchwarden who was a heroin addict and later died of an overdose. Through close contact with this family I found myself in touch with most of the heroin addicts in East London, and with some of the doctors who supplied them.

SOME HISTORICAL BACKGROUND

Between 1936 and 1953 the number of known drug addicts in the UK fell from 616 to 290, rising to 454 in 1960. The Soho district of London was important in the beginning of the change. In 1950 a raid on 'Club Eleven' in Soho produced supplies of cannabis, cocaine, opium and empty morphine ampoules. Between 1951 and 1964, 63 new addicts came to notice who were all linked with one Soho addict identified in 1951.[5] Moreover, the origin of addiction had changed. Between 1954 and 1964 there were only 14 new 'therapeutic' addicts contrasted with 436 of non-therapeutic origin. Yet the numbers of heroin addicts were still very small. In 1958 there were 442 addicts of whom 62 were using heroin, and by 1959 this had grown to 454 of whom 68 were using heroin. It was as a result of this increase that the first Brain Committee was convened in 1958. It reported to the Minister in November 1960, and the report was published in April 1961. Its conclusions have become part of drug abuse archaeology.

> After careful consideration of all the data put before us we are of the opinion that in Great Britain the incidence of addiction to dangerous drugs is still very small. . . There is nevertheless in our opinion no cause to fear that any real increase is at present occurring.[6]

The journal *Time and Tide* called it a 'smug and misleading report'.[7] Yet in 1965 the distinguished physician Henry Matthew was to defend its conclusion as the only possible one that the committee could have reached on the basis of the evidence before it.[8] If this is so, they cannot have seen much evidence. Not only was there clear evidence of an increase in heroin addiction during the years in which they were sitting, but the increase was occurring in the younger age group. In 1959 only 50 of the 454 addicts (11 per cent) were aged under 34. By 1961 297 of the 753 addicts (40 per cent) were in this age group. Most of them, and all those under 20, were addicted to heroin. In 1960 the first addict under the age of 20 appeared on the Home Office files. The number of addicts under 20 grew to two in 1961, three in 1962, 17 in 1963, 40 in 1964 and 145 in 1965.

It was this increase which led to the re-convening of the committee in 1964. In that year the Home Office noted a 'marked increase in the number of persons addicted to diacetylmorphine especially in the younger age groups'.[9] It was during these years that the 'junkies' doctors' became known. Although the 1965 report led many to assume that they were a uniformly mischievous and irresponsible group, this was not the view of those who knew the scene well. The Chief Inspector of the Home Office Drugs Branch, for example, spoke of them as 'dedicated practitioners' whose 'motives were unimpeachable',[10] while William Deedes spoke warmly of them in a Commons debate in 1968.[11] I knew most of them, and they were a mixed bunch, including two who were senile and one who was extremely dangerous. But the largest single group were very committed physicians whose only crime was that they were prepared to accept as patients a section of the community whom most doctors would not touch. They functioned in a vacuum of medical care. As one of them complained in his response to Brain: 'the problem is not to be understood or solved by hasty blame on those who are doing most of the work'.[12] For it was this small group of doctors who were maintaining the American-termed 'British system', a system which made virtually no provision for care or treatment. As a consultant wrote to one of the doctors: 'As you know, no facilities for the treatment of these cases exists'.[13]

THE SPREAD TO THE EAST END

In 1966 David Downes published the results of his research into East End delinquent subcultures. He reported that there was 'no evidence at all. . . to suggest the existence of an adolescent retreatist subculture'[14] though he noted something approaching it among the habitués of the Cable Street café quarter, and its extensions into Brick Lane and Old Montague

Street. But Downes saw East End delinquency as very different from the drug culture. He wrote:

> There is probably more change of the middle class adolescent jazz enthusiast coming into contact with the genuine retreatist culture, and indulging in marginal addictive practices such as ether or gasoline sniffing—or smoking an experimental 'reefer'—than there is of the working class adolescent 'double failure' taking to drug use. The current retreatist pattern in this country is sophisticated, 'hip' and upper class or middle class or 'student' class rather than connected with working class subcultural delinquency, though this is not to deny the probability of the drug cult spreading down the socio-economic scale.[15]

In fact this is precisely what began to happen after 1966. Most of the East End addicts who were observed between 1966 and 1970 were in social classes 4 and 5, and virtually all of them were from white working-class backgrounds.

Before the early 1960s heroin had been almost unknown in the café society of the East End. Frances Tucker, 'the Queen of Indian hemp', had been a popular figure in Cable Street where there had been a flourishing traffic in cannabis as early as the 1940s. But during 1966 and 1967 more addicts with addresses in the E1 and E2 postal districts appeared. Most of them were white, though in 1962 a curious event occurred which was to have repercussions on the East End drug culture. In that year Parkash Mara Ram arrived from India and settled in the Spitalfields district. He had been addicted for 18 years to poppy heads which have a low morphine content. Through a temporary misreading of the regulations he was unable to obtain them and turned to heroin instead. He died in 1965 but not before he had infected a small group of Indian and Pakistani men in the East End of London.[16] Ram lived in Princelet Street, E1, which at the 1961 Census had the highest concentration of Asian-born people in the whole of East London. Nevertheless, while the Asian community was to grow in the E1 district, particularly after the emergence of Bangladesh, the majority of heroin users in the East End remained white working-class males.

It is important to note the contrast with the pattern of drug

use in the American urban areas. In the USA heroin use in the
1960s was heavily concentrated in the ghetto districts, and the
vast majority of users were blacks and Puerto Ricans. 1970
was described by Dr David Smith, founder of the Haight-
Ashbury Free Clinic in San Francisco, as 'the year of the
middle class junkie', a theme which was then taken up by
Newsweek.[17] The American history is thus the reverse of that
in Britain where addiction began among the middle classes
and later spread into the inner urban areas and among the
poor, mainly the white poor. But this is to anticipate
developments which did not occur on a large scale until much
later. However, during 1966 and 1967 the increase in the
numbers of young heroin addicts continued, rising from 899
in 1966 to 1299 in 1967, a 44 per cent increase. There were
three aged 15, 38 aged 16, 82 aged 17, and 100 aged 18.
Another development at this time was the 'significant increase
in the number of addicts who have obtained their drugs
entirely from unknown sources'.[18] These words from the
Home Office report to the UN for 1965 led me to write to *The
Times* a year after the publication of Brain, and this letter,
which was given first place, sums up the situation as we saw
it from the East End of London at that time. In this letter I
pointed to three areas in which changes had occurred in the
year since the report.

> First, the widespread reluctance and refusal of GPs
> throughout London to prescribe heroin and cocaine, even
> under carefully controlled conditions, coupled with the
> opting-out of several well-known doctors, has led to a
> worsening state of affairs.
> The small group of 'junkies' doctors', whose names and
> addresses are known to everyone working in the field, have
> inherited a situation which is now beyond control. While
> some medical sources have dried up, others have exploited
> the situation.
> Secondly, it was inevitable that, given the post-Brain
> situation, the black market would develop. The latest report
> from the Home Office to the United Nations comments
> (paragraph 37) on the 'significant increase. . . in the num-
> bers of addicts who have obtained their drugs entirely from
> unknown sources'. The same report insists that 'the illicit

traffic in narcotics...is not extensive in the United Kingdom', but how long will this remain the case?

The patients in the Salter Unit at Cane Hill Hospital, in their critique of Brain, warned that 'there is already in the wings, waiting its opportunity, the efficient and well-tried Mafia organisation, eager to exploit a situation in which heroin is difficult to obtain'. There is no doubt that criminals have already moved into the black market in drugs, and many experts warn of the likelihood of professional syndicates on American lines trying to take over the controls.

Thirdly, while the relative absence of any 'drug subculture' is a characteristic of the English scene most frequently seized upon, this is becoming less true every day. The underworld is spreading to embrace kids on the 'pot and pills' fringe, spreading into new areas geographically, spreading socially and economically through sections of working-class urban delinquency.

The situation can be exaggerated and distorted, but it is serious enough. What is to be feared is that official reaction will be repressive and negative. So far the results of the Brain Report have been almost entirely negative and bad. Since Brain, the situation has got worse, not better. And perhaps most frightening of all is the fact that many of our best workers in the areas of infection are coming to feel that they are banging their heads against a brick wall. Paralysis, like addiction itself, spreads like a cancer and destroys.

I expanded the points in the letter in an article in the *Daily Telegraph* several weeks later.[19] Looking back on that letter and article almost a quarter of a century later, I would not wish to alter anything in them. Every detail has proved to be correct. But six months later an event was to take place which was to change the course of the heroin scene in Britain.

FROM LADY FRANKAU TO DR HAWES

It was well known within drug circles that the doctor referred to in Brain as having prescribed six kilogrammes of heroin was Lady Isabella Frankau of Wimpole Street. Lady Frankau had started to treat some heroin addicts in 1957, and in 1960–61 their numbers were augmented by the arrival of a group of addicts from Canada.[20] Lady Frankau saw herself as one of Britain's leading authorities on addiction, and wrote a number of articles in the medical journals.[21] In one of these she described her addicts as immature, inadequate and unstable. 'They were completely self-centred and selfish, and showed little emotion except over their own problems'.[22] By the mid-1960s Lady Frankau was legendary within the London heroin world over which she exercised considerable control. However, during 1967 she was ill, and in May she died, not having warned the Ministry of Health of her intention. Her death threw the heroin market into a state of confusion and led to the crisis which was within a year to see both new legislation and the beginnings of the treatment centres.

During the last year of Lady Frankau's life, two other doctors figured prominently in London heroin circles. One was Dr Geoffrey Dymond of New King's Road, Fulham. During 1966 Dymond prescribed for between 80 and 120 addicts, including the hard core of the East End group. In addition to his practice, he was also a police doctor. In November 1966 he announced that he was giving up seeing addicts, denying that there had been any pressure from Scotland Yard—as many addicts believed.[23] The crisis of supply created by the withdrawal of Dymond led to headlines such as 'Young drug addicts beg for "fix" at Home Office'[24] and 'Two ministries refuse help to drug addicts'.[25]

It was at this point that Dr A. J. Hawes of Fitzroy Square brought the position of the street addict into the area of public controversy. Hawes was an old man who had been treating addicts on the NHS for many years. He was a kindly eccentric who presided over an extraordinary surgery close to the Post Office Tower. He must have been the last doctor in London to employ his own pharmacist, his sister, on the premises. Hawes had seen around 1000 addicts in 10 years, and had kept detailed notes of the first 300.[26] He was a prolific writer to the press, and a letter of 1965 put the position well.

... the black market in these drugs is fed by over-prescribing doctors. I may be one of these myself, although I do my best not to be. There is no other source of supply beyond an occasional and negligible robbery at a chemist's shop. To cut off the supply by prescription would be easy; it has been done in the United States where doctors are not allowed to prescribe for addicts, with the result that the provision of drugs has become a flourishing industry and drug addiction there increases yearly. So we arrive at the curious anomaly that if we are to keep big business off the black market trade in drugs, we need a number of over-credulous, over-sympathetic, over-prescribing doctors unless we want to run the serious risk of having thousands of addicts on our hands instead of the few hundreds we have at present.[27]

Immediately after the withdrawal of Dymond, Hawes wrote a letter to *The Times* in which he issued a solemn warning of trouble ahead:

One of the prominent 'junkies' doctors' has just thrown up his addicts' practice in the past few days. I cannot blame him, but the result has been to throw about 80 heroin and cocaine addicts on to the open market which usually means the black market. . . In the past 48 hours I have had 10 new applicants for supplies whom I have had to turn away from my door—most regretfully. . . .

The most threatening portent is that addicts are telling me that there is plenty of the stuff to be had on the black market even though the source from overprescribing doctors is drying up. It looks as if big business which has been waiting in the wings for so long has now taken over the stage and is playing the lead. So we may look for an explosion in the teenage addict population as the months go by.[28]

These two letters are extremely significant and prophetic. In 1965 Hawes was warning of the consequences of a prohibitive American-style approach; in 1966, in what must be one of the first public claims for the existence of illicit heroin, he was suggesting that his earlier prediction had begun to come true.

It was after Frankau's death that Hawes' correspondence took a different turn. On 31 May he wrote to the Minister of

Health, Kenneth Robinson, inquiring about treatment facilities in the light of the disappearance of two of the main sources of supply and support for addicts. On 22 June the Ministry replied, listing nine hospitals which had 'already established out-patient facilities' and claiming that 'plans for further units' were under discussion.

The Ministry official added these words: . . . you will appreciate that until hospital facilities are available generally in London, it would be premature and unhelpful to addicts as a whole to give any publicity to the units concerned'.[29]

At once Hawes wrote to the hospitals mentioned, asking them to describe their facilities, and within a few days replies began to arrive. They were, to say the least, extraordinary. Virtually all of them denied that they had facilities other than the normal provisions of casualty departments and general psychiatric wards. Several suggested that the information given by the Ministry had been mistaken (see Appendix). One hospital clinic was run by a well-known 'junkies' doctor', one of the group cited in Brain and a vocal critic of its recommendations. Another hospital, to which Hawes had sent an addict, returned her on the grounds that 'the hospital does not at the moment usually treat drug addicts'. University College Hospital, which had sent a circular letter to all doctors on 7 July announcing the opening of its clinic, swiftly sent a follow-up letter pointing out that it could only admit 12 patients and only from the NW1 and WC1 districts![30]

By August 1967, the only NHS doctors treating significant numbers of addicts in London were Peter Chapple and Geoffrey Gray at the Chelsea Addiction Centre in Beaufort Street, Hawes, and a young doctor called Ian Dunbar who operated from Fulham and later from Notting Hill (where he set up a hippy medical practice with Dr Sam Hutt, later to be known in the music world as Hank Wangford.) But by now another figure had entered the London heroin world whose role was to be dramatic and devastating.

THE ARRIVAL OF 'DR JOHN'

It was in the spring of 1967 that the strange figure of John Petro began to appear around Soho. John Petro, originally

Piotrkowski, had come to England from Poland at the age of
11. He studied at Cambridge and at St George's Hospital
Medical School. He qualified in 1929 and was one of the first
doctors to administer penicillin in 1945. He was in general
practice with his brother in West London until the 1950s. The
Duke of Argyle is said to have regarded him as 'the most able
diagnostician in London'. But by the 1960s he had fallen on
evil days and was declared bankrupt.

Heroin addicts in London became aware of Petro's presence
in the weeks before Lady Frankau died. One explanation of
his appearance was that Lady Frankau's husband, Sir Claude,
had been his superior at St George's and had asked him to
help cope with the patients. An alternative version, common
in Soho at the time, was that he had met some Canadian
addicts in the 'Golden Nugget' casino in Shaftesbury Avenue,
and had become involved through them. Petro was a late
arrival on the scene, almost two years after the Brain Report.[31]
Soon he was to become the most notorious of the 'junkies'
doctors', although his name is missing from most books on
heroin addiction in the UK. The national press took a few
months to notice him, but on 7 July there were front page
headlines in two papers: 'Doctor holds drugs clinic in a cafe'
and 'Drugs clinic in station buffet'.[32] Petro at this time lived
in various West End hotels and ran his 'surgery' from the
buffet at Baker Street Station. Later he transferred his base to
Piccadilly Circus where he used the all-night 'Friar Tuck'
coffee bar in Coventry Street and Playland amusement arcade
which was directly opposite.

But Petro did not keep his Dangerous Drugs register up to
date, often writing the details of drugs prescribed on the back
of a cigarette packet. For a while, he 'employed' a local
stripper as a 'receptionist', but towards the end of 1967 she
was arrested and spent some time in Holloway Prison. This
gave the Drugs Squad their opportunity, and on 11 January
1968 Petro himself was arrested by Detective Sergeant David
Patrick after appearing on the David Frost TV programme. He
was charged with inaccuracies in his records. He was
remanded on bail at Marylebone Court on 12 January, and in
February he was fined £1700. He continued to prescribe, based
now at Tramway Avenue in Stratford. On 30 and 31 May 1968
the Disciplinary Committee of the General Medical Council

ordered him to be struck off the medical register, but he appealed against the decision, continuing to prescribe in the meantime. 'Struck off but still runs practice', announced the *People* on 18 August. Petro had by this time switched from heroin to methylamphetamine (methedrine). Eventually he was struck off the register on 30 October 1968, and this was confirmed by the Judicial Committee of the Privy Council on 4 December.

Soon the name of John Petro began to disappear from the pages of the national press. On 3 February 1969 the *Daily Sketch* reported that he was living on £8 a week dole money, and on 11 November the *Daily Telegraph* observed him giving injections to addicts at Piccadilly. These were probably the last references to him in any national newspaper until he died in February 1981. Petro was unique among the junkies' doctors in that he shared the life of the street addict to a high degree. As one clinic doctor commented, 'his committal to the life style was as great as any user in the clinic'.[33] He symbolised the breakdown of the 'British system' and embodied in his own tragic person its collapse.

'THE STRANGE CASE OF THE MISSING TREATMENT CENTRES'

Petro, like his predecessors, filled a vacuum in British drug policy: the virtual absence of treatment facilities. The Second Brain Report, in paragraph 22, had recommended the establishment of treatment centres 'as soon as possible', but, as Hawes's correspondence and the daily experience of workers had shown, these centres were more fictitious than real. The *Sunday Times* in 1966 contrasted 'the official double talk' with the 'daily realities of treatment'.[34] For during the period from 1966 to 1968 the Ministry of Health maintained a continuous rhetoric of claims about treatment which everyone in the field, including the Home Office Drugs Branch, knew to be absurd. As early as 3 July 1966 Kenneth Robinson said in the House of Commons: 'I am satisfied and I have already made it clear that we shall not bring in the regulations prohibiting prescription by general practitioners for addicts until we are satisfied that the hospital facilities are adequate'.[35] On 2 August he claimed that 'there are already centres for the treatment of addicts and more beds could be made available if the demand increases'.[36] However, Ministry officials, when challenged, were quick to point out that in this statement 'the Minister was not referring to any action that had been taken following the second report of the Brain Committee'.[37] No action in relation to treatment had been taken.

The following April, a month before Lady Frankau's death, Robinson said that he was satisfied that facilities were adequate,[38] and on 3 July he told the House of Commons: 'In-patient services for heroin addicts are available in all, and out-patient services in twelve, regional hospital boards. The need for expansion of services is being kept under review'.[39]

A few weeks earlier, on 20 June 1967, there had been a debate in the Lords on the Dangerous Drugs Bill. During this debate, Lord Stonham claimed that the Bill would 'help considerably in containing the general problem and bringing compassionate but real help to those who need it'. He pointed out that 'addicts are free at any time to seek treatment' though he wisely did not say where. He went on: 'I will leave it to my noble friend Lady Phillips to describe in more detail when she comes to wind up the debate our plans for a system of special treatment centres for addicts to heroin and cocaine'. But all that Lady Phillips could say was: 'I was asked to tell the House something about the treatment centres. I am not certain at this stage that it would be something your lordships would particularly want to know'.[40] Later, on 5 July, she apologised for her omission, which, she claimed, had 'almost brought down the government'. She explained that 'it seemed to me that noble Lords in the house at that time would perhaps prefer to go and have their tea'. Lady Phillips went on to claim that there were 'now in operation eleven out-patients clinics in London and plans for other centres are under urgent discussion'.[41] Nobody was ever able to discover where these 'clinics' were. They must have had some relation to the 'out-patient treatment facilities' mentioned in the Ministry's letter, most of which were non-existent. It was, ironically, two days after Lady Phillips' claim that the press discovered one actually existing 'clinic'—that run by Petro at Baker Street Station!

On 16 July 1967 the *Sunday Times* in a feature entitled 'The strange case of the missing treatment centres' quoted the replies to Hawes. The Ministry was clearly very angry about this. They had only given the names of the hospitals under pressure and did not really want anyone to know where the 'clinics' were. A few days later Lord Beswick told the Lords that it would be premature and against the interests of addicts generally to publicise the names of the hospitals with facilities.[42] Yet the numbers game continued. On 25 July Robinson claimed that there were 10 hospitals with in-patient, and 13 with out-patient facilities.[43] The *Sunday Times* continued to be unimpressed by these claims, and on 10 October 1967 Alex Mitchell wrote another report on the missing centres.

The debate rumbled on into 1968. On 15 January Peter Gladstone Smith, writing in the *Daily Telegraph*, claimed that there were plans for a hundred clinics or 'special treatment centres'. On the same day *The Times* quoted me as saying that the centres were a 'figment of the Ministry's imagination'. The Ministry line remained the same: 'It is not the Minister's policy to disclose to the public the names of the clinics providing treatment, but the names are known to the GPs who are concerned in the treatment of drug addicts'.[44] Those GPs, by now a very small group indeed, knew perfectly well that the claims were spurious, and Hawes, to the Ministry's embarrassment, continued to say so on every possible occasion. *The Times*, which had a series of letters from Hawes and myself, and which had sent two of its reporters, Ronald Faux and Stephen Jessel, to cover the realities of the drug scene, had also come to the conclusion that the Ministry's claims needed correction. A leader on 23 January entitled 'Too few drug centres' pointed out that those clinics which did exist were hopelessly overburdened and warned of the growing illicit market in heroin. Two days later this paper published a report by Stephen Jessel which pointed out that:

> claims made by the Ministry of Health concerning the effectiveness of centres established at London hospitals for the treatment of addicts have been greeted with amazement by some doctors and social workers in regular contact with addicts.[45]

On 30 January, Robinson gave a slightly fuller list of out-patient facilities, claiming that there were 15 of them,[46] and on 12 February he responded to his critic for the first time on television. Speaking on 'World in Action' on Granada TV, Robinson said:

> Now we have been criticised particularly by some of the voluntary bodies who are working in this field and I recognise that they are trying to help in this very difficult and intractable problem. I only wish that they found it possible to call attention to their own efforts without constantly denigrating the efforts of others, particularly the efforts of the government, and I would have thought that at least the reverend gentlemen that are associated with these bodies would have heard of the injunction to do good by stealth.[47]

(One assumes from his final comment that he thought the injunction was in the Bible!). Alex Mitchell on the following Sunday insisted that the clinics were 'just a myth'.[48] Robinson continued to attack the voluntary organisations. In May he said that while public comment was 'becoming more informed and responsible', there had been some exceptions. He complained of 'certain newspapers' and of 'a few people concerned with the addiction problem in a mainly voluntary capacity'. These people had been guilty of a 'consistent campaign of denigration' and 'when the facilities were established they denied their existence'.[49] The 'few people' he had in mind were clearly our group at St Anne's Church in Soho.

SCENE W1: THE VIEW FROM ST ANNE'S SOHO IN 1968

During the period from Frankau's death to the coming into operation of the new regulations in 1968, we were in a strong position, from St Anne's Church in Soho, to view what was happening at ground level to heroin addicts, and to test the Ministry's claims against the reality.

During 1967 and 1968 we witnessed not only a growth of the Soho drug scene but also significant changes within it. The

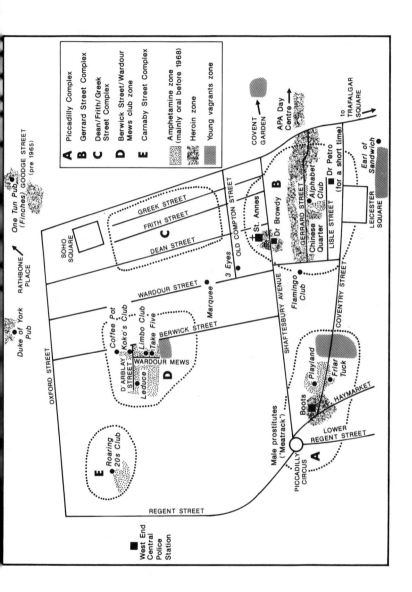

FIGURE 3.1   *The geography of the Soho drug culture c. 1968*

influx of 'flower children' into the pseudo-psychedelic world of Carnaby Street during the 'summer of love', the increase in the numbers of small coffee clubs, and the role of Piccadilly as a gathering place for a wide range of young people all meant that the population of young people in Soho increased during these years. There was a relatively short phase of LSD use during 1967. The traffic in amphetamines, which had begun in 1963 in the big discotheques, had moved more into the small clubs where the hard core of the 'pillheads' gathered. These clubs were heavily concentrated in the northern part of Soho, in the district around Berwick Street and Wardour Mews. At the 'Dilly' itself, while the Haymarket exit, where the all-night Boots' chemist was located, remained the 'junkies' corner', there were two other main groupings. These were the 'rent boys', homosexual prostitutes, who congregated at the corner of Regent Street by a stretch of railing known as the 'meat rack'; and the young drifters who met in the 'Friar Tuck' café in Coventry Street. Across the road was Playland amusement arcade which was to become a focal point for the convergence of the various groups. Nearby in the Chinese quarter of Gerrard Street was the notorious 'Alphabet Club', another centre for amphetamine users.

During this period we saw also a massive increase in the numbers of homeless young people from the north and from Scotland. It was this which led to the founding of the Centrepoint all-night shelter at the end of 1969. These young people were new to the West End, and their numbers augmented the already large numbers of Soho regulars and kids on the periphery of drug abuse.[50]

These years saw the coming together of previously distinct groups. There were many factors involved in this process, but one crucial factor was the spread of the needle culture. Before 1967 there were broadly two groups of drug takers in Soho: the junkies around Piccadilly, and the pill takers in the clubs. There was little contact between them. However, in the period between the Brain Report and the regulations of 1968, the needle culture began to spread to embrace young people within the pill scene. The crucial year was 1968 when two doctors, John Petro and Christopher Swan, unable now to prescribe heroin, began to prescribe massive amounts of methylamphetamine hydrochloride (methedrine). A government report observed that two doctors were 'responsible for virtually all of the injectible methylamphetamine misused at that time'. One doctor prescribed, in one month, 24 000 ampoules of 30 mg methylamphetamine to 100 patients.[51] The two doctors were Petro and Swan. Swan had opened his East London Addiction Centre in Queensbridge Road, Hackney, in April 1968, though his activities had begun earlier. 'He's taken over from Dr Petro' announced the *People* on 15 February. Swan was arrested in June 1968 and in January 1969 he was sentenced to 15 years imprisonment.

It was methedrine which changed the character of the Soho drug scene. It made the needle far more acceptable. It united amphetamine and opiate users. After 1968 the phenomenon of 'fixing' became an integral part of the lives of many young people. 1968 was a crucial year, the year of the needle. In that year there was a 61 per cent increase in the numbers of known addicts, a 72 per cent increase in the numbers of heroin addicts, and a 93 per cent increase in the numbers of addicts under 20. By 1968, 79 per cent of all addicts were under 25.

Soon there were reports of illicit manufacture of amphetamine.[52] But almost all of the amphetamine circulating in Soho was manufactured by Smith, Kline and French or Burroughs Wellcome. What was new was the appearance of illicit powder heroin. There had been claims that the Mafia were becoming involved as early as June 1967,[53] but this was not what happened. On 27 June another letter from Dr Hawes appeared in *The Times*. Referring back to his earlier warning of November 1966, Hawes wrote:

During the past few weeks I hear from my heroin addicts that the drug is now appearing on the black market in powder form, which has never been available before. Tablets have always been the form of the drug in this country. It looks as if my dismal prophecy of large-scale heroin merchants waiting their opportunity of a shortage in the black market which has been fed up to now by wicked over-prescribing 'junkie doctors' has come to pass. . . The next few months are going to be very interesting. The Ministry of Health does not seem to understand the implications of what they are doing. Nevertheless they soon will.[54]

On 26 March 1969 *The Times* reported that illicit powder heroin had been discovered in Britain for the first time. The reporter ironically was Norman Fowler who, 20 years later, was to be a minister in the government, responsible for picking up the pieces of the events of this period. The source of the heroin was not the Mafia of New York but the Triads of Hong Kong.

There had been no evidence of illicit heroin in Britain between 1958 and 1967. The increase was directly related to the new regulations of 1968. As supplies of legal heroin declined, so the illicit market escalated. Angela Burr has claimed that the distribution of Chinese heroin in Soho ran parallel with the prescribing of injectible heroin,[55] but she ignores the crucial dates. It was during the period that prescribed heroin became less available, and during the period of restriction, that the market in powder developed. During 1969 and 1970 the Triads moved into Gerrard Street. Since then, the heroin market has been dominated by Hong Kong (1970), Iran (after 1979) and Pakistan (after 1980).

For a time there was complacency. It seemed as if the epidemic had reached its peak and had subsided. The *Evening Standard* devoted an entire page to an article entitled 'How we beat heroin' in 1973.[56] The events since then are well known and well documented. The increase in illicit heroin has led to 'a fundamental change in the character of the British opiate black market'.[57] In the urban areas heroin addiction has become increasingly correlated with unemployment. In Merseyside in 1985 Parker found that 80 per cent of addicts were unemployed.[58] The seriousness of the problem could not have been predicted by even the most pessimistic observers of the 1960s.

A DEVOUT MEDITATION ON THE OSTRICH

The ostrich, it is said, puts it head firmly in the sand. It has also been seen to flap its wings in an apparent state of agitation, to spar with its mate or with other birds. Eventually it lays an egg. It is possible to see the history of the last 25 years of responses to drug abuse in terms of the life phases of the ostrich, though the phases overlap and there are always some who are still at the first stage.

'Heads in the sand' was an appropriate description both of the first Brain Committee and of the general atmosphere at this time. For years the Ministry of Health seemed to work on the assumption that, while the wicked, over-prescribing doctors were responsible for 'the problem', they would continue to maintain the system until the Ministry was ready with its treatment centres, and would then gracefully withdraw. The degree of incomprehension of what was actually happening on the ground, and the damage which was done during this period, are difficult to exaggerate. Much of the subsequent chaos might have been avoided had there been more recognition of the existence of a heroin problem in its early stages.

The flapping of wings has never really stopped. The period is filled with hypermanic people and movements, wild claims repeated from decade to decade as if nothing had happened in between. No issue seems to have attracted hysterical crusaders so much as that of drug abuse. Today the media focuses on 'crack'. The drug has changed; the inaccuracy, the ignorance, the hysteria remain the same. The sparring phase comes and goes, but its casualties remain. It is known in the USA and Britain as 'the war on drugs'. No war in history has so conspicuously failed to achieve its object. The recent history of drug abuse management in the USA is a history of policy failure. Yet Britain, in this as in other areas of social policy, has imitated the USA at the precise point at which its policy has been a disaster—and with the inevitable consequences. As Arnold Trebach has said, American-style tactics reap American-style 'benefits'.[59]

The egg was laid in 1968 with the establishment of a whole range of more or less permanent units and institutes for the further study of this phenomenon. Drug abuse became an industry, highly profitable. But while research proliferated, care and treatment remained at a minimal level. This has been the story of British drug 'policy': a combination of negligence, hysteria and warfare on the one hand, and of research and data collection on the other. But the accumulation of data in itself does not lead to change. And the real danger at present is that the kid at street level gets forgotten in the vast mushrooming of problem-centred activity. As I stand today on the corner of Brick Lane and Hanbury Street, a hundred yards from my office, I have an acute sense of *déjà vue*. I was here in 1965. But now it is young Bengalis, in revolt against their parents, who are showing signs of involvement in a new drug subculture in the same streets where Downes, in the early 1960s, had identified the possible beginnings of a retreatist subculture in the East End. The junkies' doctors are long gone, and the criminal syndicates are in control. The course was predictable and was indeed predicted. The tragedy is that the warnings were not heeded, and we have as a result reaped the whirlwind.

REFERENCES

1.   Kramer, John C., in D. E. Smith and G. R. Gay (eds), *It's So Good, Don't Even Try It Once: Perspectives on Heroin* (Englewood Cliffs, NJ: Prentice-Hall, 1952) p. 43.
2.   House of Commons, 7 May 1968, col. 156.
3.   *Drug Addiction*, Second Report of the Interdepartmental Committee (HMSO, 1956) para. 40.
4.   Schur, E. M., *Narcotic Addiction in Britain and America: the Impact of Public Policy* (Tavistock: 1962).
5.   Spear, H. B., 'The Growth of Heroin Addiction in the UK', *British Journal of Addiction*, 64 (1969) pp. 245–55.
6.   *Drug Addiction*, Report of the Interdepartmental Committee (HMSO, 1961) para. 24.
7.   *Time and Tide*, 15 June 1961.
8.   Matthew, Henry, in *British Journal of Addiction*, 61 (1966) p. 171.
9.   *Report of the UN* (1964) para. 40.
10.   Jeffery, C. G., cited in M. M. Glatt and J. Marks (eds), *The Dependence Phenomenon* (Lancaster: MTP Press, 1982) p. 57, H.B.
11.   House of Commons, 7 May 1968, col. 156.
12.   A physician, 'Narcotic Addiction and the Brain Committee Report', *Anarchy*, 60 (Feb. 1966) p. 38.
13.   Cited ibid p. 35.
14.   Downes, David M., *The Delinquent Solution* (Routledge, 1966) p. 215.
15.   Ibid p. 135.
16.   *East London Advertiser*, 11 June 1965. For the wider background see K. Leech, 'The East London Drug Traffic', *Social Work*, 24 (2) (Apr. 1966) pp. 23–7.
17.   Bentel, David J., and David E. Smith, 'The Year of the Middle Class Junkie', *California's Health*, April 1971, pp. 1–5; *Newsweek*, 5 July 1971.
18.   *The Times*, 9 Nov. 1966.
19.   Leech, Kenneth, 'Danger on the Drug Scene', *Daily Telegraph*, 8 Dec. 1966.

20. Spear, H. B., and M. M. Glatt, 'The Influence of Canadian Addicts on Heroin Addiction in the UK', *British Journal of Addiction*, 66 (1971) pp. 141–9.
21. Frankau, I. M., and P. M. Stanwell, 'The Treatment of Drug Addiction', *Lancet*, 24 December 1960, pp. 1377–9; I. M. Frankau, 'Treatment in England of Canadian Patients Addicted to Narcotic Drugs', *Canadian Medical Association Journal*, 90 (8 Feb. 1964) pp. 421–4.
22. Frankau and Stanwell, op. cit.
23. The *Sun*, 11 Nov. 1966.
24. *Daily Mail*, ibid.
25. The *Guardian*, 19 Nov. 1966.
26. Hawes, A. J., 'Goodbye Junkies', *The Lancet*, 1 Aug. 1970, pp. 258–60.
27. The *Observer*, 12 Sept. 1965.
28. *The Times*, 15 Nov. 1966.
29. Moyes, K. J., to A. J. Hawes, 22 June 1967.
30. Circular letters from Inner London Executive Council, 7 and 18 July 1967.
31. Tripp, Margaret, 'Who speaks for Petro?', *Drugs and Society*, 3 (2) (November 1973) pp. 12–17. On Petro see K. Leech, 'John Petro, the Junkies' Doctor', *New Society*, 11 June 1981, pp. 430–2.
32. *Daily Mail and the Sun*, 7 July 1967.
33. Tripp, op. cit., p. 17.
34. 'Narcotics and Bureaucracy', *Sunday Times*, 20 Nov. 1966.
35. House of Commons, 3 July 1966, col. 1239.
36. *The Times*, 3 Aug. 1966.
37. Smith, B. A. R., to K. Leech, 19 Aug. 1966.
38. *The Times*, 26 April 1967.
39. House of Lords, 20 June 1967, cols 1271–5.
40. Ibid col. 1316.
41. Ibid, 5 July 1967, cols 720–753.
42. Ibid, 19 July 1967, written answer.
43. House of Commons, 25 July 1967.
44. *The Times*, 15 Jan. 1968.
45. Jessel, Stephen, 'Measures Urged to Fight Drugs', ibid., 25 Jan. 1968.
46. House of Commons, 30 Jan. 1968, cols 260–1.
47. 'World in Action', Granada TV, 12 Feb. 1968.
48. Mitchell, Alex, 'Minister's Addict Clinics are just a Myth', *Sunday Times*, 18 Feb. 1968.
49. House of Commons, 7 May 1968, col. 171.
50. For a more detailed account of the Soho youth culture in this period see K. Leech, *Keep the Faith Baby* (SPCK, 1973).
51. *The Amphetamines and Lysergic Acid Diethylamide (LSD)*, Report by the Advisory Committee on Drug Dependence, HMSO, 1970, para. 50.
52. For example, The *Guardian*, 9 July 1971.
53. 'Is Mafia on the Move?', *Evening Standard*, 2 June 1967.
54. *The Times*, 27 June 1967.
55. Burr, Angela, in *International Journal of Addictions*, 21 (1) (1986) p. 86.
56. Jenkins, Simon, 'How We Beat Heroin', *Evening Standard*, 3 Apr. 1973.
57. Spear, H. B., in Glatt and Marks, op. cit., p. 51.

58.   Parker, Howard, *et al. Drug Misuse in Wirral* (University of Liverpool: 1986); and 'Heroin and the Young', *New Society*, 24 Jan. 1986, pp. 142–3.
59.   Trebach, Arnold, 'Giving Addicts the Push Off', The *Guardian*, 3 Dec. 1986.

APPENDIX

The replies from hospitals to Dr A. J. Hawes in 1967

(1) *Westminster Hospital, 7 July 1967*:
The treatment centre for Drug Addicts is at present at the 'Day Hospital', 52 Vincent Square, SW1. It is open from 9.30 am to 4.30 pm Monday to Friday, but patients are asked to telephone to make an appointment. The Telephone No. is Victoria 1537.

Yours sincerely.
House Governor and Secretary.

(2) *Harold Wood Hospital, Harold Wood, Essex, 30 June 1967*:
In reply to your letter dated 27th June last, I am afraid there has been an error in the information given to you. To my knowledge, an Out Patient Treatment Centre in respect of Drug Addiction has not been established at this hospital.

Yours faithfully,
H. J. Sallis,
Hospital Secretary.

(3) *Whipps Cross Hospital, Leytonstone, Ell., 28 June 1967*:
We have no Out-Patient treatment centre for treatment of drug addicts at this Hospital, but have agreed to treat patients who are sent here. These patients will be treated by the Psychiatric Registrar. If you will telephone the Casualty Department if you have a drug addiction case they will deal with him or her.

   10 August 1967:
The hospital does not at the moment usually treat drug addicts as has been advertised recently and I am sending her back to you at the moment.

Christina F. Palton,
Psychiatric Registrar.

(4) *Hackney Hospital, London E9, 6 July 1967*:
Further to your letter of 27th June, the Out-Patient Treatment Centre for Drug Addicts at Hackney Hospital is in the process of being established and as soon as it becomes established I will write to you with full details as requested in your letter.

Group Secretary.

(5) *St Clement's Hospital, Bow Road, E3, 5 July 1967*:
You say that the Ministry of Health have informed you that we have established a treatment centre for drug addicts. This is still on the paper stage, and neither staff nor other provisions have been granted us. I am pleased, however, to hear that the Ministry consider this as a fact which suggests that we may receive the necessary requirements in the near future.

> Yours sincerely,
> John Denham,
> Medical Director.

(6) *North Middlesex Hospital, Silver Street, N18, 7 July 1967*:
I am replying to your letter, sent to the Secretary of this Hospital, concerning Drug Addiction. This hospital has been designated for the treatment of drug addiction, but we can only deal with patients who live within our catchment area. This area consists of Tottenham, Edmonton and the Enfield district.

> S. Bockner,
> Phsyician in Psychological
> Medicine

(7) *Oldchurch Hospital, Romford, Essex, 10 July 1967*:
I would confirm. . . that there is no established Out-Patient Treatment Centre for the treatment of Drug Addiction at this hospital. We have been selected as the hospital to which addicts who are in difficulties in this area are referred by their general practitioners, and in these circumstances emergency treatment only is given in the Casualty Department. Such patients are subsequently referred to Warley Hospital for psychiatric treatment.

> Yours sincerely,
> Hospital Secretary.

(8) *St Giles Hospital, SE5, 29 June 1967*:
Dr Ollendorf who holds an Out-Patient Evening Clinic at this hospital once a week is at present in America, and I suggest he writes you on his return.

> Yours faithfully,
> Hospital Secretary.

(9) *Lambeth Hospital, Brook Drive, SE11, 11 July 1967*:
. . . discussions are at present taking place about arrangements for extending the facilities at this hospital for the treatment and maintenance of heroin addicts. The position is that an out-patient clinic for the treatment and maintenance of heroin addicts was started at this hospital more than three years ago, and we now see about 90 new cases and have about 500 attendances of old cases each year. The clinic is run in conjunction with a general psychiatric clinic and is held on Friday afternoons between 2 pm and 4.30 pm. . .

> B. S. Dobb,
> Hospital Secretary.

4 Policing the Medical Profession: the Use of Tribunals

Philip Bean

After a period during which the General Practitioners seemed to be removing themselves from the day to day treatment of drug users they are now being brought back to prominence. The reasons are clear enough: the numbers of notified drug users are increasing and the Treatment Centres are unable to cope with the demands placed on them. Moreover, many treatment centres adopt a style ill-suited to meet such changes: most Centres appear to want to operate with high treatment thresholds, that is, using detailed clinical evaluations, backed by sophisticated laboratory tests, all conducted under an appointment system. Rarely do the Centres offer the more casual drop-in system preferred by many users. Hence users are turning again to the GPs or seeking assistance as private patients. (We can leave aside for these purposes questions about the ethics of charging fees for consultation and prescribing controlled drugs to persons who often have no regular income other than State Benefits. How are these users able to pay their fees? See also HMSO, 1982). There are other reasons of course: one is that the users are preferring the drugs prescribed by the GP's. In the 1970s the heavyweight narcotics were fashionable, such as methadone, diconal or palfriam. In the 1980s there was a shift to the benzodiazepenes. Users found methadone linctus difficult to inject, and they prefer temazepam mixed with alcohol.

The problems posed by this so-called 'unplanned development' are considerable. The Advisory Council in the Misuse of Drugs sets out 'four causes for concern'. First, it says many doctors currently working with problem drug-takers lack the specialised knowledge, training and expertise that are essential for working in this difficult area. Second, that drugs supplied to problem drug users may be diverted to the black market. Third, that these doctors are placed under considerable pressure to prescribe drugs to an influx of users who seek drugs from a physician who has acquired a reputation of being a 'prescriber'. And finally, few doctors have access to support staff, for example nurses, social workers and psychologists, including facilities for adequate assessment of the needs of the problem drug takers similar to those available to doctors working in some hospital-based clinics (ibid., p. 53). The consequence of these difficulties, says the Advisory Council, is the extent to which controlled drugs are prescribed injudiciously. Not only will that lead to an increase in the amount of legally manufactured drugs available in the illegal market, but it will encourage users away from the Treatment Centres (ibid., p. 53). Mechanisms are therefore needed to regulate and control these physicians; one such mechanism is the Tribunal system.

BACKGROUND TO THE TRIBUNALS

The history of Tribunals in Britain can be divided into three periods; from 1926 to 1961, when they were included in legislation but not used, from 1961 to 1971 when they were not included, and 1971 onwards when they were included and used.

The origins of these Tribunals lies with the Rolleston Committee which recommended that Tribunals be introduced to control overprescribing or injudicious prescribing as it is now called. Earlier Regulations from the Defence of the Realm Act and later under the 1920 Dangerous Drugs Act allowed the Home Secretary to withdraw authority from any physicians to possess and supply drugs if a conviction under these Regulations had been made against the doctor in the courts. The Rolleston Committee wanted to transfer these powers to a suitably qualified medical Tribunal comprised of five members plus a legal assessor. The Committee did not think the courts had the necessary expertise to deal with what they called 'weighty technical matters' (see also P. T. Bean, 1974). The Rolleston Committee argued thus:

We consider therefore that a Medical Tribunal constituted

on the lines suggested above would afford valuable assistance to the Home Office in ensuring that possession and
supply of the drugs by medical practitioners was restricted
to that required for legitimate medical purposes, and would
enable the Deparment to deal effectively, and in a manner
satisfactory to the medical profession, with a case in which
there are strong grounds for believing that a doctor was
administering drugs for illegitimate purposes to himself or
to others.   (HMSO, 1926)

Provisions for the establishment of such Tribunals were
made under Regulations under the 1926 Dangerous Drugs
Act. The Secretary of State could refer the case of a medical
practictioner if there was evidence that the practitioner was
'supplying, administering, or prescribing any of the drugs
either to or for any other persons otherwise than are required
for purposes of medical treatment' (HMSO, 1926, S.I.996).
These Regulations were at the centre of the Rolleston
Committee's views about safeguards needed for the supply of
controlled drugs. Having introduced the so-called British
system, or rather restated some of its objectives, and allowed
the medical profession to 'supply, administer or prescribe
drugs' to users, the Tribunals were there to censure injudicious medical prescribing. The Tribunals had powers to
'withdraw the authorisation of such practitioners to be in
possession of or to supply the drugs . . . ' Leaving aside the
tricky and unresolved question of what constituted 'the
medical treatment of users' the Tribunal system was a
workable safeguard. On 12 March 1927 two Tribunals had
been set up, one for England and Wales under the Chairmanship of Sir Humphrey Rolleston, the other for Scotland.
For reasons which are still not clear the procedures were
never invoked. H. B. Spear (1982) suggests there was a lack of
suitable cases for referral, with few recorded examples of
indiscriminate prescribing, during a period in which drug
abuse was not regarded as a serious problem (see P. T. Bean,
1974). My own suspicion is that the hand of the General
Medical Council will be seen to be at work here, for the
Tribunals would have controlled the profession's prescribing
activities, almost unheard of at that time. However, the
provisions remained until 1953 when they were omitted

pending agreement with the medical profession about new rules of procedure. This coincided with the deliberation of the Franks Committee, hence long delays occurred before the machinery was reintroduced (HMSO, 1957).

Then came the first Brain Committee report in 1961 (HMSO, 1961). This Committee recommended that 'the Home Secretary should not establish medical tribunals to investigate the grounds for recommending him to withdraw a doctor's authority to possess and supply dangerous drugs'. And why not? Because the Brain Committee did not think there would be a large enough number of irregularities to justify Tribunals, and because of the expected difficulties obtaining evidence. 'There would be need for powers to take evidence on oath, witnesses who are themselves addicts are notoriously unreliable, and it might prove extremely hard to assess sufficient medical grounds in the face of possible opposing medical opinion' (HMSO, 1961).

These are very poor arguments indeed. The evidence then as now would largely depend on the number of prescriptions issued and the amounts on each prescription. But when the Brain Committee's proposals were accepted this was the end of the first period of the Tribunal system. Spear (1982) makes the point that the practical consequence of this recommendation was that for the next 12 years, until Tribunals were reinstituted by the 1971 Misuse of Drugs Act, there was no effective means other than remonstration of dealing with a doctor whose prescribing gave cause for concern.

The second phase lasted just over a decade. The mid- to late-1960s was the period which saw the largest increase in drug use, and was also the period of the greatest over-prescribing. As a result of the Brain Committee there was no machinery to deal with this. The courts did not view injudicious prescribing as a criminal offence in breach of the 1953 Dangerous Drugs Regulations. In effect any medical practictioner could prescribe as and when he wished with the only legal controls requiring that he fulfil certain minor administrative conditions such as keeping a register. Some, Spear in particular, are highly critical of the lack of safeguards available, and say the Brain Committee must stand accused of a lack of appreciation of the changes in the British drug scene and for not having the depth of vision of their predecessors in 1926 (H. B. Spear, 1982). In my view this criticism is too mild.

The second stage ended in 1971 with the Misuse of Drugs Act and the reintroduction of Tribunals. Parliament recognised that injudicious prescribing needed to be controlled and the Tribunal system might be one way of achieving that. 'Injudicious prescribing' or irresponsible prescribing as it was called was defined as 'careless or negligent prescribing or unduly liberal prescribing with *bona fide* intent' (Hansard, 25 March 1970, cols 1457–8). The Government of the day recognised too that the General Medical Council would not deal with irresponsible prescribing,—the terms 'irresponsible' and 'injudicious' are used interchangeably. It gave as one of its reasons that:

> irresponsible prescribing covers such a wide variety of possible practices. These range from infamous conduct at one extreme to poorly judged but *bona fide* intentions at the other. It is consequently not easy to see how it could be fitted into the existing machinery of the medical profession which was designed for narrower purposes. (House of Lords, 14 January 1971, cols 229–30)

Tribunals were to be part of the Government's strategy to combat irresponsible prescribing, thereby reducing spillage to the illicit system and subsequent recruitment into the user population. It was noted when the Bill was read in the House of Lords that Tribunals had been accepted by the GMC and the other medical and professional bodies concerned (ibid., vol. 230).

In this, the third stage, the powers and membership of the Tribunals are contained in Section 13 of the 1971 Misuse of Drugs Act, Schedule 3, and supplemented by the Misuse of Drugs Tribunal (England and Wales) rules, 1974 (HMSO, 1974, 85) (LI). Briefly, for these purposes the legislation states that where a medical practitioner uses his exemption under the Act in an irresponsible manner his authority to possess, prescribe, administer and supply drugs may be withdrawn by direction of the Home Secretary. (The term 'exemption' needs clarification. The import, export, production and supply of drugs is prohibited except for persons licensed by the Home

Secretary who are given exemptions. Medical practitioners are given exemptions in respect of prescribing, as are pharmacists, or veterinary surgeons in respect of their occupations.) Advice to the Home Secretary comes from the Tribunals who may recommend a physician's exemption be affected in some way, that is withdrawn completely or modified by reducing the drugs that can be prescribed. There are incidentally other Regulations in the 1971 Act which prohibit medical practitioners from prescribing heroin and cocaine except under licence from the Home Secretary. About 200 medical practitioners hold such licences, almost exclusively consultants and senior registrars working in the Treatment Centres. This restriction was another attempt at tackling the problem of irresponsible prescribing.

TRIBUNAL PROCEDURES

The powers of the Tribunals are directed towards GPs and those physicians treating drug users privately. Tribunals came into operation in 1973, and between then and 1989 44 medical practitioners have been formally dealt with by the Tribunals, or between three and four per year. There are, however, lengthy procedures to go through and various stages to negotiate.

The procedures begin as a result of routine monitoring of prescriptions by the Home Office. About 300 physicians each year are seen at this first stage. The Home Office looks for prescribing patterns which give cause for concern. Typically, the physician will be in a single-handed practice with a large number of notified drug users. Prescribing will be out of control, usually with a mixture of the new benzodiazepenes and the more heavyweight narcotics such as diconel and palfriam. When the Home Office is alerted to the position its Drug Department officers visit the physician concerned. They have by this time detailed information on the physician's prescribing patterns which often point to prescribing on demand, together with evidence about the manner and extent prescribed drugs find their way into the illicit market. Sometimes the physicians are surprised at the pattern of their prescribing unaware that they have been prescribing on demand, and that some of the drugs have gone into the illicit system. Occasionally, it seems physicians are unaware too that those drugs were controlled by the Misuse of Drugs Act.

These advisory visits have an immediate effect in about 90 per cent of the cases, with prescribing patterns changing to more acceptable levels. Each visit is followed by a formal letter from the Home Office noting the changes where appropriate.

For the 10 per cent or the 30 or so who do not change, the next step involves being given notice that they are to be formally warned and may be taken before a Tribunal. The formal warning tends to reduce this 30 to about six or seven who remain persistent prescribers. By this point the Home Office Drugs Department will have clear evidence of irresponsible prescribing. Prescriptions would have been analysed and the prescribing pattern determined. Any overlap prescribing would have been established; that is, prescribing to users who had claimed they had 'lost their prescriptions' or were 'going on holiday'. An example of overlap prescribing would be as follows:

7 August   prescribed 40 tablets of Dihydrocodeine
11 August prescribed a further 40 tablets of Dihydroco-
           deine
15 August prescribed a further 30 tablets of Dihydroco-
           deine plus 30 tablets of Temazepam

(The usual dose of Dihydrocodeine would be three or four tablets per day at the strength prescribed.)

At the formal interview stage the physician can be legally represented. A report of this formal interview is submitted by the Head of the Drugs Department to the Treasury Solicitor seeking advice about the quality of the evidence. If the Treasury Solicitor recommends a Tribunal hearing the date is set, after further consultation with an Under Secretary.

The Tribunal is headed by a lawyer, always a QC, plus four physicians. Though not a court of law it operates in like manner: the Home Office offers evidence, this is subject to cross-examination, the physician calls his/her own evidence, and so on. The physician can be legally represented. If the physician is found guilty of irresponsible prescribing the Tribunal can make a number of recommendations. It can suggest that no action be taken (it never has); it can recommend the physician be prohibited prescribing all controlled drugs, or from prescribing selected ones, perhaps allowing heroin to be prescribed in emergencies. The Secretary of State, at the Tribunal's recommendation, issues a Direction accordingly. The GMC can and often does take note of the Tribunal's decision. Sometimes it removes the physician's name from the medical register. However, in half of those six or seven cases appearing before the Tribunal the physician asks for his/her name to be removed: Tribunals can only proceed against registered medical practitioners, so the physician's action pre-empts the Tribunal's decision and powers. Thus, the process which began with about 300 being interviewed ends with three or four Directions annually from the Home Secretary.

It needs to be said that irresponsible prescribing is not a criminal offence, nor is self-medication using controlled drugs — though it may be regarded as unethical. Incredibly about 12 self-medicating physicians, usually addicted to opiates, come to the notice of the Home Office each year. Where criminal proceedings take place against a physician, such as failing to keep a register under Section 10 of the 1971 Act, or unlawfully supplying drugs or obtaining drugs by deception, the Secretary of State can issue a Direction prohibiting further prescribing without recourse to a Tribunal. About two such Directions are made each year.

TRIBUNALS AND THEIR CRITICS

The most obvious criticism of the Tribunal system is that it is protracted with a built-in bias towards the professional physician. Moreover, the whole exercise is conducted in a gentlemanly way typical of assessments of middle-class deviants (that is similar to those under the Factory Acts). This contrasts with the way others with less status are dealt with, and with those who receive the drugs as patients (P. T. Bean, 1974).

Certainly the whole exercise is protracted — extreme cases can take up to two years from the formal interview to the Tribunal — though there are powers for the Secretary of State to issue a Temporary Direction if required. Indeed the

Regulations show a set of built-in constraints (28 days to do this, 28 days to do that). The physician has ample opportunity to defend him/herself, with the final ploy to escape the Tribunal altogether by resigning from the medical register— though no physician would undertake this lightly.

There seems little doubt the system works to the advantage of the physician. On the other hand there ought to be protection from the actions of the Secretary of State and Civil Servants likewise who can be as biased and capricious as anyone else. Moreover, is it not appropriate to provide opportunities for physicians to make amends, change their ways, and return to more acceptable ways of behaving? Is that not what criminologists have long advocated? Is it not better to decriminalise and tolerate diversity rather than prosecute to achieve conformity?

At one level, yes, except that these considerations are not extended to other deviants. Nor has a case been made out for the special privileges granted to this group. And what happened to deterrence theory? Why does this not apply to physicians? Deterrence suggests it is necessary to sentence according to levels necessary to deter others. The methods described above hardly act as a deterrent—quite the reverse. Were they to do so, perhaps more physicians would take notice.

This general criticism can be put in a slightly different way. The Advisory Council on the Misuse of Drugs described the system in the mid- to late-1970s as using 'a narrow legalistic approach'. This meant 'that only those cases where there has been clear evidence of grossly irresponsible prescribing have been referred to Tribunals'. As a result said the Advisory Council, 'sanctions have rarely been available to employ against the more broadly interpreted irresponsible prescribing which is in fact both more widespread and more harmful' (HMSO, 1982 p. 61). The Advisory Council wanted to see 'irresponsible prescribing' on a continuum ranging from small amounts of over-prescribing, perhaps due to poor judgement, to the more excessive over-prescribing of a more persistent and intentional nature. It is only the latter which seemed to be dealt with by Tribunals. The Advisory Council wanted sanctions applied to all who over-prescribe, not just the gross and persistent ones. As things stand the Tribunals cannot do this, though the initial 'interview' approximates to it—without the legal sanctions of course.

In doing so the Advisory Council raised a more fundamental question, that is, what type of prescribing system is required? Is there to be a licensing system where an assessment is made of the physician's suitability to hold a licence, or should licences be granted automatically, with powers to withdraw the licence if circumstances warrant it? The British system adopts the latter view, with the exception of heroin and cocaine, and Tribunals are a product of that. Yet if one moved towards the former system the need for Tribunals would be weakened. For the question is, why restrict the prescribing of heroin and cocaine rather than many other drugs? There are two answers: first that a licensing system would distort the British system—or rather change it to make in unrecognisable, for the British system is based on the principle that all medical practitioners can prescribe unless proven otherwise. The second is that the administrative cost would soar under a licensing system where licences would need to be granted for every new condition and for every circumstance. And on what criteria? They would be difficult to determine.

On balance it seems wise, therefore, to retain the present system, relying as it does on allowing medical practitioners to make professional clinical judgements about prescribing and expecting that some will over-prescribe. The system will and can work as long as the Home Office remains vigilant, and does not act as in the early years when its legal advisors regarded Tribunals as dealing only with gross or infamous prescribing of the type featured in the 1960s. It will also work too as long as the General Medical Council retains its current flexible position: again, no longer regarding 'infamous conduct' as the only justification for sanctioning its members, but including prescribing other than in the course of *bone fide* treatment. It may not be a perfect system, but for the present it will do.

NOTE

I am grateful to Mr Peter Spurgeon, head of the Drugs Department at the Home Office for the help given in the preparation of this paper.

REFERENCES

Bean, P. T. (1974) *The Social Control of Drugs* (London: Martin Robertson).

DHSS (1982) *Treatment and Rehabilitation*, Report of the Advisory Council on the Misuse of Drugs (London: HMSO).

HMSO (1926) *Report of the Departmental Committee on Morphine and Heroin Addiction, (Rolleston Committee)* (London: HMSO)

HMSO (SI. 998).

HMSO (1957) *Report of the Committee on Administration Tribunals and Enquiries, (Franks Committee)* (London: HMSO).

HMSO (1961) *Report of the Interdepartmental Committee on Drug Addiction, (Brain Committee)* (London: HMSO).

HMSO (1974) Misuse of Drugs Tribunal (England and Wales) Rules 85 (LI).

House of Lords Debates, Misuse of Drugs Bill 14 Jan. 1971, Hansard, vol. 798, cols 1446–1560.

Parliamentary Debates, Misuse of Drugs Bill 25 March 1979, House of Lords, vol. 314, cols 221–83.

Spear, H. B. (1982) 'British Experience in the Management of Opiate', *in* M. Glatt and J. Marks (eds) (Lancaster: MTP Press).

5 Prescribing to Addicts
James Willis

The management of addiction, the investigation of its causes and natural history, remains uncertain and, in some instances, contentious. The days of medical omniscience are, quite rightly, a thing of the past although the behavioural scientists too have had some of their credibility tarnished after producing numerous theories about the causes of addiction, some impressive and carefully worked out and some frankly ridiculous. The same goes for a variety of types of treatment which have been carried out, and there is no harm in that— no honest person would claim to have a monopoly on expertise in the management of drug-related problems. Times and names have also changed—patients are 'clients' and where formerly they attended drug clinics they now enter 'health care delivery systems' staffed not by doctors and nurses but by 'carers and providers'. Roles and job descriptions too are in a state of flux. The doctor's approach ('I'm right and you're wrong') no longer commands after the failure of the penal approach ('You're wrong, and that's why you're here'). The Social Worker perspective ('You're not exactly wrong and, in any case, not to be blamed for anything—I'm examining my role and cannot say whether I'm right or wrong') has fared little better. The psychologist is perhaps in the safest situation ('I am unable to determine the parameters of rightness or wrongness, but we're working on it—come back in five years') (Willis, 1987). Doctors and behavioural scientists have often been in contention as the 'medical model' of drug management has received derisive attention—in this there is merit for the model is, in some respects, outworn. At present, however, it remains the best approach that we have, since it views addictive behaviour as being, if not illness, then something very like it, a humane and pragmatic attitude which is useful as long as it is not over-valued.

All this leaves the medical profession with the general idea that, when the dust finally settles, people still have expectations of them that must somehow be fulfilled without raising too many other professional hackles. This is termed 'clinical responsibility' by some, but 'medical omniscience' by others. The prescribing of addictive drugs to addicts is a difficult practice rejected by many but which cannot be dismissed out of hand. 'I would never prescribe methadone, I am in the business of changing people' was a comment made to the author by an otherwise reasonable person, which is as injurious in its way as saying 'let them have anything they want'. Such a comment is nowadays par for the course amongst those who no longer prescribe certain drugs since they commonly believe that they possess 'the' answer (which usually turns out to be a partial answer, if an answer at all).

In the days before and immediately after Rolleston the question of prescribing for addicts was not a serious one since addiction was a medical curiosity, more common than, say, musicogenic epilepsy but considerably less interesting. This state of affairs remained until the 1960s, when events began to move in the wrong direction. The explosion in addiction that we now see, however, is an entirely different matter, as anyone who recalls the early days of the NHS will testify. Streams of foul language from amphetamine-soaked scarecrows on the one hand, and gratuitous advice from ignorant well-meaning busybodies on television on the other, did little to boost the morale of those of us who experienced it. In the early days of the NHS drug dependency clinics there was a superabundance of very disturbed patients taking large doses of heroin and methylamphetamine, and a significant percentage were individuals with major personality disorders often compounded by drug-induced psychoses. Perhaps such patients were like the first people in this country to experiment with tobacco, that is, high risk takers ('normal' people didn't smoke). The clinics and their staff did their best to contain these people, employing maintenance prescribing, threats, cajolery, persuasion, counselling and so on, and all to little effect, it has been said. Such an assessment is less than fair to the dedicated personnel of those days, although the idea of prescribing for addicts gained a bad reputation. This is perhaps not surprising—it is difficult and everyone concerned with the management of drug dependence is looking for a cure. Even so, we must acknowledge that dependence is a chronic and a relapsing condition, circumstances well known to the medical profession (the majority of patients attending medical, neurological and psychiatric clinics are suffering from similar disorders in that respect).

Prescribing for addicts still has a place and must not be rejected out of hand—it is quite possible to define a few simple guidelines. A good starting point is to list the drugs which should never be prescribed. This point might seem obvious but it needs stating: every once in a while a rogue doctor does it and fertilises a patch of addictive behaviour. Central stimulants should never be given to anyone—no exceptions can be made (there may still be a handful of low-dose amphetamine takers remaining, but it should end there). Barbiturates must not be used except in the case of a patient prepared to enter an outpatient detoxification programme, and for no more than two weeks before entering hospital for formal detoxification. The same is true for benzodiazepine users, who should also be persuaded to enter detoxification.

So far, not so good. The real problems concerned with prescription, however, start and end with opiods, since they are the only type of addictive drug that merits serious consideration in the maintenance treatment of addiction. The reasons advanced for their use in this way are, first, to alleviate or prevent withdrawal distress and, second, to try to inhibit criminal drug-seeking behaviour, illicit drug dealing and the attendant misery thereby entailed. The first reason is not completely compelling, because withdrawal distress is not life-threatening, although it could be argued that it might endanger the well-being of others subjected to associated criminal acts, such as violence or robbery. Even so, withdrawal remains subjectively unpleasant. The second reason, that is, using prescription to attempt to interfere with the industry of drug manufacture and distribution, which makes a huge and shameless profit from human misery, certainly cannot be shrugged aside—'we are bigger than US Steel' says Meyer Lansky, the bagman of the Mafia.

Why is it that the opiod drugs are so badly regarded? It is believed that opiates began to get a bad name when it was suspected that Chinese immigrant workers on the west coast of the United States might represent a threat to the labour market. The local population seized on opium smoking as yet another ghastly manifestation of the 'Yellow Peril', despite the fact that the immigrant Chinese had always been law-abiding and decently behaved. Many writers contributed to this myth, most notably the novelist Sax Rohmer with his fiendish Oriental Doctor Fu Manchu. Fu Manchu provided the English-speaking world with the archtypical opium fiend, in spite of the fact that fashionable ladies' magazines in early twentieth-century USA displayed the 'correct' clothing to wear when smoking opium.

Other experiences of the many follies and inconsistencies involving mind-altering substances are not fictional but part of real life: the author's experience of alcohol prohibition in Saudi Arabia demonstrates this most forcibly. Worthy Western expatriates who denounced the smoking of 'dope' and the use of heroin fumed and fretted whenever the price of 'bootleg' Scotch whisky rose to £95 per bottle and telephoned one another whenever they heard that a consignment of 'good stuff' had arrived. The same persons, good men all, believed that it would be grossly immoral and bad medical practice to prescribe heroin or methadone for addicts as this would somehow be 'giving in'. Ultimately, this is what it comes down to when we look at prescribing for addicts—it appears to be too soft an option and collusion with a destructive process.

At the moment, the main area of disagreement centres on methadone maintenance, even though it is one of the most carefully evaluated treatment methods in any area (see, for example, Senay, 1985). Some see the practice as a life saver and a means of warding off criminality although others interpret it as a straight 'cop-out', wherein the doctor colludes with a 'Carry On Junkie' scenario and abrogates clinical responsibility. In spite of the contemporary distrust of the practice, the truth probably lies somewhere in between. Methadone maintenance started off in the USA in a climate of total disapproval yet was initially well-received. It appeared to promise much to people who had been, up to that time, total losers facing long term imprisonment after repeated treatment failure. Patients found themselves in work, with bank accounts and credit cards, everything that no-hoper New York addicts had believed impossible. However, the puritanical attitudes of American society soon won the day and maintenance faltered, to become submerged in bureaucratic interference masquerading as 'we know what's best for you'. This form of interference produced absurdly long waiting lists and prolonged criminality, whilst ensuring that the doctor in charge spent most of the time in paper work. Some might regard this as a disincentive and they would be correct. The orthodox notion is that addiction should be cured, although the fact remains that we are no further ahead in this respect than we were a century ago (just as we are no better at curing stomach cancer than we were a century ago).

The final idiocy of so many methadone maintenance programmes is the way in which a person may not be taken onto the programme unless he or she accepts counselling. What nonsense! At no time in history has so much counselling been available for so many conditions and to so little effect. For the addict, this requirement is hard. It is presumed that he or she must have 'problems' and these will be dealt with by counselling, to meet the 'real' needs. Methadone is a crutch which will help them to a better life, offered by some barely articulate social science graduate or a chain-smoking community psychiatric nurse. This is both insulting and absurd. If someone asks for counselling, or is obviously in need of it, then it must be given. However, to make counselling a precondition for receiving methadone is as ridiculous as insisting that someone with gonorrhoea should have counselling in regard of their psychosexual problems as a necessary requirement for receiving antibiotic therapy.

Finally, the rights and wrongs of methadone maintenance fade away into insignificance when the problem of HIV infection and its transmission by infected needles is raised. The disasterous experience of Edinburgh, where maintenance and the availability of clean needles were abandoned, is a clear example of the dire consequences of the application of rigid policies, however well intentioned. Methadone maintenance cannot therefore be allowed to go by default, or because it does not measure up to someone's half-baked notion that they alone have the answer. Being in the 'business of changing people' reflects a monstrous arrogance: the track record of psychiatry is not that much to get excited about.

In fact, methadone maintenance policies may be used validly in a number of ways. First, maintenance can be employed to hold a patient at a steady level of drug usage until such a time as it is possible to move into an abstinence-orientated programme. Second, it may be used as a long-term method of treatment aimed at patients with a prolonged history of treatment failure, where the decision to maintain on methadone is taken in the same way as the decision to maintain on insulin in the case of an insulin-dependant diabetic patient. Finally, methadone, and for that matter, heroin, can be used as a way of helping the patient to buy time, time during which the addict may be enabled to look at the options available, rather than be subjected to the blandishments of those wishing to engineer changes in life-style.

For some of us, being in charge of a drug dependency clinic must have been the worst job we have ever had. The workload can be very heavy and the experience stressful. Such stress results not only from clinical responsibility but from the ill-natured criticisms about prescribing habits that otherwise reasonable colleagues may indulge in. Maintenance prescribing of injectable heroin and methadone is a perfectly reasonable practice but has almost been driven underground by an influential minority of psychiatrists. Fortunately a degree of reality has now re-emerged with the need to control the spread of HIV infection, although it is sad that it has required a disaster to jolt the obdurate into a modicum of flexibility. The medical establishment itself is part of the problem in this regard — perhaps addiction is too serious to be left in the hands of moralising psychiatrists or behavioural scientists. Controlled availability is an acceptable policy when the alternative is the further growth of massive criminal organisations, paying no tax and contributing nothing to a vulnerable population but adulterated drugs, crime and widespread misery.

It remains obvious that, whilst addiction is frequently a chronic and relapsing disorder, persons engaged in treatment should not be deterred from aiming for a drug-free state for their patients. Any addict who becomes drug free is in a better state of physical and psychological health. The plea on behalf of maintenance for opiate addicts is a plea for time and patience in the face of self-destructive behaviour which is not easily held in check.

REFERENCES

Senay, E. C. (1985) 'Methadone-maintenance Treatment', *International Journal of the Addictions*, 20 (6–7), pp. 803–21.
Willis, J. H. (1987) 'Editorial: Reflections', *British Journal of Addiction*, 82, 1181–2.

6 Crime and Heroin Use
Joy Mott

Until the late 1970s heroin misuse or addiction was not considered to be a major source of criminal behaviour in the United Kingdom. There is, of course, a direct causative relationship between heroin misuse and some types of offence under the drug control legislation simply because, other than in cases of addiction as a result of treatment for physical disease or injury, the misuser usually obtains his first supplies of heroin illegally—most often by sharing friends' supplies however they were obtained, or by theft or forgery, or from the illicit market.

All four of the official bodies advising the Government on drug control and treatment policy between 1926 and 1982 emphasised that addiction should be regarded as a medical, or medico-social, problem. The Departmental Committee on Morphine and Heroin Addiction considered that addiction should 'be regarded as a manifestation of a morbid state, and not as a mere form of vicious indulgence' (Rolleston Report, 1926). The Interdepartmental Committee on Drug Addiction, in its first report, also considered addiction 'as an expression of mental disorder rather than as a form of criminal behaviour' (the first Brain Report, 1961). In its second report, the Interdepartmental Committee said 'the addict should be regarded as a sick person, he should be treated as such and not as a criminal, provided he does not resort to criminal acts' (the second Brain Report, 1965). The Advisory Council on the Misuse of Drugs (1982) introduced the concept of the 'problem drug taker', defined as a person who 'experiences social, psychological, physical or legal problems related to intoxication and/or regular excessive consumption and/or dependence as a consequence of his own use of drugs. . . .'.

The legislation presently in force, the Misuse of Drugs Act 1971, allows only doctors licensed by the Home Secretary to prescribe heroin (or cocaine or dipipanone) to addicts (whose addiction was not the result of medical treatment for phsyical disease or injury). Nevertheless, the medical profession has always been, and remains, able to treat heroin addicts or 'problem heroin takers' as they think fit according to their professional discretion and clinical judgement. However, longer-term or maintenance prescribing of heroin remains controversial. The Rolleston Report (1926) considered that there are 'two groups of person suffering from addiction to whom administration of morphine or heroin may be regarded as legitimate treatment'; those who were being treated by gradual withdrawal and those for whom, 'after every effort has been made for the cure of addiction' the drugs could not be completely withdrawn either because it 'produced severe distress or even risk of life', or 'experience showed that a certain minimum dose of the drug was necessary to enable the patients to lead useful and relatively normal lives, and that if deprived of this non-progressive dose they became incapable of work'.

In 1958 the Interdepartmental Committee on Drug Addiction was convened 'to review. . . the advice given by the Departmental Committee on Morphine and Heroin Addiction in 1926. . . ' The Committee's first report (1961), re-affirmed the Rolleston tenet, that the 'the continued provision of supplies (of controlled drugs) to addict patients depends solely on the individual decisions made by the medical practitioner professionally responsible for each case'. The Committee concluded that the number of heroin addicts was very small at the time. Spear (1975) commented that the report was completed before the 1960 addict statistics were available which showed an increase as compared with 1958.

Spear (1975) noted that the five-fold increase (from 68 to 342) in the number of heroin addicts known to the Home Office between 1959 and 1964, the marked change in the nature of the heroin addicted population with an increase in the number of addicts of non-therapeutic origin (that is addicted not as the result of medical treatment for physical disease or injury), together with the arrival in London of a group of Canadian heroin addicts in the late 1950s, led to the reconvening of the Interdepartmental Committee in 1964. In the second Report (1965) the Committee found that 'the major source of supply (of heroin and cocaine) had been excessive prescribing for addicts by a small group of doctors, acting within the law and in accordance with their professional judgement'. It was concerned to limit the availability of licit supplies of controlled drugs while maintaining 'the doctor's right to prescribe dangerous drugs without restriction for the ordinary patient's needs'.

The Dangerous Drug Act 1967, and the subsequent Misuse of Drugs Act 1971, implemented many of the Report's recommendations including limiting the prescribing to addicts of heroin and cocaine (later also dipipanone) to doctors licenced by the Home Secretary, making provisions for dealing with 'irresponsible prescribing', and making the notification of their addict patients a statutory obligation for doctors. It remains possible for any doctor to prescribe heroin to any patient to relieve pain due to organic disease or injury.

North American commentators have argued that 'the British system', as described by the Rolleston Report, ensured that little association would be expected between heroin use and crime in the United Kingdom 'because the British addict can maintain his habit without becoming a criminal, and the criminal is not especially exposed to addiction by the existence of a large illicit traffic or by great numbers of addicts in the underworld' (Lindesmith, 1957; see also Schur, 1963). However, some British commentators have suggested that the 'British system' was only effective when there were few heroin addicts in the population (Downes, 1977).

According to the Reports of the Interdepartmental Committee (1961 and 1965) and Spear (1969) the number of addicts to controlled drugs known to the Home Office declined from 616 in 1936 (with 88 per cent addicted to morphine and 10 per cent to heroin, 24 per cent working in medical or allied professions with an unknown but high proportion of therapeutic origin) to 454 in 1960 (15 per cent addicted to heroin of whom less than 1 per cent were aged under 20, 15 per cent working in medical or allied professions, 71 per cent of therapeutic origin) and rose to 753 in 1964 (45 per cent addicted to heroin of whom 12 per cent were aged under 20, 8 per cent in medical or allied professions, 49 per cent of therapeutic origin). From 1969 (the year after the notification of addicts to the Home Office was introduced) until 1976 the number of new addicts notified annually to the Home Office remained relatively constant, at between 700 and 900, and gave rise to little official concern. This interregnum period lasted until 1980, when the number of new addicts notified reached 1600. In 1985 6409 new addicts were notified, the highest ever number, declining to 4630 in 1988 (Home Office Statistics on the Misuse of Drugs, 1974–88).

These figures of the number of heroin addicts known to the Home Office indicate that, since the end of the Second World War, there have been two major epidemics of heroin misuse in the United Kingdom. The first epidemic may conveniently be dated as lasting from 1958 until 1971, when the Misuse of Drugs Act was passed and the NHS hospital Drug Dependence Units (DDUs) had become established, and was concentrated mainly in London and the south-east of England. From about 1976 the number of notified addicts from outside London began to rise, increasingly more new addicts were being notified by general practitioners than by the DDUs or the prison medical service, and more were being notified from the north of England and southern Scotland. The second major British heroin epidemic may be said to have been gathering momentum in the late 1970s and was officially acknowledged in 1984 by the creation of the Ministerial Group on the Misuse of Drugs (Home Office, 1985).

LICIT HEROIN (AND OTHER DRUGS) AND CRIME, 1958 TO 1971

Between 1958 and 1971 not only did the number of heroin addicts known to the Home Office increase, but the nature of the population changed dramatically. The age of new addicts began to decline, their preferred drug of addiction changed from morphine to heroin (46 per cent to morphine in 1958 and 81 per cent to heroin in 1968), the proportion of therapeutic addicts (persons who had become addicted in the course of medical treatment) fell from 79 per cent in 1958 to 14 per cent in 1968, and the proportion of 'professional' addicts (members of the medical and allied professions) fell from 18 per cent in 1958 to 2 per cent in 1964 (Spear, 1969). None of the addicts known to the Home Office in 1959 who were described as taking heroin were aged under 20, while in 1964 12 per cent were (Interdepartmental Committee 1965). During 1971 2769 addicts were notified to the Home Office of whom 30 per cent were new addicts and around 40 per cent of them were aged under 20, 69 per cent of the new addicts were described as addicted to heroin, with 8 per cent 'therapeutic' addicts, and 0.8 per cent working in the medical and allied professions (Home Office Dangerous Drug Statistics, 1971; Edwards, 1981).

Spear (1969) suggests that the soil for this first epidemic probably began to be prepared in 1949 with the theft of large quantities of morphine and cocaine, from a firm of wholesale chemists in the Midlands. The persons supplied by this thief were already known to the Home Office as receiving drugs on prescription and were using him as a source of supplementary supplies. Following his arrest there 'was no immediate, or even gradual, increase in the number of morphine addicts coming to notice and careful examination of the background history of those morphine addicts who did appear in 1950 and 1951 failed to reveal any connection with him'.

The second theft, in 1951, of large supplies of morphine, heroin and cocaine from the dispensary of a hospital near London, did lead to an increase in the number of addicts known to the Home Office. The police were able to identify 14 people who had obtained supplies from this thief of whom only two had previously come to notice as heroin addicts, although some were known to be cannabis and/or cocaine users. By the end of 1954, 63 heroin addicts became known to the Home Office who were either directly, or very probably, connected with this thief or his close associates. Of these 63 addicts, 21 were musicians and five were Nigerians of whom three were musicians. Spear remarks that, at the time, there was a close relationship between the use of cannabis and heroin and interest in popular music (bebop) played in certain clubs and cafés.

Spear (1982) notes that until 1967:

> there was sufficient over-prescribing by doctors, or under-consumption by addicts, to sustain a flourishing black market in heroin and, later, cocaine. This black market, consisting of suppliers disposing of their own legitimately acquired drugs. . . was supplemented from time to time by the proceeds of thefts from pharmaceutical warehouses, hospitals, doctors' surgeries or retail pharmacies. . . there was no evidence that illicitly manufactured heroin played

any part in the 1958–67 domestic scene. . . those arrested for unlawful possession of heroin or cocaine were invariably found in possession of pharmaceutical heroin or cocaine.

In September 1967 the first seizures of 'Chinese' heroin were made by the Metropolitan Police. This heroin was prepared for smoking but, as it was cheaper on the black market than the pharmaceutical product, it soon became popular and was used for injecting. Seized samples were generally found to contain less than 50 per cent heroin with caffeine as the usual adulterant. At this time a few doctors, including the notorious Dr Petro, began to prescribe ampoules of methedrine (methylamphetamine) and large quantities became available on the black market. Leech (1973) pointed out that it was methedrine, and not cannabis, which provided the bridge between the 'needle culture' of the heroin addicts in the West End of London and adolescent amphetamine users. Spear noted that methadone was added to the available injectable drug cocktail by the treatment policy of the newly created Drug Dependence Units, later to be joined by barbiturates and Diconal (dipipanone) which were obtained either by licit or forged prescriptions or thefts.

Thus, the 'heroin addict' of the first epidemic was often an injecting poly drug misuser who preferred to inject heroin and cocaine, and these drugs were usually prescribed in the course of treatment. Many supplemented their prescriptions from the 'spillage' of licit supplies of these drugs on to the black market, latterly with illicitly imported 'Chinese heroin', and/or licit or illicit supplies of methedrine and/or barbiturates and/or Diconal. Some case histories of such addicts may be found in Glatt *et al.* (1967) and Hepworth (1982).

Most of these addicts were to be found in London but groups of heroin users were to be found in other parts of England. The most carefully documented local outbreak occurred between 1965 and 1970 in Crawley, a town in south-east England between London and Brighton, where there were few signs of social deprivation amongst the population (de Alarcon and Rathod, 1968; Rathod, 1972; Mott and Rathod, 1976).

There were numerous descriptive accounts of the criminal histories of these 'heroin addicts' published between 1968 and 1979. Mott and Taylor (1974) and Mott (1981) critically reviewed many of the reports describing series of addict patients attending particular doctors or hospitals between 1954 and 1975, or inmates of adult and young offender penal establishments, or identified in the community. They had difficulty in describing typical heroin-using and criminal careers because there were considerable variations in the selection of the groups; definitions of the stages in their drug-using careers were either not comparable or not reported; few studies distinguished the sexes (at the time the sex ratio for notified addicts were usually three or four males to one female and there are well-known differences in the criminality of the sexes); few distinguished between native born patients and North Americans (at least one general practice treated a number of patients from the ethnic minorities); few used a standard follow-up period and few related criminal histories to defined stages of the drug-using careers.

Mott (1981 summarised the findings for the males as:

(a) about two-thirds of male opiate users had been convicted of offences before they became known to the Home Office as addicts;
(b) their re-conviction rates during follow-up periods of between two and five years while they remain in receipt of prescription for opiates may be higher than expected, when their age and number of previous convictions are taken into account, because of the proportion convicted exclusively of drug offences;
(c) while they remain in receipt of prescriptions for opiates they are likely to be convicted of drug offences and the majority of these offences will involve opiates, but the longer they continue to receive licit supplies the less likely they are to be convicted exclusively of drug offences;
(d) a reduction of licit opiate use is accompanied by a reduction in convictions for any type of offence;
(e) their non-drug offences at any time consist mainly of theft offences and they are unlikely to be convicted of offences of personal violence.

Studies of three series of females indicated that, while the criminal and drug-using careers of the sexes had some similarities, fewer of the females were convicted at any time. For example, between 70 to 80 per cent of the males were found to have been convicted before coming to notice as addicts compared with 50 to 60 per cent of the females. Like the males, the non-drug convictions of the females were usually for theft offences. Convictions for prostitution off-ences were rare even among female addicts identified in prisons. For females, but not for males, a history of convictions for non-drug offences prior to notification as an addict appeared to be prognostic of continuing opioid use (Mott, 1982).

There were attempts to identify types of heroin use in terms of their social functioning and life style, including their criminal activities. Stimson (1973), studying 128 patients of London DDUs who were being prescribed heroin at the time, distinguished four groups—Stables, Loners, Junkies and Two-worlders—on such measures. All four groups admitted to some criminal activity, with the two least criminal groups, Stables and Loners, apparently confining themselves to drug offences.

Mott (1975, 1982) concluded that all the evidence about the criminal careers of the poly-drug-using heroin addicts of the first British epidemic suggested that their drug-using and criminal careers tended to run a parallel course. Apart from drug offences, and allowing for their age and criminal histories before coming to official notice as addicts, they were no more likely to be convicted of offences than the general run of offenders. The major effect of heroin use on their criminal histories was an increase in the number of their convictions for drug offences, most of which involved opioids, and in the numbers convicted of such offences. Those who continued to attend DDUs and to remain in receipt of licit supplies of opioids appeared to have comprised of two very different groups: those who were able to combine opioid use with a stable social life and those who continued to be convicted of both drug and non-drug offences.

THE INTERREGNUM, 1972–80: THE VIRTUAL END OF LICIT SUPPLIES OF HEROIN

In the mid-1970s there was an upsurge in the illicit heroin market in London. The factors alleged to have contributed to this included the policy of the DDUs most usually to prescribe only methadone in oral doses, the success of the Metropolitan Police in dealing with the Chinese heroin market, the end of the Vietnam War requiring the South-East Asian producers to find new markets after the GIs went home, wealthy Iranian exiles using heroin as a means of getting their capital out of the country after the downfall of the Shah, and political troubles in Afghanistan and Pakistan. It seems that, initially, the illicit market was operated by amateurs, and youthful working class entrepreneurs, but professional criminals later extended their control of the cannabis market to heroin (Clark, 1980; Lewis, 1985).

Stimson and Oppenheimer (1982) described the changes in DDU treatment policy, starting in the mid-1970s: the refusal to prescribe heroin and offering only oral methadone together with 'treatment contracts', with an emphasis on abstinence as the goal of treatment. These changes were perceived by the DDU staff 'as a step in the therapeutic direction'. They comment that 'in the early days people attended a (DDU) because they wanted a regular supply of injectable drugs'. But, since the change in policy 'the people who go to clinics and who stay with them may either be those who actually seek treatment or those who, for various reasons, including pressure from other agencies such as courts, are willing to accept oral methadone'. But probably only a minority of those who did come to the DDUs stayed for long. Hartnoll *et al.* (1980) found that only 29 per cent offered oral methadone in a controlled trial conducted in one London DDU (between 1972–75) were still attending 12 months later.

During the late 1970s there was also a change in the preferred route of using heroin—from injecting to smoking, snorting or sniffing. Hartnoll *et al.* (1984) ascribed this change to the increasing popularity of sniffing cocaine or amphetamine sulphate—'sniffing one white powder. . . made sniffing another (heroin) appear a small step'. O'Bryan (1985), reporting contemporaneous interviews with young heroin users, commented:

> less extreme ways of using smack (heroin) are increasingly becoming popular. You don't have to inject to get a hit. You don't get addicted on your first exposure to heroin,

and while continuous sniffing or smoking can still lead to dependence, compared to injecting it doesn't feel addictive, it's clean, it's easy.

Clark (1980) commented on the deficiencies, by the end of the 1970s, of the funding of the statutory and voluntary treatment and rehabilitation agencies, and concluded prophetically 'if we are not going to end up with a serious smack (heroin) problem by the middle 80s, we ought to be concentrating on the health and social services side of it now'.

Despite the changes in treatment policy and the greater availability of illicit supplies of heroin, it is surprising that a study describing the criminal histories of 5000 addicts first notified in England and Wales between 1979 and 1981, and followed-up until the end of 1982, produced substantially similar results to those reported earlier by Mott and Taylor (1974). A study by the Home Office Statistical Department (1985) found that about half of the males and two-thirds of the females had not been convicted before the age of 28 (whatever their age at notification). But, of those males who had been convicted, almost three times as many had been convicted at particular ages as men in the general population. The proportion of the addicts' convictions for burglary and theft declined during the four years before, and up to two years after, notification, while the proportion for drug offences and fraud and forgery increased.

Some 6 per cent of the male addicts who had been convicted, were first convicted of an offence of personal violence compared with 12 per cent of male offenders in the general population at the same age. This proportion remained fairly constant during equivalent time periods before and after notification, so the involvement of notified addicts in violent crime had remained small and stable. It was estimated that no more than 4 per cent of 'notifiable' offences (indictable offences and the more serious summary offences) recorded by the police in England and Wales during the period 1979–82 were likely to have been committed by notified addicts.

Stimson and Oppenheimer (1982) had suggested that pressure from the courts may have been a significant reason for heroin users attending the DDUs during this time. The Home Office findings support this, since it was found that many of the new addicts had been convicted of an offence either immediately before or after they were notified.

Another study compared the criminal convictions after the age of 24 of all persons convicted of a drug offence (other than an offence involving cannabis) between 1979 and 1981 who were aged 24 or 25 at the time of the conviction, with those from a cohort of offenders born in 1953 who had been convicted after the age of 24 (only 5 per cent of the cohort). Given the earlier research findings it could reasonably be assumed that many of these drug offenders were also notified or notifiable addicts. The conviction histories of the males were very similar to those of the general offender cohort except, of course, they were more likely to have been convicted of drug offences. They were slightly less likely to have been convicted of personal violence offences and more likely to have been convicted of shoplifting or fraud offences. Apart from drug offences, there were no notable differences between the two groups of females (Slattery, 1988).

Thus, between 1972 and 1980, when heroin was very rarely prescribed to addicts attending the DDUs (where almost all the doctors licenced to prescribe it worked), the criminal histories of those new addicts who sought medical treatment and who were notified to the Home Office, were remarkably similar to those of the addicts who first came to notice between 1958 and 1971.

THE NEW HEROIN USERS: 1981 AND AFTER

By 1981 all the formal national indicators of heroin misuse (the numbers of notified heroin addicts, the numbers of seizures of heroin and the amounts seized) signalled a considerable increase in the extent of heroin misuse. There was evidence that many heroin misusers were not seeking medical treatment (and therefore would not be notified to the Home Office as addicts), that the prevalence of misuse in some parts of the country (especially Merseyside and Edinburgh) had increased dramatically, that the new misusers were as likely to smoke heroin ('chasing the dragon') as to inject it, and that many were committing offences in order to buy illicitly imported heroin of high purity (40–50 per cent) which was readily available on the black market and cheaper in real terms than it had been four or five years before (Home Office, 1985).

In response, the Government created the Ministerial Group on the Misuse of Drugs in July 1984, under the chairmanship of a Home Office Minister and including Ministerial representation from the Treasury, the Foreign and Commonwealth Office, from the Departments of Health and of Education and Science and of the Scottish and Welsh Offices. In the attempt to curb drug misuse, particularly of heroin, the Ministerial Group developed a five-point strategy, which involved simultaneously providing greater resources to reducing supplies of drugs from abroad, to law enforcement and increasing the deterrent effect of the control legislation, to prevention and to treatment and rehabilitation (Home Office, 1985; 1986; 1988).

The second heroin epidemic, like the first, was not uniformly spread through the United Kingdom but did emerge from the confines of London and the south-east of England. Pearson *et al.*, (1986) suggested that, in the north of England, there was less heroin misuse east of the Pennines that west of them and that there were marked local variations in injecting or smoking it, with injecting more common in areas where injecting of amphetamines was also practised. Pearson (1987), in 'The New Heroin Users', published verbatim interviews with some of them.

The most detailed studies of the relationship between heroin misuse and crime by the new heroin users have been conducted on Merseyside (Parker and Newcombe, 1987; Parker *et al.* 1988; Fazey, 1988). Studies were also carried out in Greater Nottingham (Bean and Wilkinson, 1988) and Glasgow (Hammersley *et al.*, 1987; 1989).

Parker *et al.* provided persuasive evidence that the exceptional rise in recorded household burglaries between 1981 and 1985 in one Merseyside borough, Wirral, paralleled the exceptional increase in the prevalence of heroin misuse amongst local unemployed young people living in the most deprived townships in the borough. It seemed likely that at least half of the adults convicted of such burglaries in the area would be heroin users. Mott (1986) had found 20 per cent of those convicted of residential burglaries in 1983 by the Wirral courts were notified addicts compared with between 3 per cent and 11 per cent in one or other of four London petty sessional divisions.

Parker *et al.* identified a substantial minority of the heroin-using offenders as young people who had grown up in high-crime areas but who were convicted for the first time after the age of 16, the typical age for first heroin use (16 was also the typical age for first heroin use in one local outbreak during the first epidemic—see de Alarcon and Rathod, 1968). This suggested, since most of them were unemployed, that for many or most of the users crime had become an economic necessity to fund the purchase of illicit supplies of heroin. There was also a larger group of heroin users who had first been convicted before they began to use heroin but whose rate of convictions for acquisitive crimes accelerated afterwards. Parker concluded that it seemed 'likely that the heroin epidemics of the 1980s, which are recruiting unemployed young adults, particularly in London and the north of England, may well be producing a stronger relationship between drug use and crime than was found in the 1960s'.

REDUCING HEROIN-RELATED CRIME—A RETURN TO THE BRITISH SYSTEM?

Some doctors working in areas where there are cheap and plentiful supplies of illicitly imported adulterated heroin readily available have argued that only the prescribing of pure pharmaceutical heroin will lure substantial numbers of misusers to seek treatment and 'keep the Mafia out' (for example Marks, 1987). Certainly the evidence from research conducted during the 1958 to 1971 heroin epidemic, when users were most often treated by the long-term prescribing of injectable heroin or methadone, suggests that such treatment can contain if not reduce the extent to which they commit acquisitive offences.

By the mid-1970s it became the practice of most of the DDUs to prescribe only oral methadone, often in reducing doses in the terms of a 'treatment contract' to new patients (Stimson and Oppenheimer, 1982). But the authors of the only controlled trial of the effects of prescribing injectable heroin or oral methadone (conducted between 1972–75) concluded that their findings '(did) *not* [emphasis added] indicate a clear overall superiority of either (treatment) approach' in terms either of achieving abstinence or of reducing illicit heroin use, or of reducing the extent to which the patients said that crime was a major form of income (Hartnoll *et al.* 1980).

More recent research has found that heroin users report committing fewer offences for money for drugs while they are receiving licit supplies in the course of medical treatment than when they are relying solely on black market supplies. Bennett and Wright (1986a) reported that the small groups of heroin users they studied in 1983/84 said they continued to use black market drugs in the year after they entered treatment. But they said they used illicitly obtained drugs less frequently and in smaller doses, during their first year of receiving treatment, whether it consisted of long-term prescribing of heroin or of oral methadone in reducing doses, than they had in the year before. Although many said they continued to steal to pay for their illicit drug others, particularly those who were receiving treatment which included the prescribing of heroin, said they usually stole things they wanted to use. Three quarters of the users who said they were obtaining all their supplies of opioids illicitly also said they committed non-drug offences exclusively to pay for drugs.

Fazey (1988) found that the patients who attended the Liverpool DDU continuously for a year (between 1985 and 1987) said they were spending, on average, half as much a week on black market drugs as they had before they attended. And, therefore, were probably committing fewer acquisitive offences.

Jarvis and Parker (1988) interviewed a small group of London opioid users in 1987 who said they were much less likely to commit offences during the periods they were receiving treatment than when they were not. Almost half of the group specifically mentioned the desire to give up crime as a reason for entering treatment, and only a few had been coerced into treatment as the result of a court order or an impending court appearance. Some comments from the former group included: 'everyday you have to shoplift in order to buy drugs before you start to feel sick. . . having a habit is a drudge'; and 'I hate crime, it's so nerve wracking but you have to do it'; and 'I've had enough of drugs and prison... I know I can do better'. Of the latter group, one woman said, 'the police threatened to take the baby away... they said if I went to court for supplying heroin the welfare would take the baby away'. On the other hand, several women said they had deliberately avoided seeking treatment because they feared the 'welfare' would remove their children.

Bennett and Wright (1986b) asked their subjects, all of whom were using heroin, and probably also other controlled drugs, whether they thought they would eventually choose to abstain from drug use with or without the help of medical treatment. About half said they probably would never abstain permanently while the remainder thought they would abstain at some time during the next ten years if some important changes occurred in their lives, most particularly, forming a stable relationship. Bennett and Wright suggested that helping addicts to come to the decision to stop using heroin was more likely to succeed in reducing heroin (or other drug) misuse and the associated crime, than a greater emphasis on law enforcement and deterrence.

In the United Kingdom heroin, and other 'problem drug takers', can decide voluntarily whether and when to seek medical treatment for their drug use or addiction. Some workers in the field suggest that the offer of relatively free and pure pharmaceutical heroin is the most effective treatment lure, while others have suggested that users are most likely to look for treatment when they feel they have had enough of the daily round of crime and shopping on the black market, and others suggest helping users to make the decision to abstain.

The advent of AIDS, with injecting drug users a high risk group, has revived controversy about the methods and aims of medical treatment for heroin misusers. But there has been very little published research on the effectiveness of the variety of treatment methods and/or prescribing regimes for heroin misusers who do present for treatment in terms of their continued drug misuse and any associated crime.

In the course of the debate Drs Robinson and Skidmore (1987) argued that 'a return to controlled availability (of heroin) is a recipe for disaster if it is not recognized that it is part of a response to managing drug abuse which involves many professional and non-professional agencies'. Spear

(1987) countered with a quotation from the Rolleston Report to show that it had not promoted maintenance prescribing of heroin (or morphine): 'it should not be too lightly assumed- . . . that an irreducible minimum of the drugs has been reached which cannot be withdrawn and which, therefore, must be continued indefinitely. . . ' Spear argued 'what those who favour a more flexible approach to the treatment of *long-term* [emphasis added] addicts are proposing is a holding, harm-reducing operation to allow the addict, with professional help, sufficient time to acquire the motivation likely to result in a permanent break with his addiction'.

The evidence summarised here suggests that more generous prescribing of heroin or methadone during the course of medical treatment will not result in the elimination of the acquisitive offences committed by heroin users. But it does suggest that such treatment could reduce the extent to which many steal to raise funds to buy black market drugs. Prescribing heroin or other opioids is not the only treatment that might reduce illicit heroin use and curb the black market but it should not be completely rejected as an option during the course of treatment. In the United Kingdom the most suitable method and goal of treatment for individual heroin users has always been, and remains, at the professional discretion and clinical judgement of the doctor treating the patient. But the evidence that the type of medical treatment offered to heroin users has implications for reducing and preventing crime cannot be ignored.

REFERENCES

Advisory Council on the Misuse of Drugs (1982) *Treatment and Rehabilitation* (London: HMSO).
Bean, P. T. and C. Wilkinson (1988) 'Drug-taking, Crime and the Illicit Supply System', *British Journal of Addiction*, 83, pp. 533–9.
Bennett, T. and R. Wright (1986a) 'The Impact of Prescribing on the Crimes of Opioid users', *British Journal of Addiction*, 81, pp. 265–73.
Bennett, T. and R. Wright (1986b) 'The Drug-taking Careers of Opioid Users', *Howard Journal of Criminal Justice*, 25, pp. 1–12.
Clark, D. (1980) 'Smack in the Capital', *Time Out*, no. 51, pp. 11–13.
De Alarcon, R. and N. H. Rathod 'Prevalence and Early Detection of Heroin Abuse', *British Medical Journal*, 1, pp. 549–53.
Downes, D. (1977) 'The Drug Addict as a Folk Devil', in P. Rock (ed.) *Drugs*

and Politics (New Jersey: Transaction Books).

Edwards, G. E. (1981) 'The Home Office Index as Basic Monitoring System', in G. E. Edwards and C. Busch (eds), *Drug Problems in Britain* (London: Academic Press).

Fazey, C. (1988) 'Heroin Addiction, Crime and the Effect of Medical Treatment', Report to the Home Office.

Glatt, M. M. *et al.* (1967) *The Drug Scene in Great Britain* (London: Edward Arnold).

Hammersley, R. and V. Morrison (1987) 'Effects of Polydrug Misuse on the Crimes of Heroin Users', *British Journal of Addiction*, 82, pp. 899–906.

Hammersley, R. *et al.* (1989) 'The Relationship between Crime and Opioid Use', *British Journal of Addiction*, 84, pp. 1029–44.

Hartnoll, R. *et al.* (1980) 'Evaluation of Heroin Maintenance in Controlled Trial', *Archives of General Psychiatry*, 37, pp. 877–84.

Hartnoll, R. *et al.* (1984) 'Recent Trends in Drug Use in Britain', *Druglink*, 19, pp. 22–4.

Hepworth, D. M. (1982) 'Addiction in Britain: Patterns of Narcotic Use in the Mid-sixties', Ph.D. thesis, London School of Economics.

Home Office (1967–71) *Dangerous Drugs Statistics* (London: Home Office).

Home Office (1974–8) *Statistics on the Misuse of Drugs in the United Kingdom* (London: Home Office).

Home Office (1985, 1986, 1988) *Tackling Drug Misuse* (London: Home Office).

Home Office Statistical Department (1985) 'Criminal Convictions of Persons first Notified as Narcotic Addicts 1979–81', Statistical Bulletin 19/85 (London: Home Office).

Jarvis, G. and H. Parker (1988) 'Does Medical Treatment Reduce Crime amongst Young Heroin Users?' Report to the Home Office.

Leech, K. (1973) *Keep the Faith Baby* (London: SPCK).

Lewis, R. (1985) 'Serious Business—the Global Heroin Economy', in A. Henman, R. Lewis and T. Malyon (eds) *The Big Deal* (London: Pluto Press).

Lindesmith, A. R. (1957) 'The British System of Narcotics Control', *Law and Contemporary Problems*, 22, pp. 141–53.

Marks, J. (1987) 'State Rationed Drugs', *Druglink*, 2, (4) p. 14.

Ministry of Health (1926) 'Report of the Departmental Committee on Morphine and heroin Addiction' (London: HMSO) (the Rolleston Report).

Ministry of Health (1961) 'Drug Addiction: Report of the Interdepartmental Committee' (London: HMSO) (the first Brain Report).

Ministry of Health (1965) 'Drug Addiction: the second Report of the Interdepartmental Committee' (London: HMSO) (the second Brain Report).

Mott, J. and M. Taylor (1974) *Delinquency Amongst Opiate Users*, Home Office Research Study no. 23 (London: HMSO)

Mott, J. (1975) 'The Criminal Histories of Male Non-medical Opiate Users in the United Kingdom', *Bulletin on Narcotics*, 27, pp. 41–4.

Mott, J. and N. H. Rathod (1976) 'Heroin Misuse and Delinquency in a New Town', *British Journal of Psychiatry*, 128, pp. 428–35.

Mott, J. (1981) 'Criminal Involvement and Penal Response', in G. E.

Edwards and C. Busch (eds) *Drug Problems in Britain* (London: Academic Press).

Mott, J. (1982) 'Opiate Use and Crime in the United Kingdom', *Contemporary Drug Problems*, Winter 1980, pp. 437–51.

Mott, J. (1986) 'Opioid Use and Burglary', *British Journal of Addiction*, 81, pp. 671–77.

O'Bryan, L. (1985) 'The Cost of Lacoste: Drugs, Style and Money', in A. Henman *et al.* (eds), *The Big Deal* (London: Pluto Press).

Parker, H. and R. Newcombe (1987) 'Heroin Use and Acquisitive Crime in an English Community', *British Journal of Sociology*, 38, pp. 331–50.

Parker, H. *et al.* (1988) *Living with Heroin* (Milton Keynes: Open University Press).

Pearson, G., M. Gilman and S. McIver *Young People and Heroin: an Examination of Heroin Use in the North of England*, Health Education Research Council Research Report no. 8 (London: Gower and Health Education Council).

Pearson, G. (1987) *The New Heroin Users* (Oxford: Basil Blackwell).

Rathod, N. H. (1972) 'The Use of Heroin and Methadone by Injection in a New Town', *British Journal of Addiction*, 67, pp. 113–22.

Robertson, J. R. and C. A. Skidmore (1987) 'Management of Drug Addicts', letter to *Lancet*, 6 June, pp. 1322.

Schur, E. (1963) *Narcotic Addiction in Britain and America* (London: Tavistock).

Slattery, J. (1988) Home Office Statistical Department, unpublished.

Spear, H. B. (1969) 'The Growth of Heroin Addiction in the United Kingdom', *British Journal of Addiction*, 64, pp. 245–55.

Spear, H. B. (1975) 'The British Experience', *The John Marshall Journal of Practice and Procedure*, 9, pp. 67–98.

Spear, H. B. (1982) 'British Experience in the Management of Opiate Dependence', in M. M. Glatt and J. Marks (eds), *The Dependence Phenomenon* (Lancaster: MTP Press).

Spear, H. B. (1987) letter to *Lancet*, 6 June, pp. 1322.

Stimson, G. V. (1973) *Heroin and Behaviour* (Shannon: Irish University Press).

Stimson, G. V. and E. Oppenheimer (1982) *Heroin Addiction* (London: Tavistock Press).

7 Lifestyles and Law Enforcement

Mark Gilman and Geoffrey Pearson

Too often there is an abject passivity implied in the lifestyle of those people who misuse drugs—typically summed up in the image of the 'smacked out' heroin addict and expressions such as 'retreatist' or 'escapist'—although this is quite false to the actual experience. In their justly celebrated paper from New York in the late 1960s, 'Taking Care of Business', Ed Preble and James Casey (1969) set the life of the street addict in a different light. The day-to-day lifestyle of a heroin user, as they described it, is one which involves a hectic flurry of hustles and economic exchanges, requiring considerable resourcefulness, economic dexterity and entrepreneurial skill and committment. When not searching for money or drugs to start the day, the heroin user was trying to avoid the police, looking for a safe place to 'get off', searching again for more money and the next bag, in an endless cycle of activity. Being a daily heroin user, according to Preble and Casey, was a job of work, a kind of work, moreover, which was seven days a week with no rest days. Even so, the street addict had a spring in his step in the more usually down-trodden streets of the ghetto. He had a business appointment to meet, had maybe just missed it. Life was a frantic whirl of friendship and emnity, business and loafing, winners and losers.

This way of life came to the streets of some areas of the North of England as an entirely new phenomenon as recently as the early 1980s, when heroin began to become available in cheap and plentiful supply in many of these localities. Heroin had been virtually unknown outside London until this time. There were small numbers of old-time users in many of the Northern towns and cities, but even so Britain's serious problems of drug misuse had been largely confined to London. What had, of course, existed in many of the industrial cities of the North was a delinquent or near-delinquent culture among young men and women in many working-class

95

neighbourhoods and council estates. This had been researched in a thorough-going way in Liverpool by John Barron
Mays in the 1950s, and later by Howard Parker and Owen Gill
in the 1970s (Mays, 1954; Parker, 1974; Gill, 1977). Although
such detailed research was not conducted elsewhere, with the
exception of David Downes' work in inner London, the central
indications from the increased interest in youthful deviance in
the 1970s confirmed the view that working-class youth
cultures and the hidden economies of working-class communities were more generally active in British cities and major
industrial towns (Downes, 1966; Cohen, 1972; Mungham and
Pearson, 1976; Hall and Jefferson, 1976; Corigan, 1979; Willis,
1977 and 1978; Brake, 1980; Jenkins, 1983).

The activities of young people which attracted concern were
rarely about property crime, except in the sense of criminal
damage and joy riding, and more likely to be centred on
hooliganism and fighting. Drug misuse was only a fleeting
focus for these concerns through the 1970s and into the early
1980s. Even so, there had been knowledge of drugs such as
amphetamines since the early 1960s ('purple hearts', 'French
blues', 'black bombers', 'uppers', 'leapers') and amphetamine
sulphate use has remained a major influence, although one
largely unexplored by social research. Hallucinogenic drugs
such as LSD and 'magic mushrooms' also began to acquire
some popularity during the late 1960s and early 1970s, and
the use of barbiturates and other 'downers' became associated
with various forms of 'poly-drug' misuse during the 1970s
(Jamieson, Glanz and MacGregor, 1984). In some areas
injecting drug subcultures appeared in various localities in the
North of England and Scotland in the course of the 1970s,
although these were always quite small, inward-looking and
reclusive. Cannabis, of course, came to be widely used in both
working-class and middle-class communities during the 1970s
and continued through to the 1980s.

In the course of the 1980s all this has changed. Somewhere
between 1979 and 1981 heroin began to become available in
cheap and plentiful supply from South West Asia, Iran,
Afghanistan and Pakistan. It was 'brown' smoking heroin, and
the practice of 'chasing the dragon' took off in many towns
and cities (Pearson, Gilman and McIver, 1986; Auld, Dorn and
South, 1986; Burr, 1987; Pearson, 1987a; Dorn and South,
1987; Haw, 1985; Parker, Bakx and Newcombe, 1988). Many

of the people who first tried the new 'smack' or 'skag' were unaware of the fact that they were taking heroin; others believed that smoking the drug was non-addictive since they had only previously known about the earlier injecting subcultures of London 'junkies' from the 1960s and the early 1970s. Where injecting subcultures had become established (around 'speed' and 'barbs') the new heroin would be more likely to be injected, rendered soluble by acidification, either with a 'Jif' lemon, citric crystals or a 'drop of vinegar'. An opiate using culture had also begun to grow in some areas where Diconal was the preference drug. There was a wide diversity of different existing drug scenes, involving their own different local knowledge of drugs and drug administration practices—for example whether powder drugs were sniffed, injected or dissolved in a glass of beer. The new heroin problem grafted itself onto that pre-existing set of diverse knowledges and subcultural practices in different localities (Pearson, Gilman and McIver, 1986).

The dominant trend was that where the new heroin became available, it was extremely popular among substantial proportions of young people. The sudden availability of heroin in so many neighbourhoods where it had been previously quite unknown resulted in localised 'mini-epidemics' among friendship networks. The arrival of heroin in abundant supply also coincided with the steep economic recession which followed the 'monetarist' budget of 1981, and it settled as just one more problem among the residents of 'multi-problem' estates— housing decay; unemployment; generalised poverty; multiracial tension and conflict; crime and the fear of crime; lack of access to transport facilities and private cars; and lack of play facilities and other amenities. It was bad news.

VILLAINS, VICTIMS AND JACK THE LAD

Against this depressingly drab social environment, the heroin habit of the early 1980s spread like wildfire in some neighbourhoods. A pattern of life which would have been entirely familiar to Ed Preble and James Casey in New York in the 1960s now became commonplace in many of the northern towns and cities:

'Like you get up, you've gotta go out, get your money, get your smack, come back, use it. . . . You're alright for ten minutes, go back out again, get money. . . you're turkeying after a couple of hours, can't get nothin', whatever, back out again. . . '   (Colin, 23 years, Manchester)

'What was your typical day like?'
'You just, get your gear, smoke it, and then. . . wonder where you'll get your next bag from and watch a bit of telly, well that's it. . . that just makes you realise and you start thinking, "God, what am I gonna do for tonight now?". . . So, like, you try and go out and get more money, and that like, so your whole day's just taken up. . . Go and do whatever you do for your money, buy your gear, get back, by then like. . . you smoke it. . . then tea-time comes around.'   (Sharon, 21 years, Merseyside)

This treadmill of activity—a seven-day a week job, as Preble and Casey had described it—was a major part of the problem which many of these new heroin users faced. In its compulsive, metronome qualities it mimicked the working day of the working man or woman in Lancashire and Yorkshire in the early 1980s.

'Getting out of that little rut you've been in for the last, y'know, twelve months or sixteen months or whatever. . . You know, getting up in the morning, going down for your gear. . . smoking the gear, what have you. . . It's just the actual boredom, you know, sitting in the house. . . Like when I do come off, I just stay in the house. . . just hibernate sort of thing.'   (Paul, 24 years, Merseyside)

'It takes time, cos for two-and-a-half years like, all you've been interested in is getting a bag. . . getting a bag . . . and you get used to that. That's a routine for you like. . . . So. . . '   (Eddie, 21 years, Merseyside)

Eventually the heroin user grows tired of this relentless activity, hustling for money, looking for drugs, the daily hectic scramble, the preoccupation with getting the timing right to avoid unpleasant symptoms of withdrawal. Of course, it is equally true that at the end of the day in any job of work, you try and put your feet up and relax. If your job is not going well, you complain that you've lost interest in seeing friends, that life is just 'bed and work', that all you do nowadays is watch TV. And it is just the same for heroin users who are growing tired of this particularly demanding routine: they sit in front of the telly, like any other person after a hard day's work, and vegetate.

This is often the point at which heroin users turn themselves in for treatment. Hence part of the reason for the emphasis on the passivity and victim status of the stereotypical drug user seen in the clinic. There is also the contribution of the 'ex-addict's tale' which is told and learned at the meetings of Alcoholics Anonymous, Narcotics Anonymous and other related self-help groups. A determinedly negative attitude is encouraged in these settings towards one's former drug use: the monkey on your back, the absence of friendship in any form, the renunciation of self-destructive behaviour. Then there is also the simplified version of events which is offered in various forms of defence, whether in terms of moral self-vindication or before the law: 'I didn't do it. It was the drug. Heroin was the boss. It wasn't me'.

One must always listen carefully to the versions of their addiction given by ex-users, or those who are trying to be ex-users. Their testimony must, if they are to convince themselves in the first place that their efforts are worthwhile, be a negative one. Otherwise, why give up? The ex-addict's tale is also cleansed of any reference to the pleasures of drug use, although the fact that drug use is pleasurable is why people do it in the first place. This denial of pleasure adds a further element of unreliability to the ex-addict's testimony, in terms of trying to understand the motives of drug use with which health education, treatment and rehabilitation services, and law enforcement must contend. The position of the ex-user is not unlike the ex-Moonie as described by James Beckford (1985), who must forget and deny the residual friendships and attachments to the old faith. Thinking of what it means to give up heroin as apostasy makes a lot of sense. It is why so many ex-users give up drugs and get religion.

The ex-user appeals to his or her former identity as that of a victim of a system controlled by villains. And many of us are

too happy to agree in thi.. The big-bucks lifestyles of the
ounce dealers with their clubs and car-wrecking firms; the guy
who did five kilos and bought a corner shop; these are
certainly different from the local herbert who knocks out £5
and £10 bags of heroin and supplies his own smoke; or the
young woman who does four hours on the street every night
to supply herself and her boyfriend with heroin. In these
terms, a contrast between villains and victims seems entirely
right. But in another way, not so.

We usually think of the structure of drug distribution
systems as a pyramid, with traffickers and economically
motivated dealers at the apex and users and user-dealers at
the base. At the apex, major traffickers are seen as evil,
motivated, rational actors who pursue the object of monetary
gain. At the base, we see users and user-dealers as sick,
irrational actors who are compelled by addiction and whose
actions are in pursuit of drugs. Therefore, in a simple logic
the apex is seen as the site for enforcement (supply-side)
measures, whereas the base is seen as a site for treatment
(demand-side) services.

The user-dealer presents something of a problem for this
model. On the one hand, he or she buys and sells drugs and
might also handle stolen goods, engaging in this activity in
order to supply their own habit—so that it might appear as
an economically rational activity. On the other hand, at this
level of drug-dealing there is no real surplus value produced
(other than drugs for self-consumption) so that the user-
dealer's behaviour is also seen to fall within the victim
category as a form of economically profitless self-harm. In
some areas, local drug subcultures themselves describe a
fundamental difference among dealers between the 'smack-
heads' who do it for the drugs, as against the 'bread-heads'
who do it for the money. In a more widely available
commonsense moral logic, the user-dealer at the messy end of
the drug distribution network is typically conceived of as a
rag-arsed victim of the heroin trade which is master-minded
by 'Mr Big' who stands for the Barons, the 'evil entrepreneurs', the 'dealers in white death'.

And yet, this is not all that there is to say. Both in terms of
how to check the flow and availability of drugs within any
given neighbourhood, and also the economics of the user-

dealer operation, there is good reason to think that this way of approaching the issue is wrong-headed. Low-level distribution networks, typically user–dealers, are the crucial means by which drugs become available within a neighbourhood—both sustaining existing drug using subcultures, and also recruiting new users. 'Mr Big' has more important business to attend to than knocking out £5 bags for the retail market, and he also has too much money invested to take such stupid risks. His trade is one characterised by high levels of necessary concealment and secrecy. The local user–dealer, however, must be visible if customers are to know his whereabouts. The user–dealer is therefore both someone who is crucial to the development of local drug epidemics, and also more easily liable to detection.

The neglect of the user–dealer as a focus for an integrated programme of enforcement and rehabilitation measures is all the more odd when we turn to the economic aspects of the lifestyle. The attribution of victim status, for example, is difficult to reconcile with even the lowest level of heroin distribution, as indicated by our fieldwork in the mid-1980s:

> Alan is a young man who lives in a run-down estate in a socially deprived area of a Northern English city. He buys 1 gram of heroin at a price of £70. He takes £25 worth for his own smoke, and knocks out the rest in fourteen £5 bags which he sells to local users. This yields an income of £70, which is then invested in 1 gram of heroin and Alan begins the economic cycle again.

Once more, there is a treadmill, metronome logic to this lifestyle. Viewed in one light, it is a rock-bottom subsistence economy, yielding no profit and no economic rationality other than mere survival. Another victim-recruit to the ruthless economy masterminded by Mr Big?

Viewed in terms of cash-flow rather than profit, however, Alan's activities look rather different. If the economic cycle is repeated daily, this involves a weekly cash-flow of £500 and a hypothetical annual cash-flow of £25 000. Where people attempt to repeat the economic cycle two or three times a day, we are looking at a cash-flow of £50 000 to £75 000 per year. This is a phenomenal economic achievement in a poor neighbourhood.

Of course, it is extremely difficult to manage and sustain a cash-flow of these proportions from such a narrow economic base. There is also always the added risk that the user–dealer (and immediate friends) begin to consume increasingly large amounts of heroin and eat into the already fragile basis of the cash-flow, so that the hypothetical annual cash-flow might remain a hypothesis. Even so, it is possible to keep economic ventures such as these afloat for a fair amount of time, and during that time, far from being a victim of the system, the user–dealer will enjoy considerable local status. Even when he is not immediately able to supply drugs, he will have a sound working knowledge of the local drug scene, in terms of availability, price structure and purity. The scale of the cash-flow means that he will always have 'a fiver' or 'a tenner' to spare, which itself can mean status among friends and acquaintances. Of course, Alan has to work hard which means that he doesn't have a lot of time to spend with friends. Which is why, when he finally turns himself in or gets arrested, he owns up to having lived a futile lifestyle, a career that went bust. Nevertheless, whether or not you or I care to think of him as an abject victim of the villainous trade of the Mr Bigs and the Drug Barons, in his own locality he is Jack the Lad.

DRUG USER CAREERS: THE CONCEPT OF 'EARLY RETIREMENT'

This image should not have been a surprise to Britain as it encountered its heroin epidemic of the 1980s. We should have been able to predict what would happen from a reading of North American sociological fieldwork from the 1960s and early 1970s—the 'stand-up cat' status described by Feldman from Boston and New York, the 'cool' hipster from Chicago in Harold Finestone's account from the 1950s, the swaggering gang-boys from Ed Preble's and James Casey's New York, the street-wise hustlers in a later Chicago described by Patrick Hughes, the 'righteous dope fiend' from Sutter's West Coast drug scene (Feldman, 1968; Finestone, 1957; Preble and Casey, 1969; Hughes, 1977; Hughes *et al.* 1971; Sutter, 1966).

Of course, not all drug users can be characterised by this inventive, entrepreneurial and economically resourceful lifestyle. There are also those who, typically counted amount the drug users who seek the assistance of clinics and other services, are in a wretched state of physical health, have considerable difficulty in supporting their habits, experience difficulties in terms of both their personal relationships and the material props of life such as housing, and lurch from one crisis to the next (cf. Jamieson, Glanz and MacGregor, 1984; Donn and South, 1985). Times change, and lifestyles change with them. It is vitally necessary, therefore, that drug policies are fashioned in such a way that they are flexible and able to adapt themselves to the different circumstances of different stages in a typical drug user's career.

It is not difficult to construct different versions of drug using careers. Perhaps the most straightforward model is one whereby the initial offer and an early phase of experimentation is followed by occasional drug use on a recreational basis, and then possibly by compulsive or habitual use:

(1) the non-user;
(2) the initial offer and experimentation;
(3) occasional use on a recreational basis;
(4) the 'grey area' of transitional use;
(5) habitual/compulsive/addictive use.

In the context of our research on heroin misuse and health education policy, we have described elsewhere how these different *statuses of involvement* with heroin (or another drug) imply different health education strategies, together with the suggestion that the *transition points* at which drug users move between these different statuses might be thought of as crucial points of intervention for health education (Pearson, Gilman and McIver, 1986). Other models of drug careers will often then go on to describe a final stage of development as 'abstinence', although we differ with this approach since drug users can (and do) quit their involvement with heroin (or any other drug) at different points, so that each status of involvement will imply its own possible *exit* towards abstinence.

For example, where a minority pursuit drug such as heroin is concerned the vast bulk of the population will neither encounter heroin, nor contemplate its use, so that they never progress beyond the status of a non-user. Or, someone in the early experimentation phase might progress no further, for a variety of reasons: 'It made me sick, I didn't like it'; 'It was too heavy a stone man, I couldn't handle that'. Someone who has progressed to occasional use, on the other hand, might see friends beginning to get into difficulties with their drug use in the form of addiction or criminal involvement and quit at that stage; 'Oh it was getting too heavy, I just kicked it into touch'; 'I didn't like the scene I was getting into, so I just packed it in'. In other words, you do not have to become addicted in order to take an exit route towards abstinence.

For those who do become addicted, reasons for giving up (or trying to give up) might also take a number of forms; pressure from family and friends; or simply a weariness with the whole drug business: 'It was just getting too much of a hassle. . . ' In other words, if, to follow Preble and Casey, heroin use is a form of work, then for some users abstinence is a form of 'early retirement'.

Different stages in a drug using career are also associated with different lifestyles. Early users are initially anxious, and then later they can become enthusiastic and energetic proselyters: 'Try this stuff, mate, it's fuckin good. . . Don't bother about all that crap on the telly, you won't get a habit'. After this early, energetic phase of occasional use in the 'grey area' of transition to addiction, drug users typically settle down to a settled routine, although things will often keep happening to de-stabilise the routine, requiring re-adjustments and re-appraisals of the situation by the user—who v‖ or decide that it is time for early retirement. At this point, his or her account of their previous drug use often has a questionable value for understanding patterns of drug misuse, since it will tend to emphasise the negative aspects of the lifestyle: in other words, the ex-addict's tale will be adopted which mirrors precisely the negative commentary of those who have opted for early retirement from conventional employ-ment careers. 'I had no time for friends, or anything but work.' 'It was getting me down, all bed and work.' 'I was turning into a workaholic.'

A crucial dimension of these 'careers' of drug involvement —from rookie and 'tea-boy', through apprentice, to handy-man, to craftsman, disillusionment and then retirement, and even possibly to a 'second career' as a heavy drinker—is that they are not merely individual 'life cycle' developments. Rather, they come about in interaction with a whole series of other impingements from both the social environment and the individual's shifting sense of identity and confirmations or disconfirmations of that identity.

One significant aspect of this social environment, which is surprisingly neglected in so many approaches to drug use and misuse, is the question of law enforcement. Drug enforcement nibbles away remorselessly at the bottom end of the drug distribution network, catching a variety of small-fry users and user–dealers through its operations, while also causing either short-term or long-term changes in the local availability of drugs, leading itself to changes in drug fashions and preferences. Pharmacology and fashion interact upon each other in helping to shape both drug preference and lifestyles. For example, a group of friends who use cannabis and enjoy having a 'draw' together discover heroin which becomes a new preference drug. At first, this is associated with a smart, cool lifestyle. But then heroin becomes scarce in their locality, possibly as a result of law enforcement activity, with different consequences for different users. So that while some of them retain their attachment to the smart lifestyle, with or without heroin, others diversify into the use of oblivion drugs such as temgesic or temazepam, coming to be known as 'garbage heads' by their former companions. The local drug scene is constantly shifting and changing, and lifestyles shift and change accordingly.

The role of drug enforcement in these processes is often haphazard, in that low-level drug enforcement trawls rarely appear to have been thought through in terms of strategic planning in the way that operations are planned and executed against major traffickers. The fact that low-level police operations are given a low priority is partly a consequence of the moral logic of the victim/villain distinction, and also that the occupational culture of the police gives a privileged status to bulk seizures as a focus for police operations whereby only a major bust is seen as good 'result'. One must also allow for a certain amount of operational throughtlessness:

'Honestly, round here the DS [drug squad] are a joke. I tell you, they use the same cars and the same fellas, over and over again. You can spot 'em a mile off. . . Even when they do try a bit, y'know, it's pathetic. Like, the fellas they use, they always have a bit of weight on 'em, you know what I mean. And when did you ever see a smack head with a beer belly?. . . [laughs]. . . 'Honest to God, they're last.'

(Maxine, 22 years, Merseyside)

We do not suggest that this is entirely typical. Nevertheless, there seems to be no reason to believe that a more strategic deployment of police resources in terms of low-level drug enforcement could not play a more emphatic role more generally as part of a concerted policy of encouraging minor drug offenders (including user–dealers) to seek assistance with their drug-related problems.[1] Indeed, law enforcement could have a crucial role to play as part of a multi-agency strategy designed both to reduce the local availability of illicit drugs and to accelerate the decision-making process by which users and user–dealers take 'early retirement'.

GETTING TO GRIPS WITH LIFESTYLES: THE MYTH OF VOLUNTARISM

The challenge for drug interventions is how to get to grips with the actually existing drug user lifestyles, which often have as much to do with fashion as with pharmacology, and which bear little relationship to the stereotype of a passive victim occupying the 'sick role'. Here, by way of introduction, are two injecting drug users, offering their comments on current health policies in the context of an evaluation of the effectiveness of the *Smack in the eye* comic which has been circulated in Manchester as an attempt to attract the interest of drug users in reducing high-risk behaviour (Gilman, 1988 and 1989). First, a view on government-funded national media campaigns which is deeply symptomatic of the way in which official policies can often be seen as actively hostile to the interests of drug users:

'. . . a lot of my mates are convinced that the AIDS adverts are just propaganda from the government to stop us enjoying ourselves. . . y'know what I mean, you can't even have a fuck now. . . They just don't believe anything from the government. . . and these guys are not idiots. . . they're people who know the score'   (Johnny, 29 years, Manchester)

Next a comment on the comic itself, which contains both a large amount of explicit pictorial material and also attempts to exploit humour to the full:

'This is the first thing I've seen that doesn't tell you to pack it in before you go blind. . . most of the other shit treats you like naughty kids. . . for fuck's sake!. . . when will they realise that we do it because we like it and we'll stop when we're fucking sick of it and not when they tell us to.'

(Ian, 23 years, Manchester)

Not only is such an actually-existing drug user unlikely to take 'early retirement' and turn himself in for treatment on a voluntaristic basis, he (or she) is also unlikely to be impressed by the current mode of televisual 'health education', involving devastatingly shot *film noir* impressions of the AIDS risk. Transmitted at 2 a.m. in the advertising slots between low-budget alternative rock videos and retro-cult third-rate B movies, these 'health education' inputs jostle against advertisements for Sun Cloche cooling beach jelly, the latest low-alcohol synthesised rum-cola Caribbean Blossom fruit drink, and Free Interest New Accent Banking Systems. Quite apart from the fact that adverts are when you 'go for a pee' when watching late-night television most drug addicts are not at their best at two in the morning. The lack of fit between what is conjured up by the fevered imaginations of 'yuppie' market researchers who have cornered the multi-million pound government 'health education' budgets in Mrs Thatcher's Britain, when set against the grim realities of drug misuse in working-class England and Scotland, is a devastating judgement on the gulf between social classes. It also fails to connect with the bottom-up appreciation of the potential risk of self-injury such as abscesses or amputations through injection— known variously as 'shooting up', 'fixing', 'jacking up', 'having a dig'—where the vocabulary of the street can be a brutal and uncompromising acknowledgement of the self-harm of an intravenous drug using habit.

This is a challenge for all forms of intervention—whether it is health education, law enforcement, or treatment and rehabilitation. These three modes of intervention, moreover, often find themselves in conflict with each other. We have dealt with how these conflicts can appear in the sphere of health education elsewhere (Pearson, Gilman and McIver, 1986) and there is now a wider appreciation of the potential conflicts which are inherent in multi-agency strategies within the sphere of the criminal justice system (Blagg *et al.* 1988; Sampson *et al*, 1988). Here, we will focus on the potential and actual conflicts between treatment and law enforcement in relation to drug misuse. Treatment services will, of course, increasingly also involve various forms of 'harm reduction' health education, whereby the aim is to reduce high-risk behaviour by drug users such as sharing injecting equipment.

In terms of the forms in which these conflicts are produced and reproduce themselves, it is not only that treatment services aim to help drug users, while enforcement agencies aim to punish them. There is also the implicit assumption in both models that a neat distinction can be made between 'victims' who are in need of treatment services and 'villains' who are the legitimate object of law enforcement. However, as we have already indicated this is a false and unhelpful assumption.

It is nevertheless very powerful, and we can begin to understand how it is produced and reproduced by the way in which drug problems make a very different impact on the routine workloads of different groups of professionals and different agencies (Pearson, Blagg and Smith, 1987). In the case of treatment and counselling agencies, for example, a large amount of their clientele are drug users who have opted for early retirement. It follows that a great many of the drug users seen by these agencies are not at all typical of the more general drug using population. The medical model of treatment, moreover, assumes that the client is a compliant individual who adopts the 'sick role' and enters into a treatment contract on a voluntaristic basis.

It is, however, highly questionable as to what proportion of those drug users who do turn themselves in for treatment have done so on an entirely voluntaristic basis. A wide range of subtle compulsions are at work—pressure from family and friends, the perceived threat of enforcement and possible imprisonment, the fear that one's children might be taken into public care if steps are not taken to 'show willing' and to enter some form of treatment. However, the medical model and associated counselling philosophies often seem to ignore these compulsions in the actual lives of illicit drug users, and proceed as if the contract between agency and client was one which had been entered into on a voluntaristic basis.

A further consequence of these assumptions is that law enforcement itself is either ignored, or regarded as no more than an obstacle to effective therapeutic engagements with drug users. Hence the refusal in the medical profession to countenance any idea of compulsory treatment for drug users. At the extreme, this view is bolstered by the argument that the problems which drug users experience are entirely a consequence of the illegality of drugs such as heroin, leading to a variety of arguments for legalisation or decriminalisation. As we know, these are arguments which have surfaced again in a number of forms in the late 1980s (Pearson, 1989b). But although arguments which would bring illicit drugs within a system of decriminalised regulation are undoubtedly interesting and sometimes intellectually compelling, the fact remains that for the foreseeable future drug services and drug workers must operate within a framework of law whereby their clients are outside the law.

What is then necessary, it seems to us, is to embrace fully the implications of the illegality of the use of indisputably dangerous drugs such as heroin and cocaine. To recognise, in fact, that within the provision of a properly devised system of community-based programmes for drug users—which would bring together within a multi-agency framework agencies such as the police, courts, probation service and the medical profession—law enforcement measures could be an effective and humane way of encouraging drug users to seek and accept help.[2]

There are two sides to this argument. The first concerns drug users themselves, and the second concerns the communities in which they live. In so far as drug users are concerned, existing drug services often seem remote and inaccessible (and often *are* remote and inaccessible) and it would be

difficult to pretend that a system of services which allows drug
users to get themselves into an utterly wretched state before
they can secure and accept help is in any way humane. Here
are two fictitious, but familiar examples of users at the point
at which they are typically referred by their general practitioners, and accepted, for methadone maintenance:

> Male, 33 years. Health extremely poor, ulcerated legs and
> numerous abscesses, very thin and in considerable pain.
> Using for 12 years. Criminal record and imprisonment in
> the past. Funds addiction by acquisitive crime including
> domestic burglary.

> Female, 30 years. Health very poor, regular groin injector,
> several open sores and abscesses. Using for 9 years. Has had
> several detox treatments in the past. Hepatitis B carrier.
> Funds addiction by prostitution.

Here are two people who should have been encouraged to
take 'early retirement' some years ago. However, the available
treatment services in their locality offered no incentive, in that
maintenance prescriptions were frowned upon. Nor did the
workings of the penal system offer anything other than a
temporary respite through incarceration. A deliberate and
explicit alignment of the criminal justice system and treatment services—by means of community-based 'diversion
schemes' which have been highly successful in the sphere of
juvenile justice during the 1980s—could hardly do a less
effective job (Children's Society, 1988).

If community-based multi-agency programmes might accelerate the process by which drug users take 'early retirement',
thus providing a more humane and effective response to the
needs of drug users, then this is an approach which might also
better serve the needs of the communities in which they live.
Serious problems of drug misuse, as these have developed
during the 1980s, have settled in a highly concentrated form
in neighbourhoods already suffering from multiple problems
of social deprivation such as unemployment, poverty and
housing decay (Pearson, Gilman and McIver, 1986; Pearson,
1987b; Parker, Bakx and Newcombe, 1988).

These clearly established associations between heroin

misuse and unemployment have been characteristically approached by social scientists and politicians, where they have been addressed at all, in terms of the impact of the social environment on patterns of drug misuse. However, we also need to take into consideration the impact of concentrated pockets of drug misuse on the social environment. And when this is done, we can see that the heroin epidemic of the 1980s simply rubbed salt into the wounds of those people compelled to live in such impoverished conditions as are experienced by many run-down neighbourhoods in the North of England and elsewhere. The interests of such people — people, moreover, who are not themselves illicit drug users — have never been addressed by therapeutically-oriented medical models which rely upon the voluntaristic enlightened self-interest of the drug user seeking treatment. And yet when these problems are counted in the balance, they must on any reckoning far outweigh the problem of drug misuse *per se* — in terms of increased levels of property crime whereby addicts supply their habits, the fear of crime and the added fear that drugs will impinge upon the lives of one's own children, and the vague but real sense of inconvenience and menace which is experienced by people who live in areas where drug use and drug-dealing are widespread.

The parents' groups and other forms of community pressure-group which flourished in the North of England in the mid-1980s were deeply symptomatic of these problems, and were not always solely concerned with the needs of drug users themselves and their families (Pearson, Gilman and McIver, 1986). One major focus for attention was why local user–dealers seemed to be allowed to do their business unchecked, when everybody in the neighbourhood knew who was doing the business and where — with the constant arrival and departure of taxis conveying people in pursuit of drugs, the rat-tat-tat on the dealer's door, and evidence of drug misuse in terms of discarded tin-foil and injecting equipment.

This groundswell of popular concern could hardly be described as a 'silent' voice in drugs discourse, because it often made its presence noisily felt. Nevertheless, it was one which went largely ignored. In so far as the clinics and other drug services were concerned, they were largely irrelevant to the problem given the traditional medical model of a compliant patient who adopts the 'sick role' and willingly enters a treatment contract. This is an arrangement which is breached, of course, in the case of mental disorder where compulsory hospitalisation is a central feature of traditional responses, and the Royal College of Psychiatrists is currently debating the advisability of a 'Community Treatment Order' for the mentally ill (Royal College of Psychiatrists, 1987; Scott-Moncrieff, 1988). With respect to drug misuse, however, although compulsion was recommended in 1965 by the second Brain Committee this has never found favour with the medical profession (Ministry of Health, 1965; Edwards, 1989). The question of some form of compulsion is nevertheless likely to return as a nagging preoccupation in the field of drug misuse, and one of the arguments in its favour will be how to provide a more effective means of community defence.

In terms of the police, justifications for perceived inaction against small-time dealers were four-fold: (a) the user–dealers were small-fry and limited police resources were being directed against larger traffickers; (b) the timing and implementation of a raid against such small dealers was difficult, in terms of yielding a sufficient quantity of drug seizure to justify the action; (c) small-scale user–dealers were entry points for surveillance operations intended to penetrate higher levels of the distribution network in accordance with the first aim of targeting major traffickers; (d) user–dealers were the 'victims' of the system and more appropriately dealt with by treatment and rehabilitation measures rather than enforcement.

Given that it is through user–dealers and small-scale distribution networks that drugs actually enter a locality, and if one allows that a paramount objective should be to prevent new users from entering the drug distribution system, each of these justifications is seriously flawed. What seems to be necessary in order to break this deadlock would be low-level enforcement measures, aligned to community-based criminal justice diversion programmes in order to make illegal drugs more difficult to obtain locally, to accelerate the process by which users enter treatment programmes, and to offer a measure of protection to the wider interests of the local non-drug-using community.

CHANGE OF GEAR: PUBLIC HEALTH, HARM REDUCTION AND 'PUNISHMENT IN THE COMMUNITY'

The Home Office Green Paper of 1988 on *Punishment, Custody and the Community*, which is concerned with the development of non-custodial alternatives for young adult offenders, offers a window of opportunity for the development of effective community-based programmes for minor drug offenders. While floating controversial proposals such as 'electronic tagging' as an alternative to custodial remand, the central emphasis of the Green Paper is to build upon the success of community-based projects in the juvenile justice system, such as Intermediate Treatment and diversion schemes, which have helped to cut by one half the number of young people under the age of 17 years in custody in the course of the 1980s. The success of these juvenile justice schemes should not be over-stated, in that the demographic changes which have reduced the size of the youthful population since the 'baby boom' of the 1960s have also played a part, and there remain wide local and regional variations in the extent to which magistrates' courts rely upon custodial sentencing—often summed up under the slogan 'justice by geography' (Children's Society, 1988; Richardson, 1988). There are also risks that community provisions such as 'community service orders' have a net-widening effect where they are used by the courts not as alternatives to custody, but in response to offenders who would not have received a custodial sentence in the first place (Marshall, 1985; Cohen, 1979 and 1985; Wilson, 1989). In spite of a growing view that these arguments on 'net-widening' and the 'dispersal of discipline' might have been over-stated (Rodger, 1988; McMahon, 1990), it will nevertheless be necessary to ensure that the expansion of community-based programmes do not have the effect of net-widening or accelerating the tariff if they are to be true alternatives to custody and are not to be counterproductive.

The proposal on 'electronic tagging' had predictably been criticised on civil liberties grounds, although more generally the Green Paper proposals have been favourably received by a wide range of relevant bodies (NACRO, 1988; Children's Society, 1989; Association for Juvenile Justice, 1989). There has, however, been an exceptionally hostile response from the National Association of Probation Officers, indicative of a strong aversion within the Probation Service to the idea that its work supervising offenders in the community should be dubbed 'punishment in the community' (NAPO, 1988). This reflects a history of opposition within the Probation Service to attempts to extend its control functions, such as the accusation that the recommendations of the Younger Report of 1974 would transform probation officers into 'screws on wheels' (Home Office, 1974; NAPO, 1975; Walker and Beaumont, 1981). NAPO's oppositional stance to the Green Paper is therefore not surprising, and although the outcome of the discussion which has ensued is far from certain, where drug-related offenders are concerned the role of the Probation Service would be crucial in the implementation of community-based programmes since the Probation Service has much more routine contact with problem drug users than do social workers in other agencies such as Social Service Departments (Pearson, Gilman and McIver, 1986; Laister and Pearson, 1988).

Nevertheless, if one sets to one side this acrimonious dispute and what can easily degenerate into linguistic quibbles about 'punishment', the Green Paper offers a real way ahead. Additional imperative against the imprisonment of offenders with drug-related problems will be the question of HIV transmission, which has already emerged as a major difficulty in some areas of Scotland, particularly on the East coast where more than 50 per cent of intravenous drug users are already HIV seropositive (Robertson *et al.*, 1986). Intravenous drug use is not only a means for the accelerated transmission of HIV, but it also forms a clear bridgehead for its dissemination within the general population. For example, whereas the male–female ratio of people known to be HIV positive in England, Wales and Northern Ireland is 15:1 in Scotland it is only 2.5:1 (Scottish Home and Health Department, 1988). The conditions of imprisonment, where drugs circulate with relative ease, are an added risk factor in that disposable syringes and needles can be used many times by many people given that needles are in short supply since they are more difficult to conceal than drugs themselves (Prison Reform Trust, 1988). It is in this context that some drug users share injecting equipment for the first time in their drug using careers, as shown by research in the Possil neighbourhood of Glasgow (Rahman *et al.*, 1989). It is difficult to imagine a scheme better designed to accelerate the dissemination of HIV.

To refuse to take preventive action against this kind of incitement to risky drug practices is unthinkable, and is what makes one all the more irritated with the response of NAPO to the Green Paper discussions. The Scottish situation very possibly offers an advance warning of the issues which are likely to be more generally felt unless effective health and social service measures are devised and implemented. It is only a matter of time before the statistics come crashing down around our ears, and those of many of our European neighbours who face identical problems of an increased prevalence of drug misuse and evidence of the accelerated transmission of HIV among intravenous drug users and through the mechanism of imprisonment.

It is in such a context that further weight has been given to the search for alternatives to custody for drug offenders by the reports of the Advisory Council on the Misuse of Drugs on *AIDS and Drug Misuse* which advances radical proposals on a variety of fronts (ACMD, 1988 and 1989). The central organising principle of the Advisory Council's recommendations is that: 'HIV is a greater threat to public and individual health than drug misuse' (ACMD, 1988, p. 1). Maintenance prescribing is now firmly back on the agenda as part of the effort to attract drug users into treatment and to sustain their continuing contact with services (Scottish Home and Health Department, 1986, p. 12; ACMD, 1988, pp. 47–8). This reverses a previous trend to prioritise abstinence as the paramount goal in treatment services, and includes a recommendation that prison medical officers should also consider the prescribing of substitute drugs such as oral methadone in order to discourage the dangerous practice of sharing injection equipment that has been smuggled into prison (ACMD, 1989, p. 65). A further direction involves the expansion of needle-exchange and syringe-exchange schemes, some of which have now been subject to careful evaluation (Monitoring Research Group, 1988). Furthermore, in order to minimise the risks of HIV transmission in prisons, the

Advisory Council endorses the recommendations of the Home Office Green Paper while arguing that 'in encouraging the greater use of existing non-custodial options, and in the development of any new options, it should be recognised that there is particular value in such disposals for drug misusing offenders' (ACMD, 1989, p. 61).

While stressing the need for adequate resources for such initiatives, together with 'substantial developments on several different fronts in addition to any changes in legislation that will be required', the Advisory Council also hints at the need for a radical rethinking of sentencing policies for offenders with drug-related problems:

> The evidence we have received so far indicates that little or no thought is currently being applied to the specific question of whether the advent of HIV-disease should influence prosecution and sentencing practice for drug misusers, and if so how. There appears to be an unchallenged assumption that the presence of asyptomatic HIV-disease should make no difference to a person's sentence. In view of the potentially serious consequences of imprisoning people who are infected with HIV, we are disturbed that no policy is being actively formulated on this.
>
> (ACMD, 1989, p. 63)

While one cannot but agree with this judgement on the apparent complacency of the government in this respect, there is nevertheless the basis for substantial agreement between the Advisory Council's views and those of the Home Office Green Paper:

> ... the chances of dealing effectively with a drug problem are much greater if the offender can remain in the community and undertake to cooperate in a sensibly planned programme to help him or her come off drugs. Such a programme would aim, in the first instance, to secure a transition from illegal consumption to a medically supervised regime designed to reduce the harm caused to the individual by drug taking and would be based on a realistic plan for tackling the addiction in the context of his or her other problems. The process might well take time, but the

programme could be varied as progress was made. Monitoring by urine tests by the agency providing the treatment could be part of the regime   (Home Office, 1988, p. 13)

Given the remarkably progressive intent of these proposals from the Home Office, NAPO's oppositional stance seems all the more bizarre. If proposals such as these were carried forward, they could become an essential part of an effective low-level drug enforcement policy aligned to treatment, rehabilitation and harm reduction strategies. Another straw in the wind is the development of arrest-referral schemes, such as that initiated in Southwark by the Metropolitan Police. It is our impression, however, that existing arrest–referral initiatives rely too much on the myth of voluntarism. Arrest–referral schemes need to be given teeth if they are to succeed, by integrating them within a clearly formulated system of agreements between the police, courts and other agencies in the way that juvenile liaison panels have been organised in many areas in the form of pre-trial diversion programmes. There will be undeniably an element of coercion in any such scheme, although this is entirely compatible with a rational-actor model of drug use such as has been implied throughout our discussion, and with the position in moral philosophy which is sometimes known as the 'disease–crime' model (Bennett, 1986; Bakalar and Grinspoon, 1984; p. 65). Stated bluntly, it is about stacking the odds through the threat of penal sanctions so that the drug user is more likely to recognise that entering some form of treatment is a rational choice: forcing people to be free, in fact. It is an ambiguous morality at best, but nevertheless a serviceable one.

If our arguments about the falsity of the victim/villain distinction and the myth of voluntarism carry any weight, then this is already the way in which many drug users opt for 'early retirement' within a context of explicit or implicit pressures and compulsions. It is a question, then, of formalising these compulsions within a clearly negotiated multi-agency strategy. The difficulties of effective inter-agency cooperation should not be minimised in that there are conflicts inherent within the system (Blagg *et al*, 1988; Sampson *et al.*, 1988). Nevertheless, these difficulties can be overcome within properly formulated multi-agency initiatives with a focus on clearly established local needs, problems and resources. According to local circumstances—such as the scale and pattern of local drug misuse—there is little doubt that police cautioning and arrest–referral schemes could be the hub around which to organise effective community-based diversion programmes which might incorporate according to local circumstances such provisions as detoxification programmes, methadone maintenance, syringe-exchange schemes, health counselling, day centre provision, community service and probation supervision. Similarly, attachments to probation orders as determined by the courts might require the offender to consult with the local clinic or engage in other forms of community-based activity. Arrangements such as these are already in *de facto* use in some parts of the North West of England, where the strategy is known jokingly in some drug-using circles as being 'Sentenced to Methadone'. And it is not such a bad thing to be sentenced to, either from the point of view of the wider community or that of the individual user who may have become tired of the metronome logic of the heroin lifestyle.

A large amount of ink had been spilled over the supposed downfall of the 'British system' of drug control as a result of the mini-epidemic of heroin misuse in London in the 1960s. However, there is still a large degree of flexibility within the British system, unlike the severely prohibitionist stance of the USA (Pearson, 1990). A major policy consideration in Britain must be not to go down the North American prohibitionist road, which has been such a total failure, evidenced by the uncontrollable drugs explosion in many North American cities in spite of the impotent 'zero tolerance' posturing currently in vogue in the USA. Indeed, it is precisely this enduring flexibility in the British system which allows the possibility of responding to what has now become a truly major epidemic of drug misuse in the British Isles and to the added threat of HIV transmission, in a way that combines a range of treatment and health education strategies within a framework of law enforcement.

The central organising principle of these policies would be that of 'harm reduction', although in a broader context than conventional health education debates. The aim would be to reduce harm on a number of fronts – to reduce the harm to the community which results both from drug-related acquisitive crime and risky behaviour which assists HIV transmission and to reduce the harm to the individual's family and friends, by stabilising his or her behaviour. And finally, to reduce the harm to the individual by involving drug users in flexible programmes which allow them to identify the harms which they would themselves like to reduce, given suitable encouragement, and to support and encourage measures to alleviate these problems. It is these possibilities which must be grasped. And given the already existing flexibility of the British system, it should not be a question of changing direction in British drug control strategies, but of changing gear.

NOTES

1. It is not possible here to develop a detailed argument about the most effective means to deploy police resources against problems of drug misuse. There are in any case general difficulties in establishing adequate performance indicators for police work (Clarke and Hough, 1984; Burrows, 1986; Horton and Smith, 1988). The difficulty is compounded by the fact that, although there is now a substantial body of British research on policing (for example, Reiner, 1985; Smith and Gray, 1985; Morgan and Smith, 1989) there has been a considerable neglect of criminological and penological aspects of drug problems in Britain, whether in terms of policy considerations or social research (Pearson, 1989a). For the present, one can perhaps say no more than that whereas evaluations of the effectiveness of drug enforcement strategies tend to prioritise operations against major traffickers and bulk seizures (Wagstaff and Maynard, 1988) there is compelling evidence to suggest that these policies have not been an unqualified success (Peltzman, 1989). Moreover, the low-level enforcement strategies deserve more focused attention, especially when aligned to multi-agency community-based programmes for offenders, as a means of getting to grips with drug problems at a neighbourhood level (Pearson, 1989b, 1989c).

2. Disadvantaged groups and consumers of public services are commonly neglected or excluded from participation in multi-agency initiatives (Sampson *et al.* 1988). Multi-agency drug strategies would undoubtedly be more effective if, wherever possible, current drug users or their representative organisations (such as 'drug users' unions') were involved in devising multi-agency programmes. One such organisa-

tion, 'Mainline' based in Manchester, has recently stated its claim for consultation in the following terms: 'As individual drug users we believe that this [consultative process] is our moral right. There are a lot of people making careers out of the drug problem—and they are not all drug dealers' (*International Journal on Drug Policy*, 1989, vol. 1, no. 1).

REFERENCES

Advisory Council on the Misuse of Drugs (1988) *AIDS and Drug Misuse*, Part I (London: HMSO).
Advisory Council on the Misuse of Drugs (1989) *AIDS and Drug Misuse*, Part II (London: HMSO).
Association for Juvenile Justice (1989) *Punishment, Custody and the Community: A Response to the Green Paper* (Birmingham: AJJ).
Auld, J., N. Dorn and N. South (1986) 'Irregular Work, Irregular Pleasures: Heroin in the 1980s', in R. Matthews and J. Young (eds), *Confronting Crime* (London: Sage).
Bakalar, J. B. and L. Grinspoon (1984) *Drug Control in a Free Society* (Cambridge University Press).
Beckford, J. (1985) *Cult Controversies: The Societal Response to the New Religious Movements* (London: Tavistock).
Bennett, T. (1986) 'A Decision-Making Approach to Opioid Addiction', in D. B. Cornish and R. V. Clarke (eds), *The Reasoning Criminal: Rational Choice Perspectives on Offending* (New York: Springer-Verlag).
Blagg, H., G. Pearson, A. Sampson, D. Smith and P. Stubbs (1988) 'Inter-Agency Cooperation: Rhetoric and Reality', in T. Hope and M. Shaw (eds), *Communities and Crime Reduction* (London: HMSO).
Brake, M. (1980) *The Sociology of Youth Cultures and Youth Subcultures* (London: Routledge and Kegan Paul).
Brettle, R. P., J. Davidson, S. J. Davidson, J. M. N. Gray *et al.* (1986) HTLV-III Antibodies in an Edinburgh Clinic', *Lancet*, vol. 1, p. 1099.
Burr, A. (1987) 'Chasing the Dragon: Heroin Misuse, Delinquency and Crime in the Context of South London Culture', *British Journal of Criminology*, vol. 27, no. 4, pp. 333–57.
Burrows, J. (1986) *Investigating Burglary: The Measurement of Police Performance*, Home Office Research Study no. 88 (London: HMSO).
Children's Society (1988) *Penal Custody for Juvenile: The Line of Least Resistance*, report of the Children's Society Advisory Committee on Penal Custody and its Alternatives for Juveniles (London: Children's Society).
Children's Society (1989) *Response to the Home Office Green Paper on Punishment and Custody in the Community* (London: Children's Society).
Clarke, R. V. and M. Hough (1984) *Crime and Police Effectiveness* Home Office Research Study no. 79 (London: HMSO).
Cohen, S. (1972) *Folk Devils and Moral Panics: The Creation of the Mods and Rockers* (London: MacGibbon and Kee).
Cohen, S. (1979) 'The Punitive City: Notes on the Future of Social Control',

Contemporary Crises, vol. 3, no. 4, pp. 339–63.

Cohen, S. (1985) *Visions of Social Control* (Cambridge: Polity Press).

Corrigan, P. (1979) *Schooling the Smash Street Kids* (London: Macmillan).

Ditton, J. and K. Speirits (1981) *The Rapid Increase in Heroin Addiction in Glasgow During 1981*, background paper no. 2, Department of Sociology, University of Glasgow.

Dorn, N. and N. South (1985) *Helping Drug Users: Social Work, Advice Giving, Referral and Training Services of Three London 'Street Agencies'* (Aldershot: Gower).

Dorn, N. and N. South (eds) (1987a) *A Land Fit for Heroin? Drug Policies Prevention and Practice* (London: Macmillan).

Downes, D. (1966) *The Delinquent Solution* (London: Routledge and Kegan Paul).

Edwards, G. (1989) 'What Drives British Drug Policies?', *British Journal of Addiction*, vol. 84, pp. 219–26.

Fazey, C. S. J. (1987) *The Evaluation of Liverpool Drug Dependency Clinic: The First Two Years 1985 to 1987*, a report to Mersey Regional Health Authority (Liverpool: Mersey Health Authority).

Feldman, H. W. (1968) 'Ideological Supports to Becoming and Remaining a Heroin Addict', *Journal of Health and Social Behaviour*, vol. 9, pp. 131–9.

Finestone, H. 'Cats, Kicks and Color', Social Problems, 1957, 5, 3–13.

Gill, O. (1977) *Luke Street: Housing Policy, Conflict and the Creation of the Delinquent Area* (London: Macmillan).

Gilman, M. (1988) 'Comics as a Strategy in Reducing Drug Related Harm', in N. Dorn, L. Lucas and N. South (eds), *Drug Questions: An Annual Research Register*, issue 4 (London: ISDD).

Gilman, M. (1989) *Comics as a Strategy in Reducing Drug-Related Harm* (Manchester: Lifeline).

Hall, S. and T. Jefferson (eds), (1976) *Resistance through Rituals* (London: Hutchinson).

Haw, S. (1985) *Drug Problems in Greater Glasgow* (London: SCODA).

Haw, S. (1988) 'The Sentencing of Drug Offenders in Scottish Courts', Drug Questions Research Conference, Institute for the Study of Drug Dependence, London, Apr. 1988.

Home Office (1974) *Young Adult Offenders, A Report of the Advisory Council on the Penal System* (London: HMSO)

Home Office (1988) *Punishment, Custody and the Community*, Cm. 424 (London: HMSO).

Horton, C and D. J. Smith (1988) *Evaluating Police Work: An Action Research Project* (London: Policy Studies Instutute).

Hughes, P. H. (1977) *Behind the Wall of Respect* (Chicago University Press).

Hughes, P. H., G. Crawford, N. Barker, S. Schumann and J. Jaffe (1971) 'The Social Structure of a Heroin-Copping Community', *American Journal of Psychiatry*, vol. 128, pp. 551–8.

Jamieson, A., A. Glanz and S. MacGregor (1984) *Dealing with Drug Misuse: Crisis Intervention in the City* (London: Tavistock).

Jarvis, G. and H. Parker (1989) 'Young Heroin Users and Crime: How Do the 'New Users' Finance their Habits?', *British Journal of Criminology*, vol. 29, no. 2, pp. 175–85.

Jenkins, R. (1983) *Lads, Citizens and Ordinary Kids: Working Class Youth Lifestyles in Belfast* (London: Routledge and Kegan Paul).

Johnson, B. D., P. J. Goldstein, E. Preble, J. Schmeidler, D. S. Lipton, B. Spunt and T. Miller (1985) *Taking Care of Business: The Economics of Crime by Heroin Abusers* (Lexington, Mass: Lexington Books).

Laister, D. and G. Pearson (1988) *Hammersmith and Fulham Drug and Alcohol Survey: Final Report* (London Borough of Hammersmith and Fulham).

McMahon, M. (1990) 'Net-Widening: Vagaries in the Use of a Concept', *British Journal of Criminology*, in press.

Marshall, T. F. (1985) *Alternatives to Criminal Courts* (Aldershot: Gower).

Mays, J. B. (1954) *Growing Up in the City* (University of Liverpool Press).

Ministry of Health (1965) *Drug Addiction: The Second Report of the Interdepartmental Committee* (London: HMSO).

Monitoring Research Group (1988) *Injecting Equipment Exchange Schemes: Final Report* (Goldsmiths' College, University of London).

Morgan, R. and D. J. Smith (eds) (1989) *Coming to Terms with Policing: Perspectives on Policy* (London: Routledge).

Mungham, G. and G. Pearson (eds) (1976) *Working Class Youth Cultures* (London: Routledge and Kegan Paul).

NACRO (1988) *Punishment, Custody and the Community: A Response to the Green Paper by the National Association for the Care and Resettlement of Offenders* (London: NACRO).

NAPO (1975) *Young Adult Offenders: An Examination of the Younger Report by the Working Party of the London Branch of the National Association of Probation Officers* (London: NAPO).

NAPO (1989) *Punishment, Custody and the Community: The Response of the National Association of Probation Officers* (London: NAPO).

Parker, H. (1974) *View from the Boys* (Newton Abbot: David & Charles).

Parker, H. and R. Newcombe (1987) 'Heroin Use and Acquisitive Crime in an English Community', *British Journal of Sociology*, vol. 38, no. 3, pp. 331–50.

Parker, H., K. Bakx and R. Newcombe (1988) *Living with Heroin: The Impact of a Drugs 'Epidemic' on an English Community* (Milton Keynes: Open University Press).

Pearson, G. (1987a) *The New Heroin Users* (Oxford: Basil Blackwell).

Pearson, G. (1987b) 'Social Deprivation, Unemployment and Patterns of Heroin Use', in N. Dorn and N. South (eds), *A Land Fit for Heroin? Drug Policies, Prevention and Practice* (London: Macmillan).

Pearson, G. (1989a) 'Drugs, Law Enforcement and Criminology', in V. Berridge (ed.), *Drugs Research and Policy in Britain* (Aldershot: Gower/Avebury, in press).

Pearson, G. (1989b) 'The Street Connection', *New Statesman and Society*, 15 Sept. 1989, pp. 10–11.

Pearson, G. (1989c) 'Low-Level Drug Enforcement: A Multi-Agency Perspective from Britain', paper presented to 'What Works: An International Conference on Drug Abuse Treatment and Prevention Research' (New York: Oct. 1989).

Pearson, G. (1990) 'Drug Control Policies in Britain: Continuity and Change', in A. J. Reiss Jnr and M. Tonry (eds), *Crime and Justice*

(University of Chicago Press, in press).

Pearson, G., M. Gilman and S. McIver (1985) 'Heroin Use in the North of England', *Health Education Journal*, vol. 45, no. 3, pp. 186–9.

Pearson, G., M. Gilman and S. McIver (1986) *Young People and Heroin: An Examination of Heroin Use in the North of England* (London: Health Education Council) (2nd edn, Aldershot: Gower, 1987).

Pearson, G., H. Blagg and D. Smith (1987) *Crime, Community and the Inter-Agency Dimension: Final Report to the Economic and Social Research Council* (London: ESRC).

Peck, D. F. and M. A. Plant (1986) 'Unemployment and Illegal Drug Use: Concordant Evidence from a Prospective Study and National Trends', *British Medical Journal*, vol. 293, pp 929–32.

Peltzman, S. (1989) 'The Failure of Enforcement', *British Journal of Addiction*, vol. 84, no. 5, pp. 469–70.

Preble, E. and J. J. Casey (1969) 'Taking Care of Business: The Heroin User's Life on the Street', *International Journal of the Addictions*, vol. 4, no. 1, pp. 1–24.

Prison Reform Trust (1988) *HIV, AIDS and Prisons* (London: Prison Reform Trust).

Rahman, M. Z., J. Ditton and A. J. M. Forsyth (1989) 'Variations in Needle Sharing Practices among Intravenous Drug Users in Possil (Glasgow)', *British Journal of Addiction*, vol. 84, pp. 923–7.

Reiner, R. (1985) *The Politics of the Police* (Brighton: Wheatsheaf).

Richardson, N. (1988) *Justice by Geography 2* (Lancaster: Social Information Systems).

Robertson, J. R., A. B. B. Bucknall, P. D. Welsby *et al.* (1986) 'Epidemic of AIDS Related Virus (HTLV III/LAV) Infection among Intravenous Drug Abusers', *British Medical Journal*, vol. 292, p. 527–9.

Rodger, J. R. (1988) 'Social Work as Social Control Re-Examined: Beyond the Dispersal of Discipline Thesis', *Sociology*, vol. 22, no. 4, pp. 563–81.

Royal College of Psychiatrists (1987) *Community Treatment Orders: A Discussion Document* (London: Royal College of Psychiatrists).

Sampson, A., P. Stubbs, D. Smith, G. Pearson and H. Blagg (1988) 'Crime, Localities and the Multi-Agency Approach', *British Journal of Criminology*, vol. 28, no. 4, pp. 478–93.

Scott-Moncrieff, L. (1988) 'Comments on the Discussion Document of the Royal College of Psychiatrists regarding Community Treatment Orders', *Bulletin of the Royal College of Psychiatrists*, vol. 12, June 1988, pp. 220–3.

Scottish Home and Health Department (1986) *HIV Infection in Scotland Report of the Scottish Committee on HIV Infection and Intravenous Drug Misuse* (Edinburgh: Scottish Home and Health Department).

Scottish Home and Health Department (1988) *Health in Scotland 1987* (Edinburgh: HMSO).

Smith, D. and J. Gray (1985) *Police and People in London: The PSI Report* (Aldershot: Gower).

Sutter, A. G. (1966) 'The World of the Righteous Dope Fiend', *Issues in Criminology*, vol. 2, no. 2.

Wagstaff, A.and A. Maynard (1988) *Economic Aspects of the Illicit Drug Market and Drug Enforcement Policies in the United Kingdom*, Home Office Research

Study no. 95 (London: HMSO).

Walker, H. and B. Beaumont (1981) *Probation Work: Critical Theory and Social Practice* (Oxford: Basil Blackwell).

Willis, P. (1977) *Learning to Labour* (Farnborough: Saxon House).

Willis, P. (1978) *Profane Culture* (London: Routledge and Kegan Paul).

Wilson, D. (1989) 'Punishment, Custody and the Community', *Criminal Justice*, vol. 7, no. 1, pp. 8–9.

8 Profits and Penalties: New Trends in Legislation and Law Enforcement Concerning Illegal Drugs

Nicholas Dorn and Nigel South

With the recent passing of the Drug Trafficking Offences Act 1986, and the two Criminal Justice Acts of 1987 and 1988, the Government and Parliament have provided the courts with new powers with which to re-assert the old saw that 'crime does not pay'. Under provisions which in certain cases enable the confiscation of assets, the courts have been empowered to deprive convicted offenders of the profits of their criminal enterprise.

Most recently, for England and Wales, the Criminal Justice Act 1988 (ss. 71–103) introduced confiscation order provisions under which the assets of someone convicted on indictment of any indictable offence (other than drug trafficking—about which more later) can be seized. The confiscation procedure under this Act is initiated where the prosecution makes an application to the court, although if it appears that the defendant would be unable to pay at least the 'minimum' amount (initially £10 000) which has been set, then the procedure is dropped (Thomas, 1989: 54).[1] These provisions are largely derived from those laid out in the Drug Trafficking Offences Act 1986, (DTOA), although as Thomas (ibid.) observes there are 'enough minor differences' between the two Acts 'to guarantee confusion if the provisions of both Acts are not kept closely in mind'.[2]

For the Government (and an Opposition which has supported these Acts), the matter of principle behind the introduction of such legislation is whether the deprivation of the liberty of wrong-doers is sufficient punishment for society to exact, if at the end of that period of suspension of liberty the offender can return to society and enjoy the fruits of their crimes. Clearly Government and others have felt that this situation needed rectifying and that punishment should involve not just incarceration but also the removal of comforts and assets from convicted offenders' domestic and business interests. The rights and wrongs of this new financial policing and punishment are by no means as clear cut as they may initially seem and are deserving of future scrutiny.

Perhaps more self-evidently of concern as a development in law, is that the concept of the burden of proof always resting with the prosecution is reversed in this legislation and defendants must prove that their assets were legally obtained, otherwise they may be subject to a Court ruling that they be confiscated. This reversal of traditional principle along with the wide-ranging power to carry out sophisticated financial investigations represents a significant change in law which has not yet been widely appreciated.

However, it is perhaps questionable as to whether provisions of this kind would have experienced such an untroubled passage into the wide body of law now embraced in the three Acts, had there not been a history of bi-partisan support for some kind of confiscation procedures. In the early and mid-1980s, such support was given a considerable boost by Governmental and popular concern about the rise in heroin use, characterised in 1985 by the all-party Home Affairs Committee as 'the most serious peace-time threat to our national well-being' (Home Affairs Committee, 1985: iii). In the rest of this paper we chart the development of this legislation and discuss some of the issues it raises.

THE DRUG TRAFFICKING OFFENCES ACT 1986: A SHORT HISTORY

From the Hodgson Committee to the Broome Report

In one sense, the idea of confiscation upon the conviction of the offender of those assets identified as having derived from involvement in serious crime, seems an overdue and logical matter for the courts to have power over. It was in this spirit of 'reasonableness' that the Howard League for Penal Reform established a committee in 1980, chaired by Sir Derek Hodgson (a High Court judge), to examine the limits on the courts which then existed. This initiative followed the outcome of the 'Operation Julie' court case—the trial at Bristol Crown Court in 1978 of a group of manufacturers and distributors of LSD. This case revealed the inability of the courts to confiscate the assets of persons convicted of major drug offences. After a trial which had attracted considerable public attention, the judge imposed long prison sentences and then, in addition, 'made an order, confirmed by the Court of Appeal, for the forfeiture of certain assets. . . purportedly exercising a power given by section 27 (1) of the Misuse of Drugs Act 1971' (Hodgson, 1984:3).

As the Hodgson Committee report observed:

> Huge profits have been made and the prosecution was able to trace some £750 000 of those profits to assets in the criminals' hands. . . The power given to the Court under the Act was to 'order anything shown to the satisfaction of the Court to relate to the offence to be forfeited'.
>
> A further appeal was made to the House of Lords against the orders for forfeiture and the House 'with considerable regret' found itself compelled to allow the appeals. Among the reasons given for allowing the appeal the House held that Parliament had never intended orders of forfeiture 'to serve as a means of stripping the drug traffickers of the total profits of their unlawful enterprises'.   (Hodgson, 1984:3)

What the provisions of the Misuse of Drugs Act *could* allow was seizure of, as it were, the *tools of the trade*—but not the profits derived from that trade. Thus the House of Lords held that the power available under the Act could only be used:

> where it was 'possible to identify something *tangible* that can fairly be said to relate to any such transaction such as the drugs involved, apparatus for making them, vehicles used for transporting them or cash ready to be or having just been handed over for them'.   (Ibid.; emphasis added)

Property held abroad was also held to be untouchable by an English court and furthermore, the forfeiture provisions which did exist under S.27 (1) of the Misuse of Drugs Act 1971 could not apply anyway because the defendants were charged with *conspiracy* to commit various offences under the Act rather than with actually having *committed* particular offences.[3]

Considerable dismay in both conservative and liberal quarters followed, and although ultimately it was a Conservative view of how this state of affairs should be rectified that prevailed, it was the liberally orientated Hodgson Committee that provided the most thoughtful contribution with the publication of its report in 1984. This proposed new powers to enable courts to confiscate assets identifiable as the proceeds of crime and to freeze the assets of a defendant pending trial so that they could not be disposed of prior to any subsequent conviction. The liberal composition and intentions of the committee were reflected in its concerns to emphasise that punishment should not be the principal consideration in introducing new legislation but rather that redressing wrongs should also be aimed for through, for example, victim compensation and the restoration of property to its rightful owners.

In the view of the Committee:

> Orders for the payment of money or transfer of property should be taken into account in calculating the sentences. Our approach to these orders has positive roots in our belief in the intrinsic value of redressing a wrong but it also has negative foundations. Prison is expensive, degrading and mainly harmful. In our view, particularly when, as in most property crimes, offenders do not present a danger of violence, it ought to be used much more rarely than it is. (Hodgson *et al*. 1984: 36)

From another constituency—the senior police officers' body ACPO (Association of Chief Police Officers)—came another influential, if rather more secretive, document. This was the Broome Report (ACPO Crime Committee, 1985), named after its chairman, Ronald Broome, the Chief Constable of Avon and Somerset. Among other matters, this Committee considered the legislation and powers that the police felt would be necessary to undertake financial investigations that 'chased' the drugs money at the same time as the operational tiers of Divisional, Force and Regional officers were chasing the drugs.

As the ACPO committee was aware, the ears of the Government were by no means closed to such proposals. When the Committee observed that the recommendations of the Hodgson report fell far short of the measures that would be required to be truly effective against major dealers, it did so with the knowledge that the Home Office had already outlined its own proposals for measures to freeze assets prior to trial, to implement confiscation on conviction and make the laundering of money from drug trafficking an offence. Such indications of Government support were unsurprising in the early 1980s when no criminal more than the drug trafficker came to represent for Mrs Thatcher and her Home Office Ministers the epitome of the heartless criminal profiteer. Her pledge was 'We will get you'—and, she might have added, 'and everything you own'.

The Home Affairs Committee, 1985

In 1985 the Home Affairs Committee considered evidence about the rise in illegal drug use in Britain and drew threatening parallels with the crisis situation they described in the USA. Echoing the rhetoric of the American 'War on Drugs' they asserted that:

> Western society is faced by a warlike threat from the hard drugs industry. The traffickers in hard drugs amass princely incomes from the exploitation of human weakness, boredom and misery. . . the ruthlessness of the big drug dealers must be met by equally ruthless penalties once they are caught, tried and convicted.

> The American practice, which we unhesitatingly support, is to give the courts draconian powers in both civil and criminal law to strip drug dealers of all the assets acquired from their dealings in drugs. Drug dealers must be made to lose everything, their homes, their money and all that they possess which can be attributed to their profits from selling drugs.   (Home Affairs Committee, 1985: iv–vi; Stimson, 1987: 44; Rutherford and Green, 1988: 21)

As is clear, the Home Affairs committee were fairly unequivocal in their support for financial penalties. Hence, by mid-1985, the recommendations of their interim report, of the Hodgson and Broome reports and no doubt the contributions of many others, sat well with aspects of Government thinking on this issue and helped to shape the Drug Trafficking Offences Bill, published in November 1985.[4] It should however be emphasised, although it came as no great surprise, that in the formulation of the legislation a number of key stipulations to be found in the Hodgson Committee report were lost. These conditions included the idea that any confiscation of assets should, to some degree at least, be grounds for reduction of prison sentence and that confiscation should only be used in cases of large sums of money, over £100 000, and not be used against persons with low level involvement. Instead the introduction of the DTOA was endorsed by both Conservative and Labour spokespersons in terms of the power of confiscation orders being an *additional*, not partially alternative, sentence.

In fieldwork interviews carried out in 1988/9, senior police officers and Customs staff have enthusiastically acknowledged that the Drug Trafficking Offences Act has given them a very wide range of powers and capabilities and conceded that they have felt some surprise at the untroubled passage which the Act received. Indeed if the issue of concern had been anything but drugs, which according to the Home Secretary, Mr Douglas Hurd, the world was 'awash with', then it is highly probable that Parliament would have given the Bill considerably more scrutiny and entered into a rather more critical debate about its content. However, the all-party accord on the threat of the 'drugs menace' allowed the Bill through from hasty drafting and reading to swiftly enacted Act.[5]

In brief summary then, the Act introduces and makes distinctions between the terms 'drug trafficking' and 'drug trafficking offence' (S.38 (1)); the former definition is 'more broadly drawn' than the latter and 'applies to activities carried out anywhere in the world' (Bucknell and Ghodse, 1989: 57). This means that when assessing the proceeds of drug trafficking then any proceeds beyond the jurisdiction of the court are nonetheless to be included (S.2) and similarly that 'the Act applies to property situated anywhere in the world'

(S.38 (3)). . . 'if the defendant does not make arrangements for it to be brought within the jurisdiction for realisation, he will suffer an *additional* period of imprisonment under the default procedure. . .' (ibid.; emphasis added). Under S.38 of the Act a drug trafficking *offence* can mean any of a variety of offences under the Misuse of Drugs Act 1971, the Customs and Excise Management Act 1979, the Criminal Law Act 1977, or the Criminal Attempts Act 1981.

The Act has introduced powers of confiscation for the courts to use, and enables the police and customs to undertake detailed financial investigations. It is worth noting, not least because it is regarded by many as unnecessary and a mistake, that a financial investigation is mandatory in all cases brought under the Act. The imposition of any consequent confiscation order is seen as a fitting *further* punishment for drug trafficking, on top of any prison sentence. Even more against the grain of the recommendations of the Hodgson Committee report is the provision that failure to pay any levied amount over £10 000 will attract an *additional* prison sentence. New offences of prejudicing an investigation (S.31) and of assisting traffickers (by 'laundering', concealing, any assets) (S.24) were also created with sentences of up to five and 14 years respectively.

According to one report, by late 1988 the Act had been used to 'freeze' (place under restraint) approximately £15 million of alleged traffickers' assets pending the outcome of trials and some £5 million had been confiscated following conviction (Stockley, 1988: 298). By June, 1989, according to Home Office Minister Mr Douglas Hogg, confiscation orders to the value of £11 million had been made, (*Hansard*, 9 June 1989: 524).

IMPLICATIONS, PROBLEMS AND PROSPECTS

Unsurprisingly, the availability of such powerful new legislation has brought changes in investigative techniques both as envisaged and as the result of innovation and adaptation. It has also opened up a whole new arena for debate around the resourcing of the police service which resonates strongly with trends that are clear in the Government's thinking about how to introduce private enterprise and non-state sources of funding into the operation of the criminal justice system.

Police and Customs operationalisation of their powers under the DTOA has resulted in the formation of Drug Profits Confiscation Teams or Units in police forces and a Drugs Financial Investigation Branch in HM Customs and Excise.

The role of coordinating drugs intelligence has been given to the National Drugs Intelligence Unit (NDIU), based at Scotland Yard. This was developed out of the former Central Drugs Intelligence Unit, following one of the recommendations of the Broome report and the publication of the Government's strategy document *Tackling Drug Misuse* (Home Office, 1985). The 'raison d'etre of the (unit) is to gather, collate, analyse and disseminate drugs intelligence, whether emanating from within the United Kingdom or abroad, and to provide the essential link between the two enforcement agencies, police and customs' (Stockley, 1988: 297). Part of this link is provided by NDIU hosting a joint police/customs financial intelligence section which 'is the central point for receipt of disclosures of suspected accounts. . . held by banks and other financial institutions' and which disseminates financial intelligence to police and customs investigators (Stockley, 1988: 298).

However, all is not necessarily rosy cooperation and instances of rivalry between the two services and between drugs personnel in different police forces have not been unknown—although a variety of respondents in recently conducted interviews suggested that relations probably have improved. But equally, it has also been observed that the kudos attached to success in operations which net large amounts of money remains one potential source of conflict— and the question of the disposition of assets seized is another matter which has been exciting considerable interest. As one serving officer has recently observed of the operation of seizure legislation in the USA (where assets confiscated can be used by the law enforcement agency responsible for their seizure):

(the system works well in the main but) it has the potential of bringing its own divisive problems which however isolated must not happen here. Consider a few examples:
There is a tempation for investigators to be increasingly

selfish with their intelligence in the hope that by not cooperating with other forces they avoid sharing the spoils of success. The reality is to minimise any chance of success at all.

After initial cooperation there have been isolated cases of fierce disputes over who initiated the case and who takes the credit and the major share of an asset seizure.

It is not unknown for a unit to suffer severe management pressures for bigger seizures to ease other financial problems within the organisation.

Police authorities or City Hall begin to include past, or even worse, projected future seizures, into a police budget.

There are moral and ethical questions surrounding the concept of using the money of unknown victims to finance police operations which should be adequately funded by central and local Government.   (Saltmarsh, 1989: 392)

To Whom should Confiscated Assets Go?

The 'big question' upon which the above dangers are contingent is, of course, *where* should the money and property that is seized *go*? Many in the police and Customs services say that, logically, it should be channelled back to them to assist with further drug/crime investigations and in addition, with a view to attempting to reduce the demand for illegal drugs, it should go toward local drug-related projects, community responses, advice agencies, treatment and rehabilitation facilities and so on.

The view of the Government—at present at least—is that such revenue should go to the Consolidated Fund (that is the Treasury). It would seem that this issue had recently been the subject of some behind the scenes Ministerial negotiation and one recent incident displayed uncertainty from the Government about what principles it was trying to adhere to in this matter. In this case, the US Drug Enforcement Administration had, in 1988, urged the Metropolitan Police to apply for a share of the drug-linked assets that had been confiscated in the USA as the result of a joint operation resulting from the police's investigation of laundering of money from the Brinks–Mat bullion robbery. Uncertainty followed as to whether procedures existed to enable this and also over whether the money could or could not go to the Metropolitan Police—as the DEA wanted—or whether it had to go to the Treasury. Eventually, when it began to seem likely that the DEA would withdraw their offer, the Home Secretary reached agreement with the Treasury that the Met could accept the £32.5 million. However the lack of a mutual legal assistance treaty between the UK and the USA meant that the US government then vetoed the offer. The swift action to remedy matters that was promised by the Home Secretary clearly indicated— according to one Home Office official quoted in *Police Review* (20 January 1989)—that 'Mr Hurd was eager to permit British police to be rewarded for successful drug investigations and would press for mutual assistance treaties with "friendly states" '. Resolution of the matter was not to be found so easily, however, and one month later *Police Review* (17 February 1989) was quoting another Home Office official as saying that: 'The Government is eager to introduce legislation to allow drugs assets seized abroad to be sent back to Britain, but unfortunately that enthusiasm does not translate into getting the money back to the police'.

An appetite for a share of assets seized abroad has been whetted but how the shares might be apportioned remains a contentious issue.[6]

This situation has been the subject of recent discussions between ACPO and the Home Secretary and the Government's latest view, as outlined to Parliament by the Home Office Minister Mr Douglas Hogg, is that:

> It is undesirable to give a police force or any enforcement agency a pecuniary interest in an inquiry, and I fear that it would distort policing policies.
>
> The Home Office is considering the possibility of a central pot, to use jargon, to assist with exceptional expenditure. General drug policing needs should be reflected in bids made by police authorities to my Right Hon. Friend the Home Secretary, which will be considered by the Inspectorate in the normal way. I do not believe that there is a substantial shortfall in our enforcement effort.
>
> (*Hansard*, 9 June 1989: 523)

The eventual arrangements will be a significant development whatever shape they may take. The 'central pot' may, in the end, leave many dissatisfied—and indeed may please no one. Yet it would seem a positive sign if the government has recognised that channelling funds realised from seized assets directly into the coffers of those police and customs units responsible for the seizures, could have unforeseen and negative consequences.

For example, it might be noted that the DEA (the US Drug Enforcement Administration) generally 'makes a profit' (in so far as most years they seize more assets than they cost in Government funding)—and *specialist* police agencies might be expected to become self-financing along such lines. Expensive, out of the ordinary, police operations could come to routinely require the input of this 'private', non-state, money. This could lead to the direction of investigative efforts more and more against what can be expected to be 'profitable' crimes that will yield a high return of seized assets. Such developments would be in the interest of neither Government nor the police and Customs services—to say nothing of the broader public interest.

However, whilst the issue of what to do with confiscated assets is less than straightforward, there are perhaps concerns in relation to civil liberties and principles of justice that may be a little more clear-cut.

Some Issues Relating to Civil Liberties and Principles of Justice

It has been noted by many commentators that the whole area of drugs law enforcement raises concerns over the erosion of civil liberties which can follow from precedents set and actions taken under the banner of fighting 'the good fight' against drugs (Rutherford and Green, 1988: 13). The specialist techniques required by drugs investigators are precisely those which arouse most anxiety—they are covert, undercover, rely on rumour, hearsay, and the dubious integrity of informers, they involve the interception of personal communications whether by mail or telephone, they involve keeping people under observation, dignified by the term surveillance—and so on. For the drugs investigator these are indeed *necessary* tools —but it is certainly easy to see why it is legitimate and equally necessary to express concern about any extension of such practices or the legal powers which enable them.[7]

The content and implications of the empowering legislation must also be held up to scrutiny. As the Editorial of the *Criminal Law Review* noted in commenting upon the Drug Trafficking Offences Act:

> It is worth pointing out that among the supposed principles of English criminal justice which suffer reversals in this Act are the presumption of innocence, the principle of *mens rea* for serious offences, and the principle that offenders should be dealt with only for the offence(s) before the court.
>
> (*Criminal Law Review*, 1986: 577)

It might also be observed that the Act has done nothing to reduce the reliance of the state on imprisonment as a means of punishment. Instead it has introduced a powerful financial penalty that is *additional* to imprisonment and has created new offences which also carry prison sentences. Further, whilst the Act is commendable in facilitating the pursuit of the funds of those who may be adept at hiding them in offshore banks and other financial havens, as Rutherford and Green observe, 'No account is taken of the defendant's means or the needs of his family or other commitments'.[8]

It is still early days in the operation of the DTOA, but it is widely agreed that it is a complex piece of legislation and that interpreting it is a matter that has led to some confusion and difficulty in the courts. There is then ample potential for mistakes to be made in the application of this Act and perhaps also, where they follow it closely, the Criminal Justice (Scotland) Act 1987 and the Criminal Justice Act 1988.

CONCLUSION

In terms of the trends and concerns which have led to the DTOA and similar legislation, it may, in conclusion, be useful briefly to identify some potential negative and positive outcomes.

One negative consequence for law enforcement may follow from the repeated raising of the penalties of imprisonment for drug offences—now up to life imprisonment for serious cases of trafficking. This is likely to have had a negative effect on the ability of law enforcement to break into distribution networks at points where it would count. This follows as successful entrepreneurial dealers, who fear the financial effects of the DTOA as well as higher prison penalties, get ever more cautious, security conscious and violent in their efforts to impede the passing of information about their activities to the police. As successful law enforcement efforts rely heavily on good 'information received' this seriously diminishes the chances of initiating investigations that will 'pay off'.

At the same time, this situation also results in negative consequences for the small-scale user–dealer who is correspondingly easier to apprehend than larger drug distributors, because financial investigation with a view to the imposition of a confiscation order is *mandatory* under the DTOA and there is no minimum level of £10 000 that a person convicted must be capable of paying before a confiscation order is made (as there is under the CJA). Thus a judge, if so inclined, can confiscate any, and indeed all, assets which the defendant cannot show to have been legitimately acquired and *not* to be the proceeds of drug dealing.

As noted earlier, the reasonable intentions underlying the Hodgson Committee's support for asset confiscation measures were jettisoned by the Government. In much the same way that voices of disquiet were raised when the inadequacy of the Misuse of Drugs Act 1971 was highlighted by the 'Operation Julie' case, leading to Hodgson, Broome, the Home Affairs Committee and ultimately the DTOA, so, since the passage of the DTOA, alarm has been registered at the draconian cast of the Act and its interpretation. The pendulum of redress has swung much too far for some commentators. It may also be the case that those who have most welcomed the DTOA will come to have doubts of their own as the Act produces unintended side-effects. If the threat of loss of liberty with lengthier sentences is combined with the potential loss of all property and assets, the question must be asked not only as to whether this is a just punishment but also whether it is a sensible one? If it fails to act as a deterrent, then its effect is more likely to be an unwanted and harmful hardening of the drug distribution business. Increased resistance of the business to police investigations and increased levels of violence to ensure the silence of informers and maintain a competitive edge will be the likely consequences.[9]

Perhaps in future, a more positive view could be taken if commentators with a committment to critical but constructive dialogue with law enforcement and other agencies could be afforded the access to, and the resources to monitor and influence, the development of legislation such as the DTOA and its use in practice. And, returning to the starting point of this paper, whilst the introduction of the recent Criminal Justice Act 1988 might bring with it some matters to be cautious about, it might also be a positive development if its use in certain specific directions could be encouraged, for example against white collar crime (to recoup losses from fraud, embezzlement and the like).[10] A similar measure was taken in the USA against the assets of junk bond dealer Michael Milken who was charged with securities fraud and insider trading. Government prosecutors used anti-racketeering legislation more usually applied against drug traffickers, to freeze assets suspected of being accumulated illegally (Brummer, 1989: 19). In the past, the lack of legal measures available or action taken against white collar/financial crime has long been an evident sign of the imbalance of justice. In the new measures enabling the policing of criminal profits there is scope for a rational and just approach to the policing of serious crimes, perhaps redressing some of this imbalance. The danger is that law enforcement agencies may flex their powerful new muscles, scare their serious criminal targets beyond their arm's reach and end up merely raising the price that civil liberties have paid in the 'war on drugs and crime'.

NOTES

A revised version of a paper originally presented to the British Sociological Association conference, 'Sociology in Action', Plymouth Polytechnic, March 1989.

1. Similar provisions to confiscate the assets of 'terrorist' groups are to be introduced in the reading of the Prevention of Terrorism Bill.

2. For example, the confiscation order provisions (that is allowing for confiscation of assets) applicable under the DTOA are mandatory and initiated by the sentencer; they apply only in Crown Court; there is no minimum limit on a confiscation order under the DTOA; and the definition of any benefit which might have accrued to a person includes 'any payment or other reward' which, as Thomas (1989; p. 54) observes 'clearly includes rewards in any other form (such as sexual favours conferred directly or indirectly)'. By contrast, confiscation procedures initiated under *either* the Criminal Justice (Scotland) Act 1987 or the Criminal Justice Act 1988 are discretionary, following from an application from the prosecution. In some cases the confiscation order provisions of the CJA 1988 apply in the magistrate's court; confiscation orders may not be made for less than £10 000 and the definition of obtaining a 'benefit' supposes that the offender must 'obtain property' or 'derive a pecuniary advantage as a result of or in connection with the offence' (Thomas, *ibid.*). This definition is somewhat different to the wording of the 1986 Act and, unhelpfully, no definition of 'pecuniary advantage' is given. To add a little further confusion, under both the DTOA 1986 and the CJA 1988 the court is required to complete the whole process of considering and making a confiscation order (where applicable) before sentence can be passed. This can slow the business of the courts considerably. However, 'the corresponding Scottish legislation (Criminal Justice (Scotland) Act 1987). . . allows the court to pass sentence before the matters relating to confiscation have been settled: there is no need in Scotland to adjourn sentence pending the outcome of the proceedings relating to confiscation' (Commentary, *Criminal Law Review*, November 1988, pp. 779–80).

3   Note that this is no longer the position in law as S.70 of the Criminal Justice Act 1988 has amended S.27 (1) of the Misuse of Drugs Act 1971 to enable its application to offences such as attempting and conspiring to commit drug trafficking offences. 'R v. Cuthbertson no longer states the current law' (Bucknell and Ghodse, 1989, p. 51).

4   The Home Office Minister, David Mellor acknowledged the help and influence of the Home Affairs Committee (see Home Affairs Committee 1986, p. 22), whilst the Home Secretary, Douglas Hurd referred—albeit rather dismissively—to the Hodgson Report during the second reading of the Bill.

5. It should be noted that bipartisan support for punitive drug legislation is not new. The Misuse of Drugs Act 1971 was introduced as a Bill by the Labour Government and then steered through the next Parliament in a similar form by the new Conservative Government.

6. It might be speculated that in practice, if financial reward for success in an investigation is an influential factor but the Government continues to direct all confiscated assets to the Treasury, then some erosion of the power of the DTOA may occur simply by reduction in its use. In discussing a number of cases handled by HM Customs and Excise between 12 January 1987 and 1 January 1988, Rutherford and Green (1988, p. 27) report that 'the separation between confiscation

and sentence has caused severe problems, including lengthy delay on remand. The costs involved can outweigh the value of the confiscation order. As a result a senior court official reported that there was a movement away from confiscation towards costs for the prosecution and the original forfeiture powers. The point was made that any assets that are confiscated go to the Treasury whereas prosecution costs go to Customs and Excise.'

7.   A similar, uncomfortable ambivalence is honestly and neatly captured in Gary Marx' recent study of undercover police strategies in the USA:

> . . . The undercover tactic is compelling and controversial partly because it can be a means for both protecting and undermining our most cherished values.
>
> In a democratic society, covert police tactics, along with many of the other surveillance techniques, offer us a queasy ethical and moral paradox. . . . We are caught on the horns of a moral dilemma. In Machiavelli's words: '(Never) let any state ever believe that it can always adopt safe policies . . . we never try to escape one difficulty without running into another; but prudence consists in knowing how to recognise the nature of the difficulties and how to choose the least bad as good'. Sometimes undercover tactics may be the least bad. Used with great care, they may be a necessary evil. The challenge is to prevent them from becoming an intolerable one.   (Marx, 1988, p. 233)

8.   Although it may be pointed out that, although:

> traffickers' wives have no right to representation in the assessment of trafficking proceeds, . . . (nonetheless) to implement restraint or confiscation orders police must obtain a High Court order which is sent to anyone affected.
>
> At this stage wives can challenge the order by arguing that some of the assets were obtained by them independently of their husband's illegal activities. To help argue their case they are entitled to legal aid.   (D. Sgt. Mike Lloyd, Avon and Somerset police,
> cited in *Druglink*, Jan./Feb. 1989, 4)

Nevertheless, critics of the DTOA would still be dissatisfied that there are no safeguards or provision for assistance with such a challenge embodied in the Act.

9.   We discuss related issues further in N. Dorn and N. South forthcoming, 1991.

10. Part vi of the Criminal Justice Act 1988 which came into force on 3 April 1989, provides powers to recover the proceeds of other (non-drug trafficking), serious, profitable crimes.

REFERENCES

ACPO Crime Committee (Broome Committee) (1985) '*Final Report of Working Party on Drugs Related Crime*', unpublished.

Brummer, A. (1989), 'SEC Levies Heavy Fine on Drexel', *Guardian*, 14 Apr. p. 19.

Bucknell, P. and H. Ghodse (1989), *Misuse of Drugs and Drug Trafficking Offences Act, Supplement no. 3 (Cumulative)*, The Criminal Law Library, no. 2 (London: Waterlow).

Criminal Law Review (1986), 'Editorial', *Criminal Law Review*, Sept., p. 577.

Criminal Law Review (1988), 'Commentary on R v. Bragason', *Criminal Law Review*, Nov., pp. 778–81.

Dorn, N. and N. South (1990), 'Drug Markets and Law Enforcement', *British Journal of Criminology*, in press.

Dorn, N. and N. South (forthcoming, 1991), *Policing the Drugs Distribution Business* (London: Routledge).

Hodgson, D. *et al.* (1984), *The Profits of Crime and their Recovery* (London: Heinemann).

Home Affairs Committee (1985), *Misuse of Hard Drugs*, Interim Report, House of Commons, 1984–5, HC 399.

Home Affairs Committee (1986), *Misuse of Hard Drugs*, First Report, House of Commons, 1985–6, HC 66.

Home Office (1985) *Tackling Drug Misuse: A Summary of the Government's Strategy*, (1st edn) (London: HMSO).

Marx, G. (1988), *Undercover: Police Surveillance in America* (Berkeley: University of California Press).

Police Review (1989), 'Treasury Blocks Forces Receiving Drugs Assets', *Police Review*, 17 Feb., p. 5.

Rutherford, A. and P. Green (1988), 'Illegal Drugs and British Criminal Justice Policy', *paper presented to conference on Drug Policies in Western Europe*, Tilburg University, The Netherlands, 39 May–3 June; forthcoming in H. Albrecht and A. Van Kalmthout (eds), *Drugs Policies in Western Europe* (Freiburg: Max Planck Institute).

Saltmarsh, G. (1989), 'Cleaning up with Dirty Money', *Police Reivew*, 24 Feb. pp. 392–3.

Stimson, G. (1987), 'The War on Heroin: British Policy and the International Trade in Illicit Drugs', in N. Dorn and N. South (eds), *A Land Fit for Heroin?: Drug Policies, Prevention and Practice* (London: Macmillan).

Stockley, D. (1988), 'National Drugs Intelligence Unit', *Police Journal*, Oct., pp. 295–303.

Thomas, D. (1989) 'The Sentencing Provisions (of the Criminal Justice Act, 1988)', *Criminal Law Review*, Jan., pp. 43–55.

Part II
Contemporary Policy Themes

9 Epidemiology of Contemporary Drug Abuse

John Giggs

In the Oxford English Dictionary (OED 1989) epidemiology is defined as 'That branch of medical science which treats of epidemics'. This definition is unsatisfactory on two counts. Firstly, it presents a very dated and circumscribed view of the range of subjects studied by epidemiologists. Secondly, it is misleading because it conveys the impression that the field is solely the concern of medical scientists. It is certainly true that scientific epidemiological studies arose in the nineteenth century in response to community-wide epidemics of acute infectious diseases (Barker, 1973) and that such research is still important (for example, Cliff *et al.* 1987; Scientific American, 1988). However, for the past 50 years or so the impact of the majority of infectious diseases has diminished considerably, while the scope of the subject has broadened to include all diseases. Epidemiology is now the basic science of public health, embracing all morbidity and mortality. Furthermore, medical scientists have been joined by a growing number of experts from other disciplines—history, the social sciences, demography and statistics. Their different perspectives have further broadened the scope of the subject. Thus a recent dictionary of epidemiology defines the discipline as: 'The study of the distribution and determinants of health-related states and events in populations, and the application of this study to control of health problems' (Last, 1982). Consequently it could be argued, with some justification, that *all* the chapters in the present book constitute aspects of the epidemiology of drug abuse!

Among the multitude of health problems which have been the subjects of epidemiological study, substance abuse has long occupied an important place. Thus the *British Journal of Addiction*, the longest established journal in its field, was established in 1884. A century later these problems are still being addressed. During this time, social and institutional responses to substance abuse in Western countries have changed dramatically (Conrad and Schneider, 1985; West and Cohen, 1985). The voluntary (that is non-therapeutic) and sustained use of drugs is now categorised as mental disorder and classified specifically as *volitional* or *dependency* disorder (American Psychiatric Association, 1980, p. 163; Mule, 1981; West and Cohen, 1985). The merits and demerits of the medicalisation of substance abuse and other forms of social deviance have been debated elsewhere (for example, Conrad and Schneider, 1985; West and Cohen, 1985; MacGregor, 1989) and are amplified in other chapters of this book. However, for the epidemiologist these issues are important, if only for the fact that they have determined the kinds of data that are available and the research strategies employed to analyse the subject.

Epidemiological research into human health problems has typically focused upon five major themes:

(a) Analysing the natural history of the specific health problem (that is, its changing incidence and/or prevalence) in the population of a clearly defined geographical area (for example, a country or a city and its various parts).

(b) Measuring the ways in which the health problem are related to the spatial, ecological and social characteristics of the area in which it is located.

(c) Identifying, firstly, the demographic, social and behavioural attributes of the individuals who experience the specific health problem and, secondly, the group processes which help to determine the temporal and spatial patterns observable in the affected population and the wider society.

(d) Monitoring and evaluating what is being done about the problem (for example, legal/political/health care responses) and recommending what could be done in the future.

(e) Assessing the success (or failure) of the policies directed towards the problem.

This chapter provides an overview of epidemiological research into the first three of these themes, for several of the other chapters in this book address themes four and five. Further, attention is focused chiefly upon epidemiological studies of the illegal narcotic drug scene in the UK.

TEMPORAL AND SPATIAL DIMENSIONS OF DRUG ABUSE IN THE UK, 1973–88

Research by historians and social scientists has established that drugs have been devised and used since prehistoric times, apparently in every society and continent (Reed, 1980; Pearson, 1989; Plant, 1989). Drug use has, therefore, always been endemic in every society. However, most drug users participate only intermittently, moderately and in socially and culturally prescribed settings. In contrast, a minority uses drugs in socially unacceptable ways (for example, illegally or in excessive quantities, either episodically, or for protracted periods).

In the UK the non-medical use of what are defined as Class 'A' drugs (chiefly heroin and cocaine) has long been proscribed by law. Given the illegal nature of the activity, official statistics inevitably seriously underrepresent the real scale of the problem. This is especially true of the crucial supply side of the equation for, as Plant (1989, p. 53) recently observed: 'there are no routinely gathered statistics which indicate levels of production, sale, or consumption of substances such as heroin and cocaine. In contrast, such information is available in relation to alcohol, tobacco, and legally produced prescribed drugs'. However, data for the number of drug seizures, the kind and quantity of illegal drugs seized by the police and the Customs, are published annually by the Home Office (Home Office, 1987). This information could form a useful indirect indicator of trends in illicit drug supply. Statistics relating to illicit drug use are also published annually by the Home Office. Persons cautioned or found guilty of any offences (for example, trafficking, unlawful production, simple possession) under the *Misuse of Drugs Act* (1971) constitute one important indicator. In addition, the

Home Office register of notified narcotic addicts provides valuable information on the changing numbers of new and former addicts, their gender and age.

Although these three official data sets record only a fraction of the total illegal drug supply and consumption market, this does not mean that they have no value as bases for epidemiological analyses. Similar problems beset researchers in the field of criminology (Herbert, 1982) and analysts of infectious diseases. Thus Cliff, *et al.* (1986) in the preface to their magisterial study of influenza epidemics, recognise the indifferent quality of much 'influenza' data, but argue that: 'our philosophy has been pragmatic in the sense that to ignore the data, whatever their limitations, would be to overlook major potential sources of information about the disease; in other words, we see our business as one of lighting candles rather than cursing the darkness'. Moreover they 'note the large number of robust statistical methods which have been developed specifically to deal with dirty data'.

Despite their limitations, these measures of illegal drug supply and use in the UK have all shown broadly similar trends since the early 1970s (Figure 9.1). There were steadily rising numbers during the 1970s, massive increases from around 1980, followed by modest falls in numbers from the mid-1980s. This 'wave-like' temporal profile is similar in form to that found for most communicable diseases and has, therefore, prompted several epidemiologists to describe the upsurge in illegal drug abuse in the UK as an 'epidemic' (for example Pearson, 1989; Plant, 1989). It would be valuable to analyse the trends in drug seizures, offences and notifications (that is of new and known illegal drug uses), not just nationally, but also regionally. This would certainly be feasible, for the necessary annual statistics are available not only for the whole of the UK, but also for the four member countries and for the 52 police force areas (PFAs) found within the UK (Home Office, 1987).

Some examples of the potential for epidemiological research are given briefly here. The first uses the data relating to newly notified narcotic drug addicts (that is, to the *incidence* of illegal narcotic drug use). Figure 9.2 charts the growing numbers of new registered narcotic addicts in the UK as a whole and in five sample regions for the period 1973–85.

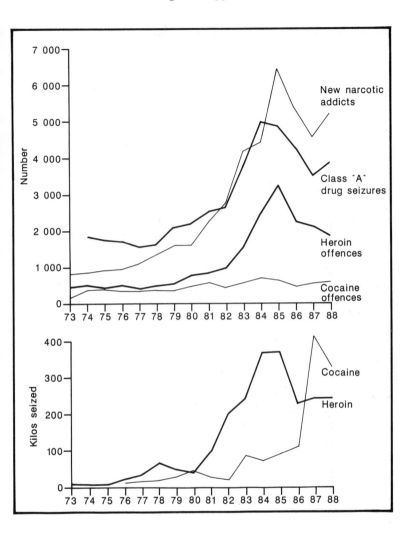

FIGURE 9.1   *Selected dimensions of the UK's drug epidemic: 1973–88*

Simple visual comparison suggests that the profiles for
Greater London (that is the combined Metropolitan and City
PFAs) and the Metropolitan Ring (that is, the combined
Essex, Hertfordshire, Thames Valley, Surrey, and Kent PFAs)
are broadly comparable with that for the entire UK. In
contrast, the profiles for the three neighbouring provincial

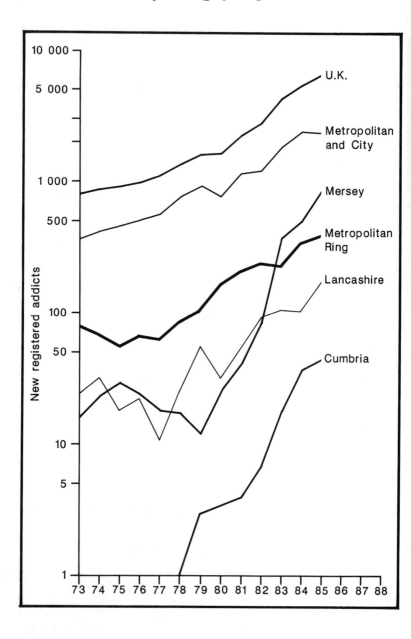

FIGURE 9.2 *Numbers of new registered narcotic addicts in the UK and selected regions*

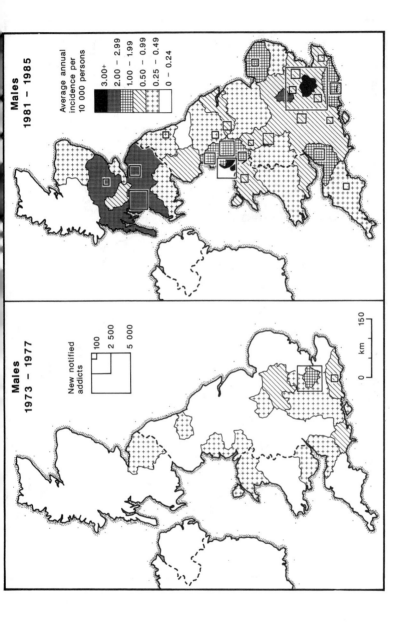

FIGURE 9.3 *Male narcotic drug addicts: distribution and incidence by police force areas in the UK: 1973–77 and 1981–85*

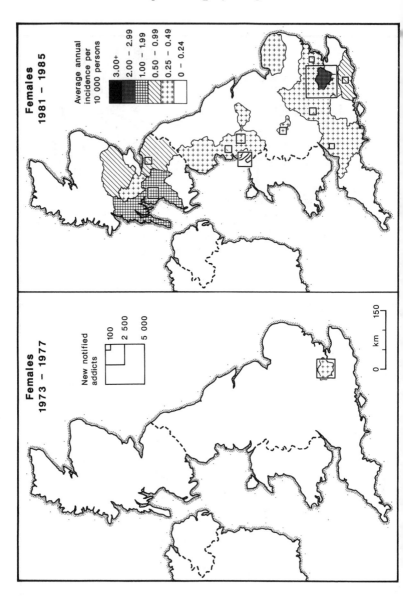

FIGURE 9.4　*Female narcotic drug addicts: distribution and incidence by police force areas in the UK: 1973–77 and 1981–85*

PFAs located in northwest England (that is Cheshire, Lancashire, and Cumbria) differ markedly from the national picture. It is clear that there are marked spatial variations in both the timing and rate of growth in numbers of new narcotic drug abusers.

Using appropriate statistical methods, it would be possible, firstly, to identify regions with common patterns of increases in drug abuse and, secondly, to model diffusion patterns of drug abuse within the UK. More simply, the spread and retreat of the epidemic over time and space could be examined by mapping the reported incidence of drug abuse on a year-by-year basis. Such an exercise is obviously impractical here, but the merits of the strategy are exemplified in Figures 9.3 and 9.4. During the current epidemic's formative years (defined here as 1973–77) there were only 4607 new narcotic drug abusers in the UK and just over half of them (51.7 per cent of the males, 50.4 per cent of the females) were living in London. The average annual incidence was consequently very low throughout the country, peaking in London at 1.28 per 10 000 adult males and only 0.36 for females. In none of the 50 PFAs outside London did the incidence rate for females exceed 0.25 per 10 000 adults, compared with 18 for males. Outside London, secondary peaks in the incidence of illegal drug use for males were found in three areas—Sussex, Dorset, and Cambridgeshire/Northamptonshire. Most of the 18 PFAs with rates above 0.25 have coastal locations and it is tempting to infer that their distribution is a function of contemporary import supply routes for narcotic drugs. This conclusion is probably overly simplistic, given the considerable size of most of the areas and, more importantly, the lack of data on the actual spatial patterning of those supply routes. Furthermore, 33 of the UK's 52 PFAs border the coast and only 13 of these had incidence rates in excess of 0.25 per 10 000 adult male residents.

During the middle years of the 1970s, therefore, there were comparatively few new notified narcotic drug addicts in the UK, and their spatial distribution was both highly localised and of very low intensity. In the 1980s this picture was transformed. Between 1981 and 1985 the epidemic apparently peaked, for 21 030 new addicts were notified to the Home Office, compared with only 4707 during 1973–77. Moreover, the epidemic appeared to have spread almost countrywide, especially among males (Figure 9.3). During the period only one PFA outside London (that is Sussex) recorded more than 100 new male addicts: in 1981–85 the number had risen to 23. Although London experienced a near fourfold increase in numbers, even greater increases occurred in its neighbouring 'satellite' PFAs, and especially in northwest England (for example, Mersey and Greater Manchester PFAs), and in central Scotland (chiefly Strathclyde PFA). As a consequence of this massive provincial upsurge in illegal drug abuse, London's share of the nation's new male addicts fell from 51.7 per cent (1973–77) to 39.9 per cent (1981–85). Among females the spread of the epidemic was both less diffuse and less intense (Figure 9.4). Thus London still accounted for 48.2 per cent of the nation's new female addicts in 1981–85, compared with 50.4 per cent during 1973–77. Nevertheless, 10 provincial PFAs now recorded numbers in excess of 100 compared with none for 1973–77.

In 1985 the UK's epidemic wave of new narcotic addicts peaked at 6409. Thereafter numbers dwindled to 4593 cases during 1987, then rose to 5212 in 1988. The geographical characteristics of the current phase in the epidemic can be portrayed in much finer detail than was possible hitherto, because the Statistics Department of the Home Office began to publish data for the 216 District Health Authorities in 1987. Figures 9.5–9.7 show the distribution of new narcotic addicts in the UK during 1987–88. It is evident that the problem was highly localised, with the bulk of the cases (Figure 9.5) occurring in just three regions: Greater London (and especially inner London–Figure 9.7), northwest England and central Scotland. Outside these clusters isolated peaks were found in some DHAs along the South coast, and in several provincial capitals—notably Bristol, Norwich and Birmingham.

Average annual incidence rates per 10 000 adults were also calculated for 1987–88, using the OPCS (1987) and GRO (1987) mid-year resident population estimates for the 216 DHAs. The results of this analysis are given in Figures 9.6 and 9.7. The map of the UK narcotic drugs scene in the late 1980s (Figure 9.6) resembles an archipelago, comprising 11 islands of contrasting size, shape and relief. The largest 'islands' of drug abuse were located in central Scotland, northwestern

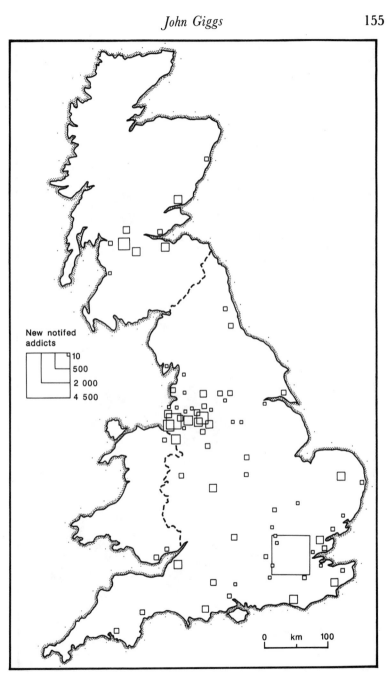

FIGURE 9.5 *Distribution of new narcotic drug addicts by Health District Areas in the UK: 1987–88*

The Epidemiology of Drug Abuse

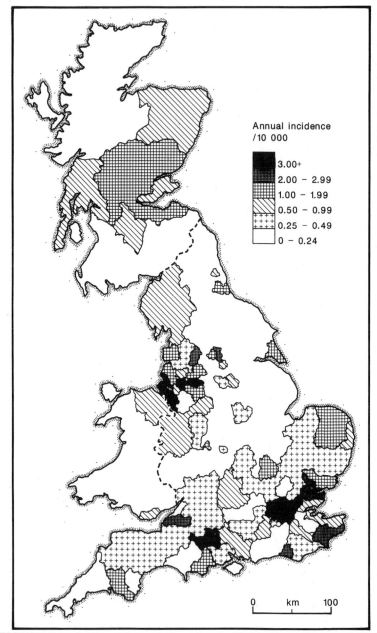

FIGURE 9.6   *Incidence of narcotic drug abuse by Health District Areas in the UK:*
1987–88

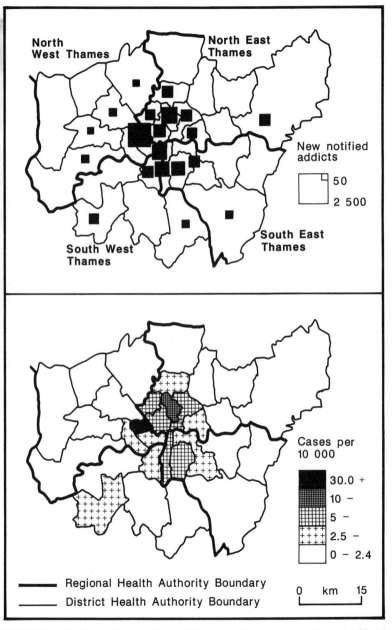

FIGURE 9.7 *New Narcotic Drug Addicts: distribution and incidence by Health District Areas in Greater London: 1987–88*

England and southern England. The details of local spatial variations in drug abuse within central Scotland are obscured because the DHAs there are much larger than their English counterparts. The second 'island' extended from Cumbria in the north, to Shropshire and Birmingham in the south. For much of its length it is bounded to the east by the Pennines. At its centre were DHAs with rates in excess of 5 per 10 000 residents (Liverpool, South Sefton, Wirral, Chester, Warrington and Central Manchester). The third 'island' of narcotic drug use was the largest, covering almost the whole of England south of a line extending from the Severn Estuary to the Wash. Within this large territory there were many 'peaks' and 'troughs' in the incidence of drug abuse. Of the 61 DHAs in the UK with average annual incidence rates in excess of 1 per 10 000, 30 were found in southern England. Greater London alone (Figure 9.7) accounted for 21 of these, peaking at 35.7 per 10 000 adult residents in Paddington and North Kensington DHA. Even so, Greater London's share of the nation's new known narcotic addicts had continued to fall. During 1987–88 the capital had 35.8 per cent of the total cases, compared with 51.4 per cent during 1973–77, the formative years of the epidemic.

The three major 'islands' of narcotic drug abuse in the UK were separated by a 'sea' which covered the Southern Uplands of Scotland, eastern England, the southern Midlands and most of Wales (Figure 9.6). Here the incidence of narcotic drug abuse was almost everywhere below 0.25 per 10 000 adults. This surface was broken by just eight small 'islands', only three of which had incidence rates in excess of 1 per 10 000 —Durham, Hull and West Leeds DHAs.

The geographical analyses presented above appear to be the first to chart the actual growth and spread of a drug epidemic in this country. In contrast, several researchers have sought to determine the incidence or prevalence of narcotic drug abuse in specific British cities during the 1980s. There are regrettably few studies which trace the development of narcotic epidemics within British cities. The rapid increase in the prevalence of heroin addiction has been documented for Glasgow by Ditton and Speirits (1981, 1982) and Haw (1985). Parker *et al.* (1987, 1988) have reported similar trends for Wirral, Merseyside. In contrast, Peveler *et al.* (1988) found

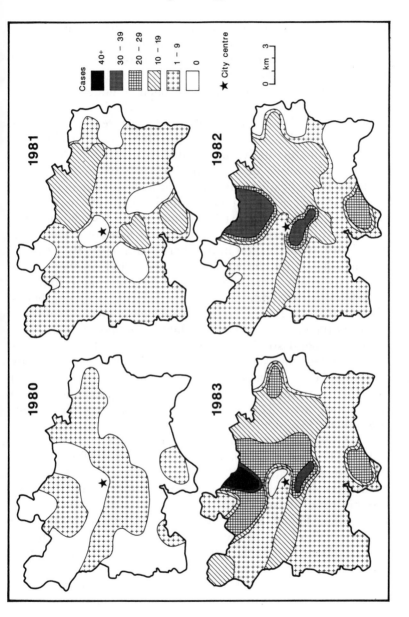

FIGURE 9.8 *Distribution of Referrals to Drug Clinics in Glasgow: 1980–83*

that the prevalence of heroin misuse in Oxford during 1984–85 was little different from that of 1969. Haw's (1985) study of Glasgow is of particular interest because she has mapped the distribution of cases within the city for four consecutive years (1980–83) and four data sets: offences under the Misuse of Drugs Act (1973), all referrals to Drug Clinics, drug related admissions to General Hospitals, and drug related Hepatitis B. Unfortunately, it was not possible to determine the numbers of unique individuals and then map them. Nevertheless, it is possible to demonstrate how the spatial spread and localised intensification/diminution in a drug epidemic within a large urban area might be mapped. Figure 9.8 is adapted from four of Haw's maps (that is maps 3.6–3.9) showing the distribution of referrals to drug clinics in Glasgow. The rapid spread and intensification in numbers is dramatic. By 1983 the neighbourhoods on the southern, eastern and northern sides of the city centre were characterised by quite large numbers of referrals. In addition, two suburban neighbourhoods (Easterhouse in East Glasgow, Castlemilk on the southern fringes of the city) were reporting large numbers of referrals.

Such temporal studies are rare. More typically, researchers have adapted the static, or 'snapshot' approach, typically collecting data for a single year. This information is then used to calculate prevalence rates for the 'at risk' population of the entire study area. This strategy has been adopted in studies of Southern Tyneside (Pattison *et al.* 1982), Bristol (Gay *et al.* 1984), Brighton (Levy, 1985), Wirral (Parker, *et al.* 1987, 1988), Oxford (Peveler *et al.*,1988) and Nottingham (Bean, *et al.*, 1987; Giggs *et al.*, 1989; Giggs, 1990). In a few cases, researchers have also measured and mapped prevalence of narcotic drug abuse for the constituent parts of their study areas. Thus Parker *et al.* (1987, 1988) calculated prevalence rates for each of the 48 townships of Wirral. In Nottingham's 97 Basic Data Zones, the prevalence of Class 'A' drug abuse ranged from 75.0 per 10 000 persons aged 15–44 years in one zone to zero in several (Giggs *et al.*, 1989). In contrast, some workers have focused upon the drug abuse problem in selected parts of large urban areas, notably Hartnoll *et al.*, (1985), Southwark Council (1985) and Burr (1989) in London, Bucknall *et al.* (1986) and Robertson (1987) in Edinburgh. Pearson *et al.* (1987) have provided a rare *comparative* study of heroin abuse in selected parts of Greater Manchester, Merseyside, and South Yorkshire.

These detailed locality-based studies of drug abuse are especially valuable because their authors have not relied solely upon official statistics (that is upon notifications to the Home Office). It has long been recognised that Home Office records seriously understate both the incidence and prevalence of narcotic drug abuse. Thus a survey of heroin and methadone misuse in Oxford in 1969 (Arroyave *et al.*, 1973) found that less than 30 per cent of identified opioid users were known to the Home Office. Consequently, researchers now routinely use the *multi-agency* enumeration method to estimate the local prevalence of narcotic drug abuse. Thus Peveler *et al.* (1988) used 11 sources in their survey of heroin misuse in Oxford. Only 5 per cent of the cases identified for Oxford were known to the Home Office, whereas 43.5 per cent of the Class 'A' drug users identified in Nottingham had been notified to the Home Office (Bean *et al.* 1987).

ECOLOGICAL STUDIES OF DRUG ABUSE

Epidemiologists have established the existence of profound spatial variations in the prevalence of narcotic abuse at a variety of spatial scales—national, regional, intra-urban and local (that is neighbourhood). In doing this they have answered the first question commonly asked by geographers (that is 'Where')? Several epidemiologists have then sought to answer the next question usually asked by geographers: 'Why There?'. In seeking to answer this question a few researchers have analysed the relationships between the spatial patterning of rates of drug abuse and selected social and environmental (for example housing) attributes of the areas in which it is most prevalent. Faris and Dunham (1939) first popularised this strategy in their classic study of the ecology of mental disorders in Chicago. They identified all cases of drug addiction (without psychoses) admitted to 'institutions for the insane' during 1922–34, and calculated rates per 10 000 adults for 120 'subcommunity areas' within the city. The rates ranged from zero in several areas to 68.2 in one. Almost 50 per cent of the cases were in the 'rooming house' and 'hobo' areas in the centre of the city. In contrast, the suburban 'single home' areas had only 4.4 per cent of the cases. Faris and Dunham (1939, p. 122) suggested that 'like persons with alcoholic psychoses, drug addicts come mainly from the zone of transition where it is, of course, easier to obtain an in-group solidarity and maintain contacts with other addicts and "dope" peddlers'. The example set by Faris and Dunham has since been emulated and refined in numerous spatial studies of mental and physical illnesses (Giggs, 1988; Jones and Moon, 1987), crime and delinquency (Herbert, 1982), and other social problems (Herbert and Smith, 1979, 1989).

Despite these substantial methodological and empirical precedents, there is a real dearth of empirical analyses of the ecology of drug misuse in the UK. Parker *et al.* (1987, 1988) have correlated the prevalence rates of known opioid use (for all users and for users aged 16–24) with seven measures of housing and socio-economic deprivation for the 48 'townships' in Wirral District, Merseyside (1981 population: 339 000). All the correlations were statistically significant, and especially that for unemployment. However, four of the townships were exceptions to the general trend, having high rates of known opioid use but low rates of unemployment. The authors suggest that two of these middle-class townships (that is, Wallesey and Bebington) may owe their high rates of known opioid use to the fact that they abut the more typical areas of high opioid use and high unemployment which border the Mersey estuary. In geographical language, the high rates of opioid use in these two townships might simply be a function of *contagious* diffusion (Pyle, 1979). In contrast the second pair of middle-class townships possessing high rates of opioid use (that is, West Kirby and Heswall) are located on the western side of the District and are comparatively remote from the eastern focal area of drug taking. However, these two townships have the highest population in Wirral, after Birkenhead. The appropriate explanatory mechanism would therefore appear to be *hierarchical* diffusion (Pyle, 1979). In this model, an epidemic would originate in the largest city in a region and then diffuse progressively through time to successively smaller settlements in the urban hierarchy. Although the evidence is not discussed, Parker *et al.* (1987, 1988) have shown that there is a size effect in operation within

Wirral District, for they also correlated the two rates of known opioid use with the population size of the 48 townships, and obtained statistically significant positive coefficients.

Pearson *et al.* (1986), in a study of heroin use among young people in the north of England, showed that the problem was highly localised and scattered in form. Thus heroin use was serious in some towns and cities, but not in others. Similarly, within cities, equally dramatic spatial variations in the prevalence of heroin use were apparent. Thus in selected neighbourhoods with serious heroin misuse in Greater Manchester, Merseyside and South Yorkshire, the authors found very high rates of unemployment, one-parent families, and lack of access to a car. Moreover, within these neighbourhoods, there were pockets of substantially greater heroin use and social deprivation. In a subsequent essay, Pearson (1987 a) has described the strong links between prevalence of heroin use and multiple deprivation in some inner city neighbourhoods and in run-down council estates.

For Greater Nottingham (1981 population: 472 285), Giggs *et al.* (1989) have measured the relationships between known adult Class 'A' drug abuse and two measures of deprivation —unemployment, and a composite index of multiple deprivation based on 14 variables used by Nottingham County Council (1983). For the 97 zones within the study area the positive correlation coefficients were significant at $p < 0.0001$. Similar results were obtained when the rate for drug abuse was correlated with three types of crime: burglary, criminal damage, and assault and wounding. In a second analysis of Class 'A' drug abuse in Greater Nottingham, Giggs (1990) selected 40 variables (drawn mainly from the 1981 census) and used Principal Components Analysis and non-hierarchical cluster analysis to group the study area's census tracts into 14 distinctive. sets of 'social areas'. Poisson probability mapping subsequently identified statistically significant variations in the numbers of Class 'A' drug addicts living in several of these social areas. Only two of the three low status inner city social areas and only one of the four low status, council estate, area types had significantly more addicts than could be expected by chance. In contrast, among the five middle-class area types, three had significantly fewer addicts than could be expected by chance, and one had a significant excess of cases. However, this 'atypical' middle-class area was located directly next to the low status, inner city neighbourhoods, where the greatest number of drug addicts were resident. Stepwise regression analysis of the drug abuse rates and component scores for the 14 social areas identified significant links with Component I (labelled 'poor social and material resources') and Component III (which identified high rates of young people and areas of predominantly private rented nineteenth-century terraced housing).

These few studies of the intra-urban ecology of drug abuse are not strictly comparable in terms of the variables, spatial units, and statistical methods employed. Nevertheless, the findings are remarkably similar and tell us several important things about the nature of narcotic drug abuse in British cities during the 1980s. Firstly, there are massive spatial variations in the prevalence of drug abuse over quite small distances within large urban areas. Secondly, there are strong statistical associations between levels of illicit drug use and various measures of social and material deprivation. Thirdly, several apparently atypical neighbourhoods have been identified. Thus some decaying inner city neighbourhoods and council estates (in both inner city and suburban areas) have high rates of deprivation, but low rates of narcotic drug abuse. Additionally, some middle-class neighbourhoods have high rates of illicit drug abuse. Pearson and his colleagues (Pearson *et al.*, 1986; Pearson, 1987) have suggested that a critical factor explaining these three major features of the geography of narcotic drug abuse is probably drug availability. The very existence of drug abusing populations in particular localities, neighbourhoods, towns and regions within the UK is, therefore, likely to be a function of the existence of drug supply and distribution networks.

The findings of these few ecological studies of narcotic drug abuse are valuable. The evidence certainly suggests that further studies are required. Ideally, the problem should initially be examined simultaneously in a set of urban areas, using a standard set of variables (that is, identical measures of both drug abuse and socio-environmental attributes) for a common set of areal units (for example electoral wards or enumeration districts). Using such a strategy it would be possible to establish whether the existing findings are common to all urban areas, or whether these vary as a result of such factors as: size of settlement, regional location within the UK, and the distinctive demographic, social and economic attributes of individual towns (Moser and Scott, 1960). This comparative and cross-sectional analysis should then be repeated at a later date, so that the effects of temporal influences could be determined.

This discussion of the merits of ecological analyses of the narcotic drug abuse phenomenon must be concluded with a note of caution. The identification of systematic relationships between illicit drug abuse and unfavourable environmental factors does not necessarily mean that specifically *causal* links have been identified. This fact must be emphasised, because these analyses are based on aggregated data (that is, rates for areas), not upon information about the specific attributes and circumstances of individuals. Despite this interpretative limitation, ecological analyses have many positive features (Giggs, 1980, 1988; Herbert, 1982; Smith, 1984).

DEMOGRAPHIC, SOCIO-ECONOMIC AND BEHAVIOURAL ATTRIBUTES OF BRITISH NARCOTIC DRUG ABUSERS

The upsurge in illicit drug abuse in the UK during the late 1970s and early 1980s has generated a wave of epidemiological studies of the problem. Most of this research has focused upon identifying and characterising the drug abusers themselves. Comparatively few of the findings have come from official, government funded, agencies. In this respect the UK differs markedly from the USA or Canada, where regular national surveys are commonplace (West and Cohen, 1985). For Britain most of the information which we possess concerning the 'high risk' groups *vis-à-vis* illicit drug abuse has come from comparatively small-scale, localised, and cross-sectional surveys. Given the illegal nature of the problem under review, these surveys rarely obtain all the required data from illicit drug users, so that calculation of precise rates (for example, age specific rates) is often impossible. Meaningful comparisons between studies of different localities are frequently hampered by this problem.

The majority of drug users are young people, with few aged 35 years and over. There are, however, considerable temporal and spatial variations in the age structure of the illicit drug-using population. Thus the Home Office statistics for new notified narcotic drug users show that the proportions aged under 25 years fell considerably from 1973 (75.6 per cent for males, 73.6 per cent for females) to 1988 (56.5 per cent for males, 51.5 per cent for females). In contrast, during the heroin epidemic in Glasgow (when the numbers of heroin addicts referred to drug clinics and psychiatric services grew from 76 in 1980 to 430 in 1983) the proportion aged less than 25 years increased from 44.7 to 67.6 per cent (Haw, 1985). Comparisons of the opioid-using addicts identified in seven intra-urban studies during the mid-1980s reveals that the proportions of users aged under 25 years ranged between 76.2 per cent in Wirral (Parker *et al.*, 1987) and only 10.8 per cent in Nottingham (Bean *et al.*, 1987).

Equally wide variations exist in terms of the gender of the drug using population. In common with most forms of 'problem' behaviour—notably crime and delinquency, alcohol abuse, and cigarette smoking (Herbert, 1982; West and Cohen, 1985), the majority of British narcotic drug abusers are males. Thus in 1985 the ratio for total known narcotic addicts was 2.36 males to each female: for new notified narcotic addicts the ratio was 2.5:1. However, the disparity between the sexes has narrowed substantially since the epidemic commenced. In 1973 the ratios were 3.0:1 and 3.95:1 respectively, for all known narcotic addicts and for new known narcotic addicts. During the course of the present epidemic, therefore, the proportions of females in the total known narcotic drug addict population rose from 24.6 per cent in 1973 to 29.8 per cent in 1985. Among newly notified narcotic addicts, in contrast, the proportions were 20.2 per cent in 1973 and 28.5 in 1985.

The upsurge in numbers of female addicts has not been spread evenly across the UK. In both absolute and proportional terms the greatest increases relative to males occurred in southeast England and central Scotland. Among new narcotic addicts notified during 1981–85, females comprised over 30 per cent of the total in 15 of the country's 52 Police Force Areas (PFAs). Nine of these formed a single extensive region centred on London and three were located in central Scotland. In contrast, in only seven PFAs did the proportion of females fall below 20 per cent of the total new addicts. The lowest figures were reported in Fife (14.3 per cent), Staffordshire PFA (17.3 per cent), and Cleveland and Humberside PFAs (both 17.6 per cent). Within this broad regional variation, finer details are provided by the small set of 'multi-agency' and locality-based prevalence studies. For the mid-1980s the ratios of male to female addicts ranged from only 1.8:1 in Camden and Islington in London (Hartnoll *et al.* 1985), 2:1 in Bristol (Gay *et al.* 1984), 2.7: in Brighton (Levy, 1985), to 3.6:1 in Wirral (Parker *et al.* 1987) and Glasgow (Haw, 1985).

Our knowledge of the social attributes and circumstances of narcotic drug addicts is derived mainly from only a small number of the total addicts identified in a few detailed prevalence studies. Thus Parker *et al.* (1987) provided data on the marital status and family setting of 219 opioid users known to the local drugs councils and 197 known to the local detoxification unit, out of 1305 known opioid users in Wirral. Similiarly, Bean *et al.* (1987) were able to obtain this information for only 83 of the 170 Class 'A' drug users found in Greater Nottingham. Clearly we have no way of knowing whether these small samples are representative of the entire narcotic drug using population. In the two Wirral samples most of the addicts were single (that is, 78.1 per cent of the drug council cases, 71.6 per cent of the detoxification unit cases). In contrast only 29.9 per cent of Nottingham's interviewed addicts were single. The profound difference between the two localities almost certainly reflects the markedly different age profiles of the drug addicts. In Wirral 76.2 per cent of all opioid addicts were aged less than 25 years, whereas 89.2 per cent of all Nottingham's opioid addicts were aged 25 years and over. The age differential would also probably explain the fact that only 10 per cent of Wirral's addicts lived alone, compared with 25.3 per cent of the Nottingham cohort.

Of the few well-surveyed social attributes of illicit drug users, employment status appears to be the most significant. The best evidence comes from a study of a large sample of young people in Lothian, Scotland (Plant, 1985; Peck and Plant, 1986). Additional evidence has come from studies of

Wirral (Parker *et al.* 1987, 1988) and Nottingham (Bean *et al.* 1987), where the majority (that is, 81 per cent and 89 per cent respectively) of the addicts interviewed were unemployed. Among Nottingham's addicts, 80 per cent had been unemployed for over 12 months. Only 2.4 per cent of the interviewed addicts in both Wirral and Nottingham were engaged in non-manual employment. The literature on narcotic drug abuse and unemployment has been reviewed most recently by Peck and Plant (1986), Plant (1989) and Pearson (1989). In addition to reviewing the findings of local cross-sectional surveys, Peck and Plant (1986) also analysed annual data for the UK from 1970 to 1984, using three variables: average annual unemployment, cautions and convictions for offences concerning drug misuse, and the numbers of narcotic drug addicts notified as being in treatment. Partial correlation analysis identified significant and positive correlations between unemployment and both drug misuse offences and addict notifications.

Unemployment is inextricably linked with poor educational attainment and other measures of poor social circumstances in the lives of most narcotic addicts (Plant *et al.* 1985; Pearson *et al.* 1986, Pearson, 1987; Bean *et al.* 1987). Although the rise of mass unemployment may have been the single most important factor in the genesis of the narcotic drug epidemic during the late 1970s and the 1980s, it would be wrong to stereotype the addicts as being exclusively ill-educated and unemployed. Pearson (1989, pp. 313–14) has shown that, since the mid-1960s, even the rich, the famous, and the powerful have not remained untouched by problems stemming from the use of illicit drugs. Indeed, his list might be extended to include, during the 1980s, the conviction of the Duke of Westminster, and the drug-induced death, at Oxford University, of the daughter of Paul Channon, Minister of Transport.

Many epidemiologists have sought to discover when, how, and why narcotic addicts began their drug-using 'careers'. It is evident that most first started when very young. Several surveys of self-reported drug use during the 1980s have shown that substantial proportions of secondary school leavers and young adults have reportedly engaged in smoking, using alcohol and illicit drugs (Bewley *et al.* 1980; NOP Market

Research 1982; O'Bryan, 1985; OPCS 1985, 1986; Plant *et al.* 1985; Peck and Plant, 1986; Williams, 1986; Pearson, 1987). The research in Lothian is particularly interesting because a large cohort of young people were interviewed on two successive occasions (that is, at ages 15 and 16, then at ages 19 and 20). It was shown that the prevalence of drug abuse in the cohort had more than doubled over the four year period (Plant *et al.* 1985; Peck and Plant, 1986). Furthermore, heavy drinkers among the 15 and 16 year-olds were particularly likely to have used illicit drugs during the following four years. Unemployment was also strongly linked with drug use among the 19 and 20 year-olds.

More recently, Swadi (1988) has reported the first comprehensive epidemiological study of drug and substance abuse among British adolescents. During 1986 3333 self-report questionnaires were completed by children aged 11–16 at six state schools in Inner London. The survey revealed disturbingly high levels of drug and substance abuse. Thus 18.7 per cent were currently smoking cigarettes, with the prevalence rate rising progressively from 5 per cent in 11 year olds, to 31 per cent in 16 year olds. The prevalence of smoking was significantly higher among girls. Alcohol consumption was even more widespread, for 63.3 per cent of the total cohort had 'ever used' alcohol and 10.9 per cent drank once a week or more. Illicit drugs and solvents had been used at least once by 20.5 per cent of the adolescents, and 5.8 per cent had tried hard drugs. Heroin had been tried by 1.6 per cent of the school children, and cocaine by 1.8 per cent. More seriously, 53.8 per cent of those who had tried heroin and 25.4 per cent of those who had tried cocaine were using the drugs at least once a week. It was also found that there were no significant gender differences in the frequency of use of individual substances except for solvents and cocaine, where girls predominated.

It is evident that many adolescents and young people (perhaps more than a third) experiment with smoking, drinking and illicit drug use. They generally begin because of encouragement from their friends or from curiosity. Thus among interviewed Class 'A' drug addicts in Nottingham, 66.3 per cent reported that they had first obtained illicit drugs from relatives or friends (Bean *et al.* 1987). Comparatively few young people first experiment with opioids, although Wirral appears to be an exception to this generalisation (Parker *et al.* 1987, 1988). Most begin (and end) their flirtation with illicit drugs by using cannabis, amphetamines or other Class 'B' drugs. A minority subsequently become regular users and addicts to drugs (but see Plant, 1989, pp. 59–60). In the Nottingham cohort, 77 per cent of Class 'A' drug users had first used cannabis or amphetamines, and only 2.4 per cent had first used opioids. However, at the time of interview, 60 per cent were using opioids. Almost all the interviewed addicts were now heavily involved in drug taking, with 81 per cent claiming daily use and only 3.5 per cent using drugs one day a week or less (Bean *et al.* 1987).

Most authorities agree that the present British narcotic drug epidemic differs from past outbreaks in several important respects (see Pearson *et al.* 1986, Pearson 1987, 1989; Plant *et al.* 1985, Plant 1989). Firstly, the reasons for current illicit drug abuse are extremely varied, but recreational use is now a major component. Secondly, the present epidemic is characterised by a substantial proportion of young addicts who have been described as 'poly-drug' users, or 'multiple-drug' users. That is, they are heavy users of several drugs (including alcohol and tobacco). Thus in Nottingham it was found that many heroin addicts frequently also used such 'lower order' drugs as amphetamines, and cannabis (Bean *et al.* 1987).

Thirdly, the present epidemic is distinctive because of the immense variety of drugs that are now available for illegal use. Moreover, there are substantial temporal, spatial and social variations in the particular drugs used, methods of consumption and even the contexts in which they are consumed (for example, Pearson, 1987). Although heroin has been the mainspring of the epidemic for most of the decade, its use now appears to be waning. This decrease may be attributable to the greater use of cautioning of drug offences by the police, or the fact that heroin is simply becoming less fashionable among drug users (Fraser and George, 1988). During the past two years large quantities of imported cocaine have entered the country (Figure 9.1). Formerly the favoured drug of the affluent minority, cocaine (and its potent variant 'Crack') has been drastically reduced in price to widen the market. It is now being sold and used in London (roughly 75 per cent of the total supply—*Sunday Times*, 15 January 1989), Liverpool and the East Midlands. There has also been a resurgence in the use of amphetamines and of LSD, in a new synthetic form called Ecstasy (*Observer*, 2 October 1988). This 'designer' drug has become a central part of the new 'Acid House' fashion that is spreading from London to nightclubs and other venues all over the country. Several other drugs, normally only available on prescription, are being dissolved in water and injected (for example, the tranquilliser temazepam, and the pain reliever dihydro-codeine).

A fourth distinctive feature of the present epidemic is the 'footloose' lifestyle of many addicts. Although the phenomenon has never received the attention that it deserves, the high levels of residential mobility found among drug addicts have undoubtedly contributed to the rapid spread of the epidemic. Alarcon (1969) has provided a fine example of the impact of *relocation* diffusion (see Pyle, 1979). The genesis of the heroin epidemic in Crawley New Town during 1966 and 1967 was attributable to outside initiators. Alarcon showed that just two in-migrant addicts accounted for no fewer than 48 confirmed cases in the town's population. In a recent study of HIV and drug misuse in Edinburgh, Brettle *et al.* (1987) showed that 44 intravenous drug misusers (IVDMs) who attended the city's screening clinic had shared needles with other addicts in 17 other localities in the UK (ranging from Wick in the north of Scotland, to Stonehenge in the south of England) and in three European cities (that is, Amsterdam, Rotterdam and Paris). In a recent newspaper article on 'crack' (*Sunday Times* 15 January 1989) it was stated that customers travelled from all over the country to buy the drug at the centre of the Milton Court Estate (dubbed locally as 'Crack City') in Deptford, south London.

An analysis of the 'residential histories' of the 170 Class 'A' drug addicts found in Greater Nottingham confirmed both the scale and diversity of the phenomenon (Giggs, 1990). Only 32.5 per cent had not changed address in the 12 months prior to being first interviewed. Nearly half of the addicts could be classed as long distance movers, for 14.5 per cent had lived in Nottingham for less than 12 months and 32.4 per cent were known to have left the city after the first interview. Seven of the addicts (4.1 per cent) claimed to have had no fixed abode in the city for the previous 12 months; six addicts (3.5 per cent) had moved home within the same neighbourhood, and 22 addicts (12.9 per cent) had moved to other neighbourhoods within the city. Nearly all of the moves occurred within Nottingham's lowest status residential areas.

CONCLUSIONS

Epidemiological research during the 1980s has taught us much about the present epidemic of illegal drug use in the UK. Even so, we still do not know nearly enough about the specific themes discussed in this chapter. Certainly there are both insufficient data and analyses to enable epidemiologists and others (for example, the legal, political, and health care agencies) to make effective and unbiased decisions about the various strategies which might be implemented to both reduce existing levels of drug addiction and discourage people (especially adolescents) from becoming addicts in the future. Given the present British system of drug control, the situation is unlikely to change for the better. Epidemiologists recognise that drug use is endemic (that is normal) in every society (for example, Pearson 1989; Plant 1989) and that only a minority of drugs users will become drug-dependent through sustained use. However, designating the non-medical use of one set of drugs illegal, while permitting the sale of others (notably alcohol and tobacco) is illogical, not least because the inimical economic, social and health costs of alcohol and tobacco abuse are monumental when compared with those for illicit drug abuse (West and Cohen, 1985). Furthermore, it is curious (to say the least!) that a subject which has engendered such a sustained 'moral panic' among politicians, the media, and the wider society, should be so ill-served in terms of funding for both official documentation and epidemiological research.

REFERENCES

American Psychiatric Association (1980), *Diagnostic and Statistical Manual of Mental Disorders*, 3rd ed (Washington, DC: APA).
Arroyave, F., D. Little, F. Letemendia and R. De Alarcon (1973) 'Misuse of

Heroin and Methadone in the City of Oxford', *British Journal of Addiction*, 68, pp. 129–35.

Barker, D. J. E. (1973) *Practical Epidemiology* (Edinburgh: Churchill Livingstone).

Bean, P., C. K. Wilkinson, J. A. Giggs and D. K. Whynes (1987) *Drug Taking in Nottingham and the Links with Crime*, Report to the Home Office Research and Planning Unit (Nottingham University).

Bewley, T., M. Johnson, J. Bland and M. Murray (1980) 'Trends in Children's Smoking', *Community Medicine*, 2, pp. 186–89.

Brettle, R. P. *et al.* (1987) 'Human Immunodeficiency Virus and Drug Misuse: the Edinburgh Experience, *British Medical Journal*, 295, pp. 421–4.

Bucknall, A. B. V. and J. R. Robertson (1986) 'Deaths of Heroin Users in a General Practice', *Journal of the Royal College of General Practitioners*, 36, pp. 120–2.

Bucknall, A. B. V., J. R. Robertson and J. G. Strachan (1986) 'Use of Psychiatric Drug Services by Heroin Users from General Practice', *British Medical Journal*, 292, pp. 997–9.

Burr, A. (1989) 'An Inner-city Community Response to Heroin Use', in S. MacGregor (ed.), *Drugs and British Society: Responses to a Social Problem in the 1980s* (London and New York: Routledge).

Cliff, A. D., P. Haggett and J. L. Ord (1987) *Spatial Aspects of Influenza Epidemics* (London: Pion).

Conrad, P. and J. W. Schneider (1985) *Deviance and Medicalisation: from Badness to Sickness* (Columbus, Ohio: Merrill).

De Alarcon, R. (1969) 'The Spread of Heroin Abuse in a Community', *WHO Bulletin on Narcotics*, 21.

Ditton, J. and K. Speirits (1981) 'The Rapid Increase of Heroin Addiction in Glasgow during 1981', Background Paper no. 2, University of Glasgow.

Ditton, J. and K. Speirits (1982) 'The New Wave of Heroin Addiction in Britain', *Sociology*, 16 (4), pp. 595–8.

Evans, D. J. and D. T. Herbert (eds) (1989) *The Geography of Crime* (London: Routledge).

Faris, R. E. and H. W. Dunham (1939) *Mental Diseases in Urban Areas* (University of Chicago Press).

Fraser, A. and M. George (1988) 'Changing Trends in Drug Use: An Initial Follow-up of a Local Heroin using Community', *British Journal of Addiction*, 83, pp. 655–64.

Gay, M., J. Parker, Y. Poole and R. Rawle (1984) *The Interim Report: Avon Drug Abuse Monitoring Project* (Hartcliffe Health Centre, Bristol).

Giggs, J. A. (1980) 'Mental Health and the Environment', in G. M. Howe and J. A. Loraine (eds) *Environmental Medicine*, 2nd edn (London: William Heinemann Medical Books).

Giggs, J. A. (1988) 'The Spatial Ecology of Mental Illness', in C. J. Smith and J. A. Giggs (eds), *Location and Stigma: Contemporary Perspectives on Mental Health and Mental Health Care* (Boston: Unwin Hyman).

Giggs, J. A., P. Bean, D. K. Whynes, and C. K. Wilkinson (1989) 'Class A Drug Users: Prevalence and Characteristics in Nottingham', *British Journal of Addiction*, 84, pp. 1473–80.

Giggs, J. A. (1990) 'Drug Abuse and Urban Ecological Structure: the

Nottingham Case', in D. W. Thomas (ed), *Spatial Epidemiology*, London papers in Regional Science Series (London: Pion).

Hartnoll, R. L., R. Lewis, M. Mitcheson and S. Bryer (1985) 'Estimating the Prevalence of Opioid Dependence', *Lancet* 16 Jan., pp. 203–05.

Haw, S. (1985) *Drug Problems in Greater Glasgow* (Glasgow: SCODA).

Herbert, D. T. (1982) *The Geography of Urban Crime* (London and New York: Longman).

Herbert, D. T. and D. M. Smith (eds) (1979) *Social Problems and the City* (Oxford University Press).

Herbert, D. T. and D. M. Smith (eds) (1989) *Social Problems and the City: New Perspectives* (Oxford University Press).

Home Office (1987) 'Statistics of the Misuse of Drugs, United Kingdom, 1986', *Statistical Bulletin*, 28/87 (and personal communication).

Jones, K. and G. Moon (1987) *Health, Disease and Society* (London: Routledge & Kegan Paul).

Knox, P. (1987) *Urban Social Geography* (London: Longman and New York: Wiley).

Last, J. M. (ed) (1982) *A Dictionary of Epidemiology* (Oxford University Press).

Levy, B. (1985) *Prevalence of Abuse of Substances in the Brighton Health Authority Area* (Brighton Drug Dependency Clinic, Brighton, Sussex).

MacGregor, S. (ed) (1989) *Drugs and British Society: Responses to a Social Problem in the 1980s* (London: Routledge).

Moser, C. A. and W. Scott (1960) *British Towns: a Statistical Study of their Social and Economic Differences* (London: Oliver and Boyd).

Mule, S. J. (ed) (1981) *Behaviour in Excess: an Examination of Volitional Disorders* (New York: Free Press).

NOP Market Research (1982) *Survey of Drug Use in the 15–21 Age Group undertaken for the* Daily Mail (London: NOP Market Research).

O'Bryan, L. (1985) *Adolescent Research Project: Interim Report to the DHSS*, Drug Indicators Project, Birkbeck College, London.

OED (1989) *Oxford English Dictionary*, 2nd edn (Oxford: Clarendon Press).

OPCS, Office of Population Censuses and Surveys (1985) *Smoking among Secondary School Children* (London: HMSO).

OPCS, Office of Population Censuses and Surveys (1986) *Adolescent Drinking* (London: HMSO).

Parker, H. J., R. Newcombe and K, Bakx (1987) 'The New Heroin Users: Prevalence and Characteristics in Wirral, Merseyside', *British Journal of Addiction*, 82, pp. 147–57.

Parker, H. J., K. Bakx and R. Newcombe (1988) *Living with heroin: the Impact of a Drugs Epidemic on an English Community* (Milton Keynes: Open University Press).

Pattison, C. J., E. A. Barnes and A. Thorley (1982) *South Tyneside Drug Prevalence and Indicators Study* (Newcastle upon Tyne: Centre for Alcohol and Drug Studies, St Nicholas Hospital).

Pearson, G. (1987) 'Social Deprivation, Unemployment and Patterns of Heroin Use', in N. Dorn and N. South (eds) *A Land Fit for Heroin?* (London: MacMillan).

Pearson, G., M. Gilman and S. McIver (1986) *Young People and Heroin: an Examination of Heroin Use in the North of England* (London and Aldershot:

Health Education Council and Gower).

Pearson, G. (1989) 'Heroin Use in its Social Context', in D. T. Herbert and D. M. Smith (eds), *Social Problems and the City: New Perspectives* (Oxford and New York: Oxford University Press).

Peck, D. F. and M. A. Plant (1986) 'Unemployment and Illegal Drug Use: Concordant Evidence from a Prospective Study and National Trends', *British Medical Journal*, 293, pp. 929–32.

Peveler, R. C., R. Green and B. M. Mandelbrote (1988) 'Prevalence of Heroin Misuse in Oxford City', *British Journal of Addiction*, 83, pp. 513–18.

Plant, M. A., D. F. Peck and E. Samuel (1985) *Alcohol, Drugs and School Leavers* (London: Tavistock).

Plant, M. (1989) 'The Epidemiology of Illicit Drug-use and Misuse in Britain', in S. MacGregor (ed), *Drugs and British Society: Responses to a Social Problem in the 1980s* (London and New York: Routledge).

Pyle, G. F. (1979) *Applied Medical Geography* (Washington, DC: V. H. Winston).

Reed, J. L. (1980) 'Drug Dependence in Contemporary Societies', in G. M. Howe and J. A. Loraine (eds), *Environmental Medicine*, 2nd edn (London: William Heinemann).

Robertson, J. R. (1987) *Heroin, AIDS and Society* (London: Hodder and Stoughton).

Scientific American (1988) *What Science Knows about AIDS*, Oct., pp. 1–112.

Smith, C. J. (1984) 'Mental Health and the Environment: Geographical Approaches' in H. Freeman (ed), *Mental Health and the Environment* (London: Churchill Livingstone).

Southwark Council (1985) *Report of the Working Party in Drug Misuse* (London: Southwark Council).

Starr, P. (1982) *The Social Transformation of Medicine* (New York: Basic Books).

Swadi, H. (1988) 'Drug and Substance Abuse among 3333 London Adolescents', *British Journal of Addiction*, 83, pp. 935–42.

West, L. J. and S. Cohen (1985) 'Provisions for Mental Disorders', in W. W. Holland, R. Detels, G. Knox and E. Breeze (eds), *Oxford Textbook of Public Health*, vol. 2 (Oxford University Press).

Williams, M. (1986) 'The Thatcher Generation', *New Society*, 21 Feb. pp. 312–15.

10 AIDS and British Drug Policy: History Repeats Itself. . . ?

Virginia Berridge

There appear to have been some radical changes in British drug policy since the advent of AIDS. Since the discovery of the HIV virus among British drug users at the end of 1985, the pace of policy change has been rapid. Two major reports on AIDS and Drug Misuse have followed, together with £17 million for the development of drug services. At least 100 needle exchanges offering new for used syringes are the most tangible public expression of new developments, underlining the view that the danger of the spread of AIDS from drug users into the general population is a greater threat to the nation's health than the danger of drug misuse itself. British drug policy and in particular the visible manifestation of a harm-minimisation approach in the form of needle exchanges, has attracted worldwide attention. Some commentators have as a result argued that AIDS has changed the direction of British drug policy.

> The only instance of AIDS overriding established policy objectives has been in the field of drugs. . . . The Government had abandoned its previous stance of augmenting its restrictive and punitive policies on drugs now that AIDS had come to be seen as the greater danger.[1]

Others have been more cautious. Gerry Stimson comments:

> these new ideas appear as a distinct break with earlier ones, but as with many conceptual and practical changes, the possibilities are inherent in earlier ideas and work. It is perhaps a matter of emphasis and direction, rather than abrupt rupture with the recent past.[2]

Susanne MacGregor is also more sceptical. 'Are we now entering a new fourth phase in British policy and practice

176

regarding drugs, or are we seeing merely a modification to the third phase?'[3]

This paper aims to look at the question of the 'newness' of British drug policy post-AIDS. How far has drug policy been radically changed under the impact of AIDS? How far has AIDS been simply a vehicle whereby developments inherent in existing policy have been achieved more quickly than might otherwise have been possible? From a longer term perspective, how much is really new at all; how far do recent changes merely exemplify some very long-standing themes and tensions in British drug policy?

One historical analogy is with the debates around the impact of war on social policy. Historians have in recent years begun to look more closely at the impact of the First and Second World Wars on social and health policy in particular. They have questioned the view that war was the only catalyst for radical change. In the Second World War, for example, the 'national consensus for social change' appears to have been less than unanimous; and the roots of the National Health Service, established in 1948, can be found not just in wartime change, but in pre-war debates and blueprints for health care. What war did was to enable this to happen more quickly and in rather a different fashion (the nationalisation of the hospitals, for example, rather than local authority control) than might otherwise have been the case. War served, too, to lay bare the deficiencies of the existing system. The chaotic overlap of hospital services and structures pre-war was quickly rationalised in the emergency Medical Service in the war; war served to overcome vested interests and opposition to change, but essential continuities with the pre-war service remained.[4]

AIDS, too, fits into this paradigm. Like war, it evoked a period of political emergency reaction which was at its peak from 1986–87, but which, in the case of drugs, spilled over into 1988 with the government reaction to the Advisory Council on the Misuse of Drugs Part I report on *AIDS and Drug Misuse*. Many of the actions of central government in this period had a wartime flavour—the creation of an interdepartmental Cabinet committee chaired by William Whitelaw, Deputy Prime Minister, the 'AIDS week' on television in February 1987, when both television companies joined together on a war time model; the Commons emergency debate in November 1986.[5]

DRUG POLICY IN THE 1980S: BEFORE AIDS

How far did this emergency reaction stimulate genuine new departures? To analyse this question in relation to drug policy, it is first necessary briefly to sketch in developments in the preceding years. Drug policy in Britain has been characterised historically in terms of four distinct phases. The first, in the nineteenth century, saw gradually increasing professional controls inserted into a system of open availability of opiate drugs.[6] A more stringent reaction established during the 'cocaine epidemic' of the First World War, heralded a new phase of policy.[7] The 1920 Dangerous Drugs Act marked a penal reaction to drug use; but the Rolleston Report of 1926 reasserted what became known as the 'British System' of medical prescribing of opiates, a system of medical control operating within a more penal framework of national and international controls.[8] It was not until the late 1960s that a new and third phase began. The development of a drugs subculture, over-prescribing by a number of London doctors, were among the factors leading to a change in policy. The second Brain Committee report in 1965 led to changes in drug policy, in particular the limitation of the prescribing of heroin and cocaine to doctors licensed to do so by the Home Office; treatment of addiction was re-located in the 'clinics', hospital-based drug dependency units. These initially operated as prescribing centres, in the belief that 'competitive prescribing' would undercut and curtail the development of a black market in drugs. Changes in clinic policies in the 1970s, however, brought a decline in opiate prescribing and a rise in more active treatment methods, based on short-term methadone prescribing or on no prescribing at all.[9]

In the early 1980s, drug policy again entered a new phase. What were the main changes which characterised it? Firstly, a 'new' drug problem began to emerge. At the beginning of the 1980s, the numbers of addicts notified to the Home Office underwent a sharp increase although the numbers had in fact been rising more slowly since the mid-1970s. The 3425 addicts notified in 1975 had risen to over 12 000 by 1984. At the same time the amount of heroin seized by Customs rocketed—from under 50kg in 1980 to over 350kg in 1984. The real price of heroin in London is estimated to have fallen by 20 per cent between 1980 and 1983. The number of people involved in drug-related offences also rose steeply—from under 500 in 1975 to 2500 in 1984. Beneath this worrying surface rise in drug-related indicators there was also a realisation that the numbers of addicts or drug users was in reality far higher than the number notified to the Home Office—a multiplier of between five and ten was suggested. Customs and police between them probably at best seized only a tenth of the drugs coming into the country; a significant black market in drugs had developed. After some years of calm, Britain was clearly in the throes of a 'new drug problem'.[10]

This coincided with the emergence of drugs as a concern for politicians. Crucially however, they became not a political issue, but one of political consensus. From about 1984, the Conservative government took a direct interest in the formation of drug policy. In 1984 an interdeparmental working group of ministers and officials, the Ministerial Group on the Misuse of Drugs, was established, for the first time bringing together the 13 departments, from the Home Office and Department of Health to the Welsh Office and Overseas Development Administration, with an interest in the subject.[11] The Group is chaired by a Home Office Minister; this chairmanship, undertaken firstly by David Mellor, and then by Douglas Hogg, has proved to be far from a political liability. David Mellor during his tenureship of the office adopted a high political profile as the public exponent of the 'war on drugs'. This reawakened political interest in drugs was reflected in the Commons Select Committee System also with reports from the Social Services Committee (1984–85) and the Home Affairs Committee.[12] The latter, reporting in 1986, commented that:

> drug misuse, especially of hard drugs like heroin and cocaine, is still one of the UK's most distressing and difficult problems. Drug dealers still make princely profits and threaten us all, including our children, with a nightmare of drug addiction which has now become a reality for America.[13]

There were some signs that drugs might emerge as an issue for political division between the parties. In 1985, David

Owen, leader of the Social Democratic Party, gave a lecture in which he cited research evidence linking drug use with youth unemployment, and deprivation.[14] But the incipient debate did not develop. In the 1987 general election the SDP/ Liberal Alliance manifesto did not mention drugs and an election leaflet on health policy gave the subject no more than a mention. Labour's manifesto was likewise silent. Any argument was, as one commentator noted, 'about how *much* rather than *what* should be done'.[15] Some commentators have seen the 1980s as characterised by the politicisation of drug policy.[16] Drugs in fact never became a party political issue, but a Conservative issue with some degree of all-party consensus.

The public face of Conservative political interest was a policy focused on a strong penal response to drugs, on both domestic and international fronts. In 1985, the government published the first version of its strategy document for drugs, *Tackling Drug Misuse*.[17] The strategy had five main aspects, three of which were penal in orientation. Its aims were:

(a) reducing supplies from abroad;
(b) making enforcement even more effective;
(c) maintaining effective deterrents and tight domestic controls;
(d) developing prevention;
(e) improving treatment and rehabilitation.

In the same year, the Commons Home Affairs Committee in its interim report called for continued enforcement of the law; the stationing overseas of additional customs and police intelligence liaison officers; harsher penalties for trafficking offences; help for crop eradication and substitution schemes; legislation to attack and seize the profits of traffickers; and changes in banking law to impede the disposal of money derived from drug trafficking.[18] Much of this was put into effect. The Drug Trafficking Offences Act 1986 (in force since 1987) provided (with all party support) comprehensive powers for tracing, freezing and confiscating drug money, along with measures to stop the laundering of drug money. The Controlled Drugs (Penalties) Act 1985 increased the maximum penalty for drug trafficking from 14 years to life. The National Drugs Intelligence Unit was set up in Scotland Yard to provide a national link between police and Customs. The eight regional crime squads outside London developed 17 dedicated 'drugs wings'; in London, the strength of the Central Drug Squad was nearly doubled. For customs, the number of specialist drugs investigators tripled in the 1980s; nine of these were posted overseas to aid foreign law enforcement agencies. At the level of supply the British government pledged £3.4million in 1987 for a five-year crop substitution/rural development project in Pakistan and money was provided for law enforcement in Bolivia and Ecuador after a visit by David Mellor in 1986. Drug policy assumed new visibility at the level of international control. Increasingly, too, it acquired a European dimension. Britain had chaired the Pompidou Group (the Council of Europe Co-operation Group to Combat Drug Abuse and Illicit Trafficking in Drugs) since 1984. The arrival of a single European market in 1992 brought questions of drug control to the fore.

Clearly a penal reaction largely out of favour since the 1920s was back in fashion. But what was the relationship between political rhetoric and policy practice, in particular within Britain? Here the evidence about the extent and impact of the penal wing of policy was more equivocal. Research on trends in sentencing in Scotland showed that low-level drug offences were indeed receiving longer custodial sentences.[19] But mostly the operation of penal policy was the subject of hearsay rather than sustained investigation. A drop in heroin seized in 1986 was more than matched by increased seizures of cocaine; both were the result of fewer seizures of larger quantities. There was discussion of police tactics at the local level, but little by way of analysis of how policy was actually operating at that level—or indeed at the level of larger-scale distribution.[20] There was, for example, no investigation of prosecutions under the Drug Trafficking Offences Act. An economic study of the cost-effectiveness of expenditure on police and customs drug enforcement work underlined the lack of empirical data on which to base any assessment.[21] The penal response remained a powerful rhetorical symbol; what it meant in practice was rather more uncertain.

HEALTH POLICY ON DRUGS: A TIME OF CHANGE

One aspect of policy which it did symbolise was the decline of a primarily medical response to drugs. British drug policy, as established in the 1920s, had a twin-track approach of penal control, symbolised by the lead role in policy taken by the Home Office, but also of a medical reaction, underpinned by the departmental interest of the Ministry of Health. Since the 1926 Rolleston Report British drug policy had been based on a medical response to drug addiction, symbolised in that report by its reaffirmation of the disease model of addiction and by a doctor's clinical freedom to provide maintenance doses of opiate drugs as a form of treatment. The Rolleston Committee, although arising out of Home Office concern, was established as a Health Ministry Committee, and serviced by the Ministry, in particular by its doctor–civil servant secretary, E. W. Adams. But the resultant 'British system' of medical control operated as part of a legal system based on penal sanctions and international controls as laid down in the 1912 Hague Convention and the 1919 Versailles settlement.[22] How the balance operated could vary over time.

In the 1980s, that balance did begin to drift towards a penal response. But the 'British system' had in fact been in decline well before the Conservative government introduced its package of penal measures in 1984–86. The shift in the health side of drug policy had begun in the mid-1970s. It was marked by a number of factors; a decline in medical prescribing of opiate drugs and of the clinics as centres for the treatment of drug addiction; a change in the characterisation of drug addiction; the rise of the voluntary sector and of drug treatment as part of primary health care. Perhaps most important of all, it had seen the consolidation of a new 'policy community' round drugs and the emergence (or re-emergence) of the concept of harm-minimisation as an objective of policy. It is worth looking briefly at all of these developments. The specialist model for the treatment of drug addiction within the National Health Service as exemplified by the clinic system did not long adhere to the original blueprint. Between 1971 and 1978, the amount of heroin prescribed fell by 40 per cent.[23] Increasingly injectable and oral methadone were used, following the American example;

short-term treatment contracts based on withdrawal replaced longer-term prescribing. The clinics were effectively treating only addicts who were highly motivated to come off drugs. This, coupled with cuts in funding and resources, ensured that the clinics, by the early 1980s, had become what Mike Ashton called a 'backwater of our social response to drug abuse'.[24] Withdrawal from prescribing was a central feature of the medical response. This change of tactic was enshrined in the *Guidelines of Good Clinical Practice* distributed to all doctors in 1984, which emphasised the limited role prescribing had to play.[25] The weight of professional opinion against prescribing was demonstrated by the case of Dr Ann Dally, brought before the General Medical Council in 1987 for technical offences involved in prescribing in her private practice.

The 'medical model' of addiction as a disease requiring specialist treatment was disappearing in practice – and in theory as well. The older concept of addiction had given place, in official parlance at least, in the late 1960s, to the concept of dependence, enshrined in an official World Health Organisation definition.[26] But in the 1980s, this changed to the concept of the problem drug taker, paralleling similar developments in the alcohol field. The change in definitions received official sanction in the 1982 Advisory Council on the Misuse of Drugs Report on *Treatment and Rehabilitation*, which declared:

> most authorities from a range of disciplines would agree that not all individuals with drug problems suffer from a disease of drug dependence. While many drug misusers do incur medical problems through their use of drugs some do not. The majority are relatively stable individuals who have more in common with the general population than with any essentially pathological sub-group. . . . There is no evidence of any uniform personality characteristic or type of person who becomes either an addict or an individual with drug problems.[27]

Accompanying this change in definitions was an emphasis on a multi-disciplinary approach, based on regional and district drug problem teams and local drug advisory committees. Although medical personnel would continue to take the lead, the involvement of other agencies, local authority, police and voluntary agencies was actively sought. The voluntary agencies in particular had already been playing a more prominent role in the provision of services since the late 1970s. The Treatment and Rehabilitation report encouraged a partnership between them and the statutory services. In 1983, the Department of Health mounted a Central Funding Initiative for the development of new community-based services. Fifty-six per cent of grants were administered through health authorities; 42 per cent through the voluntary sector.[28] The aim was to displace the old hospital-based London-focused specialist treatment system. A senior Department of Health civil servant recalled:

> . . . Brain had bunged clinics into London. . . . The most important thing was to try and get a few more services up and running. . . . We had to get the voluntary and hospital services working together. We had to say to generalists and generic workers that the problems of drug users are the same as others—get on and deal with this homeless person and forget he's a drug user.[29]

This approach met resistance from a variety of quarters, from some of the London clinic establishment and from some voluntary agencies, suspicious of incorporation.

But the first half of the 1980s was marked also by the formation of a new 'policy community' around drugs. Richardson and Jordan have used this concept to delineate the way in which the central policy-making machinery is divided into sub-systems in departments (organised round areas such as alcohol or drugs).[30] Close relationships can develop between these subsystems and outside pressure groups, involving shared policy objectives and priorities. For drugs, the 1980s saw a shift from a primarily medical policy community to one which was more broadly-based, involving revisionist doctors, the voluntary agencies, researchers, and, most crucially, like-minded civil servants within the Department of Health. The change can be characterised through the changed membership of the Advisory Council on the Misuse of Drugs, the main expert advisory body on drug policy. In the 1980s, it recruited to an originally mainly medical membership, representatives of the voluntary agencies, of health education, social science research, the probation service and of general practice.[31] The increase in drug use in Liverpool and the Wirral attracted much attention; non-medical researchers and service workers there were of key importance in advocating the thesis of the 'normalisation' of drug use. But doctors also played a key role there; and it was in the Manchester area that revisionism received its clearest expression. The Regional Drug Dependence consultant introduced a 'new model service' based on satellite clinics, community drug teams and a regional training unit.[32] Developments such as these were actively encouraged by civil servants in the Department of Health.

This new policy community took the conclusions of the *Treatment and Rehabilitation* report as its bible. There were differences over questions of implementation and practice. The 1982 report's recommendations were, for example, criticised for establishing the regional drug problem team as basically the staff of a specialist service, headed by a consultant psychiastrist, rather than a genuine multi-disciplinary and agency partnership; and there were also differences over questions of prescribing. But another policy objective, that of the minimisation of harm from drug use, found general support. This was an aim which had long received support from within the voluntary sector of drug services and also from doctors critical of the clinic's non-prescribing policies and their consequent policy objective in the 1980s. In 1984, the ACMD's report on *Prevention* abandoned earlier divisions into primary, secondary and tertiary prevention in favour of two basic criteria: (a) reducing the risk of an individual engaging in drug misuse; (b) reducing the harm associated with drug misuse.[33] But such objectives remained difficult to enunciate publicly in relation to drug use. They certainly lacked political acceptability. When, in 1981, the Institute for the Study of Drug Dependence published a pamphlet, *Teaching About a Volatile Situation*, advocating harm-minimisation techniques (safe sniffing) for glue sniffing, there was an outcry which nearly brought an end to the Institute.[34] There was still a yawning gap between the 'political' and 'policy community' view of drugs. This gap was epitomised in the furore surrounding the government's

decision to mount a mass media anti-heroin campaign in 1985
–86. This essentially political decision ran counter to received
research and internal policy advice which concluded that such
campaigns should not be attempted and were potentially
counterproductive.[35]

To sum up, 1980s drug policy pre-AIDS had a dual face—
a 'political' penal policy with a high public and mass media
profile; and an 'in-house' health policy based on a rhetoric of
de-medicalisation and the development of community services
and harm-minimisation. The relationship between policy and
practice in both wings was paradoxical—and worthy of
further research. For the penal response, data about its
operation, let alone its effectiveness, was largely absent. And
although a network of non-specialist services outside London
was developed, it was notable how much this de-medicalising
shift in policy was still dependent on medical support.[36]
Medicine might, as Jerry Jaffe commented in his 1986 Okey
Lecture, no longer sit at the top of the table, but the new
system could not have moved forward if doctors and doctor
civil servants had not wanted it.[37]

THE IMPACT OF AIDS: THE IMMEDIATE RESPONSE

What has been the impact of AIDS upon an area of policy
already in a state of flux? Most obviously the nature of the
problem presented by drug use has changed. Late in 1985
reports from Edinburgh revealed a prevalence of HIV
antibody seropositivity among injecting drug misusers which
was considerably higher than in the rest of the United
Kingdom and also higher than in parts of Europe and the
United States.[38] The issue of potential heterosexual spread
was not new. The blood transfusion question and the spread
of the virus among haemophiliacs had in 1983/4, raised the
question of the spread of the virus into the general
population.[39] But drugs made this more urgent. A Scottish
Committee chaired by Dr D. McClelland, Director of the
South East Scotland Regional Blood Transfusion Service, was
set up to review the Scottish situation and to report on how
to contain the spread of HIV infection and allay public
concern. The report of this committee, published in September 1986, foreshadowed many of the more publicised state-

ments of the later ACMD reports.[40] It enunciated harm-minimisation as a primrary objective. The threat of the spread of HIV into the general population justified a response based on the minimisation of harm from drug use and on attracting drug users into contact with services.

There is. . . . a serious risk that infected drug misusers will spread HIV beyond the presently recognised high risk groups and into the sexually active general population. Very extensive spread by heterosexual contacts has already occurred in a number of African countries. . . . There is. . . an urgent need to contain the spread of HIV infection among drug misusers not only to limit the harm caused to drug misusers themselves but also to protect the health of the general public. The gravity of the problem is such that on balance the containment of the spread of the virus is a higher priority in management than the prevention of drug misuse.

Substitute prescribing and the provision of sterile injecting equipment to addicts were two major means by which these ends were to be achieved.

Members of the new policy community began to voice these objectives more openly. David Turner, coordinator of SCO-DA, the Standing Conference on Drug Abuse, the national coordinating body for the voluntary drug sector, commented at an AIDS conference in Newcastle in 1986, 'it is essential that no risk-reduction option is rejected out of hand because it appears to conflict with a service's stated goal of abstinence'.[41] Reports of Dutch harm-reduction strategies and needle exchange projects became more frequent. Social researchers joined in. Russell Newcombe of the Wirral Misuse of Drugs Research Project in Liverpool, argued;

Drug education policy-makers and practitioners should be giving serious consideration to how the reality of drug use in the '80s' is best tackled. The question they should ask themselves is: would it be preferable to reduce the incidence of illicit drug use while not promoting safer forms of drug use, or would it be more realistic to give greater priority to the reduction of harm from drug use? The emerging AIDS epidemic has rapidly brought this question to the forefront of the debate. It is my view, and increasingly the view of others who work with drug users or young people, that it is high time for harm-reduction.[42]

These objectives were, as before AIDS, shared by civil servants in the Department of Health. 'We're going to get harm minimisation much more quickly' commented one senior non-medical civil servant in the autumn of 1986.[43] Another saw it as the opportunity:

> to go out and push out a bit further. Almost fortuitously the fact we'd already shifted our policy. . . was. . . a fertile seed bed from which we've been able to develop. . . . We'd be weeping in our tea now. . . . The pre-existing development of community services enabled us to get harm-minimisation approaches off the ground more rapidly than if we'd been rooted in the old hospital based approach to drug misuse.[44]

The urgency of the situation enabled what had been a stumbling block to the unspoken objectives of drug policy pre-AIDS—political and media opposition to any suspicion of 'softness' on drugs—to be quietly overcome. Research was an important legitimating factor. In December 1986, Norman Fowler, Secretary of State for Social Services, announced the intention to set up a number of pilot needle exchange schemes (building on some already in operation, in Liverpool and Swindon, for example). Assessment of effectiveness in preventing the spread of the virus was an important consideration. There were doubts in the Cabinet Committee on AIDS (set up in October 1986) about the provision of syringes; and early in 1987 a project to monitor and evaluate the pilot schemes was established at Goldsmiths' College. In May 1987, the ACMD set up its own working group on AIDS and drug misuses, chaired by Ruth Runciman, a non-medical member of the Council. Of the working group's 13 members, six were non-medical. Part of the ACMD's report, ready in the Autumn of 1987, was not published by the government until March 1988, causing disquiet among some members of the working party.[45] The Report, like the McClelland Commmittee before it, declared the danger of the heterosexual spread of the virus to be a greater menace than the danger of drug use itself. It called for a range of harm-minimisation strategies, most notably needle-exchange and over the counter sales of syringes by pharmacists. Prescribing, too, was seen as an option to attract drug users into services. But the initial political reaction was lukewarm. Although the goal of harm-reduction was accepted by Tony Newton, Minister of Health, in his statement to the Commons on 29 March 1988, only £1 million was provided for the development of services and the further results of evaluation were awaited. The response from Michael Forsyth, Scottish Health Minister, saw central funding of the two pilot schemes still in operation at an end —and a generally negative response to the particular critic-isms of the Scottish situation in the ACMD Report. It seemed as though policy would founder on the rocks of political opposition. The summer of 1988 saw intense pressure from civil servants for a more positive response from ministers which brought a turn-around in the autumn, aided by research results from the Goldsmiths' group which showed that users did change to lower risk behaviours (although a disappoint-ingly small proportion of attenders stayed on to achieve them).[46] David Mellor, the new Health Minister, announced an extra £3 million for the provision of services in England. The money was specifically to enable services to expand and develop in such a way as to make contact with more drug misusers in order to offer help and advice on reducing the risk of HIV infection. Only £300 000 was allocated to Scottish services, despite the disparity in numbers of HIV positive drug users there by comparison with England. Further money followed for 1989/90 with an extra £5 million available for the development of drug services. Coming on top of pre-existing AIDS allocations, the extra funding since 1986 gave health authorities at least £17 million to spend on drug services; money was being provided, too, on a recurrent basis. In Scotland the 1989/90 figure of £2.1 million for drug services was less significant than the doubling of the general AIDS allocation to £12 million. For some English projects funded by the earlier CFI, the money came just in time.

THE 'NORMALISATION' OF DRUG POLICY THROUGH AIDS

What then had AIDS really meant for drug policy? At the level of policy formulation it has clearly, on the war-time model, meant the public establishment of the previous largely unspoken aims of policy. Drug policy in general and services in particular have ostensibly come out of the ghetto and the process, instigated pre-AIDS, of integration into the normal range of services, has been intensified. One of the clearest analyses of the ethos of the new approach instanced changes in assumptions about the nature of the problem; and the nature of the task is now more clearly seen, in this analysis, to be poly-drug workers rather than medical specialists. Services, too, rather than testing client's motivation with long waiting lists and abstinence-oriented treatment philosophies, must become user-friendly (including the potential provision of opiates).[47] The message of government advertising on drugs has changed, too, away from the mass shock approach to targeted harm-minimisation. A senior medical officer commented:

> AIDS may be the trigger that brings care for drug users into the mainstream for the first time ever. . . . The drug world can come 'in from the cold' through AIDS. . . . it's a golden opportunity to get it right for the first time.[48]

Drugs, so it is argued, have become a problem of public health rather than a question of individual pathology. Gerry Stimson argues:

> HIV has simplified the debate and we now see the emergence of what I will call the public health paradigm. Rather than seeing drug use as a metaphorical disease, there is now a real medical problem associated with injecting drugs. All can agree that this is a major public health problem for people who inject drugs, their sexual partners, and their children.[49]

AIDS, so it seems, has gone some way to achieving the normalisation of drug use. In declaring prescribing to be a legitimate option, it has appeared to deal with the prescribing question which had bedeviled drug policy in the 1970s and 1980s. The new 1980s policy community around drugs has been strengthened by the support of some key politicians. References to normalisation and attracting drug users to services now appear in Hansard as well as the pages of the in-house drug journals.[50] The media have been diverted away from heroin into the cocaine issue. For some members of the policy community AIDS has opened up the wider agenda of the liberalisation of drug policy. AIDS has, for some members of the drug policy community, been a type of new dawn.

A NEW DEPARTURE FOR DRUG POLICY?

Policy is clearly in a state of flux and it would be unwise in the early 1990s to attempt to lay down definitive statements about either present or future directions. The rest of this paper will simply raise a number of questions about the 'new drug policy' in the light of an historical perspective. In particular it will draw attention to questions of the implementation of policy and the power relationships within policy; to the continuing war on drugs; it will question how new the 'new public health' model for drugs really is; and will speculate on the long-term impact of policy change.

The nature of the implementation of policy is important: for the rhetoric of policy and its practice can differ significantly.[51] There is relatively little information as yet on how policy is being implemented in practice within services apart from within needle-exchanges. Clearly the impact of the pre-existing local situation is important. One study of the response of Edinburgh agencies, for example, instances increased medical involvement primarily through the medium of the infectious disease specialism rather than psychiatry, which had traditionally in Scotland had little to do with drug users.[52] AIDS in some respects appears to have brought a revival of medical involvement in drug use. It has brought doctors back more centrally into drugs through the emphasis on prescribing as an option and the focus on the role of the general practitioner. There is also a new emphasis on the general health of drug users. A consultant commented:

What's disturbing is that I have had to change positions. I hadn't seen doctors as being that important in services. . . . There were nineteen CDTs in X, each one autonomous and funded by the NHS, but only one headed by a doctor and the others would be headed by a community nurse, a social worker, a voluntary worker. . . . Now I've started arguing strongly that all drug services need a lot of doctor input. . . . The impact of AIDS means an urgent need for medical care. . . . Drug services will have to do routine health checks and be proactive in selling it.[53]

Such views were echoed at an official level. A joint Royal College of Psychiatrists and Department of Health conference in 1989 on new models of services for drug misusers highlighted 'an extreme shortage of trained psychiatrists' to guide the future development of these services. The need to cater for HIV positive drug users—potentially using methadone and AZT—led some drug services to establish specialist clinics aimed at that group. The need, underlined by the McClelland and the two ACMD Reports, of contacting drug users not normally in contact with services has served to elevate the notion of treatment which has resumed its place as an unchallengeable good. The role of the voluntary sector in drug services has also been affected. Ben Pimlott's comment that the Thatcher government, with its rhetoric of voluntarism, had seen the virtual abolition of the voluntary sector, may have been exaggeration, but it did contain an element of truth.[54] The voluntary sector, in drug services as in AIDS more generally, was drawing closer to the statutory sector, and was often funded by it. Even within the voluntary sector, drug use, because of HIV, had become associated with illness. 'They champion the drug users' rights to treatment and to use drugs if they want because they have an illness and need a script. . . . The voluntary sector ends up holding a disease model.'[55] This focus on illness coincided with and complemented pre-existing tendencies in drug policy, for example the increased prominence of private addiction clinics which emphasised the old disease concept; and a revived emphasis in research into the bio-chemical and genetic basis of alcohol and drug dependence. So far as the power relationships in policy-making went, the situation had changed little from the pre-AIDS position. Without the support of influential and centrally placed doctors, the 'new departures' in policy could not have been sustained. Drug policy-making after, as before AIDS, has exemplified the influence of doctor civil servants as important in policy-making, a tradition going back to Dr E. W. Adams, a Ministry of Health civil servant and secretary of the Rolleston Committee in 1924–26.[56]

THE 'WAR ON DRUGS' CONTINUES

The twin-track nature of British drug policy also remains in existence post-AIDS. Penal policy still remains, albeit modified at the local level. Britain still adheres to a system of international control of drugs. The Department of Health has, through AIDS, taken a more public stance as the spokesman for certain aspects of drug policy. But the Home Office remains the lead department and the overall trend of penal policy at the international level remains as before. In June 1987, the United Nations convened an international conference on Drug Abuse and Illicit Trafficking in Vienna, followed in November by a conference on drug abuse and illicit trafficking in the western hemisphere. Tim Rathbone, chairman of the Commons All Party Committee on Drug Abuse and delegate to the later conference, commented that there was general consensus, among other aspects of drug policy, on:

the need to maintain a hard legal and penal line on supply and to match that with more and better cures for possession and use than are presently offered within penal systems; the growing urgency of even better multinational controls, co-ordination and co-operation in tackling and reducing illegal distribution, including improved legal powers to trace, seize and confiscate the assets of drug traffickers.[57]

Increasingly, drug control is assuming a European dimension. In 1989, the Home Office signed an agreement committing the UK and Switzerland to cooperation in tracing and freezing the proceeds of drug trafficking as a direct development from the 1986 Drug Trafficking Offences Act; and negotiations were under way with other European countries. Within Britain at the local level, policies do appear to have changed, with police cooperation in the establishment of needle exchanges, police participation in local drug advisory committees, and links between police and services.[58] But the advent of cocaine as a policy issue has served to legitimate the penal response. Cocaine could potentially, too, impinge on the legitimacy of harm-minimisation as a policy. By the end of the 1980s then, penal drug policy may have been modified at the local level; but, as an overall objective, it remained firm. One senior Conservative politician in 1989 saw drug control as 'increased controlled availability at home and stronger prohibition round the edges'.

THE 'NEW PUBLIC HEALTH' APPROACH?

The 'public health' approach to drugs engendered by AIDS had, like other aspects of policy, clear historical antecedents. One observer commented in 1988 on the parallels between the Advisory Councils part 1 report on AIDS and Drug Misuse and the Brain Committee's report on drug addiction in 1965.[59] Like the ACMD, Brain also justified change in drug policy on public health grounds—addiction was a 'socially infectious condition', a disease which 'if allowed to spread unchecked, will become a menace to the community'. And the remedies suggested by Brain—including notification and compulsory treatment— were classic public health responses. The balance required in drug policy in the 1980s between minimising the harm from drug use but not thereby promoting drug use is parallelled by Brain's attempt to graft the public health objective of preventing infection on to a system geared to individual treatment; drug workers had to prescribe opiates to undercut the black market, but not so much that the market was supplied and new addicts created. There have always been tensions in drug policy, not simply between penal and medical forms of control, but between different forms of medical input. In the nineteenth century, for example, the earlier 'public health' focus on opium adulteration, on child doping or working-class industrial opiate use gave place to medical theories of addiction and disease.[60] Roy MacLeod has pointed to the focus on individual pathology rather than an environmentalist approach in late nineteenth-century discussions of inebriety.[61] Likewise Brain's public health focus in 1965 was modified in practice to a focus on active medical treatment. There has always been an implicit tension between preventive and curative approaches, in this as in other areas of health policy. There are more general parallels between drug policy in the 1960s and the 1980s which cannot be explored here. The 'public health' paradigm itself, too, is worth closer examination—for 'public health' has not been an unchanging absolute. Its definition and remit has changed in the twentieth century, as the nature of state intervention in social issues has itself shifted.[62] Social hygiene with its emphasis on individual responsibility for health was the reformulated public health of the 1900s; the 1970s and 1980s public health has, in its emphasis on individual lifestyle and on prevention, revived these earlier social hygienist concerns. Drug policy, both pre-and post-AIDS, with its emphasis on health education, on the role of the voluntary sector, on the drug user as a 'normal' individual responsible for his or her own actions and health, has epitomised some key elements of the redefinitions. Certainly the 'public health paradigm' of post-AIDS policy is nothing new.[63]

THE LONG TERM IMPACT OF POLICY CHANGE

The question of the long-term impact of policy change should also be considered. How long will the revived 'public health paradigm' persist? It would be an unwise historian or policy scientist who attempted to predict what the long-term balance of policy might be—de- or re-medicalisation; an individualistic public health approach shifting subtly to an individualistic medicalised approach? The analogy of war and policy change with which this article began does offer some suggestive indications. The 'public health' response to alcohol in the First World War with state control of the alcohol industry and limited pub opening hours only partially survived the war.[64] The 'hard-line' emergency response to drugs at the same period was moderated in the 1920s.[65] War does lead to change—but long standing themes and tendencies also express and re-assert themselves. This article has suggested that, despite the apparent revolution in the public rhetoric of drug policy achieved by

AIDS, many aspects of post-AIDS policy were already inherent in drug policy in the 1980s, most obviously the goal of harm-minimisation and the 'normalisation' of drug services. Other themes, the 'new public health' approach, for example, have an even longer history. Even harm-minimisation itself is only a re-statement in different circumstances of the principles enunci-ated in the Rolleston Report of 1926.[66]

> When, therefore, every effort possible in the circumstances has been made, and made unsuccessfully, to bring the patient to a condition in which he is independent of the drug, it may . . . . become justifiable in certain cases to order regular-ly the minimum dose which has been found necessary, either in order to avoid serious withdrawal symptoms, or to keep the patient in a condition in which he can lead a useful life.

Indeed the overall impression is of some long-standing tendencies—the role of medicine, the penal approach—even the revival of the nineteenth-century role of the pharmacist[67] which have not been undermined and may even have been enhanced by the impact of AIDS. Whatever the future of drug policy in the post-AIDS years, it will not escape from its history.

NOTES

I am grateful to Philip Strong for comments on an earlier draft and to the Nuffield Provincial Hospitals Trust for financial support for the research on which this paper is based. My thanks are due to Ingrid James for secretarial assistance.

1. Fox, D. M., P. Day and R. Klein, 'The Power of Professionalism: AIDS in Britain, Sweden and the United States', *Daedelus*, 118 (1989), pp. 93–112.
2. Stimson, G. 'AIDS and HIV: The Challenge for British Drug Services', *British Journal of Addiction* (forthcoming).
3. MacGregor, S. 'Choices for Policy and Practice', pp. 171–200 in S. MacGregor (ed), *Drugs and British Society. Responses to a Social Problem in the 1980s* (London: Routledge, 1989).
4. For discussion of these issues, see C. Webster, *The Health Services Since the War. Vol. I: Problems of Health Care. The National Health Service before 1957* (London: HMSO, 1988).
5. Berridge, V. and P. Strong, 'AIDS Policies in the UK: a Preliminary Analysis' (forthcoming) in E. Fee and D. Fox (eds), *AIDS: Contemporary History* (Princeton University Press).

6. Berridge, V. and G. Edwards, *Opium and the People: Opiate Use in Nineteenth Century England* (London: Yale University Press, 1987).

7. Berridge, V. 'War Conditions and Narcotics Control: the Passing of Defence of the Realm Act 40B', *Journal of Social Policy*, I (1978), pp. 285–304.

8. Berridge, V. 'Drugs and Social Policy: The Establishment of Drug Control in Britain, 1900–1930', *British Journal of Addiction*, 79 (1984), pp. 17–29.

9. MacGregor, S. 'Choices for Policy and Practice'; P. Bean, *The Social Control of Drugs* (London: Martin Robertson, 1974); G. Edwards, 'Some Years On: Evolutions in the "British System", in D. H. West (ed.), *Problems of Drug Abuse in Britain* (Cambridge: Institute of Criminology, 1978); H. B. Spear, 'The Growth of Heroin Addiction in the United Kingdom', *British Journal of Addiction*, 64 (1969) pp. 245–55.

10. Stimson, G. 'British Drug Policies in the 1980s: A Preliminary Analysis and Suggestions for Research', *British Journal of Addiction*, 82 (1987) pp. 477–88.

11. Home Office, *Tackling Drug Misuse: A Summary of the Government's Strategy* (London: Home Office, 1986).

12. Social Services Committee, *Fourth Report of the Social Services Committee: Misuse of Drugs with Special Reference to the Treatment and Rehabilitation of Misusers of Hard Drugs* (London: HMSO, 1985).

13. Home Affairs Committee, *First Report from the Home Affairs Committee, Session 1985–86: Misuse of Hard Drugs* (London: HMSO, 1986).

14. Owen, D. 'Need for a Scientific Strategy to Crub the Epidemic of Drug Abuse in the United Kingdom', *Lancet*, 26 October 1985, p. 958.

15. Election '87, 'What the Parties said about Drugs', *Druglink*, 2, (5) (1987), p. 7.

16. For example, G. Stimson, 'The War on Heroin: British Policy and the International Trade in Illicit Drugs', pp. 35–61 in N. Dorn and N. South, (eds), *A Land Fit for Heroin? Drug Policies, Prevention and Practice* (London: MacMillan, 1978).

17. Home Office, *Tackling Drug Misuse*, see note 11.

18. Home Affairs Committee, *Interim Report. Misuse of Hard Drugs* (London: HMSO, 1985).

19. Haw, S. and D. Liddell, 'Drug Problems in Edinburgh District. Report of the SCODA Fieldwork Survey' (London: SCODA, 1989).

20. Dorn, N. 'The Agenda for Prevention', in V. Berridge. (ed), *Drug Research and Policy in Britain: a Review of the 1980s* (Gower/Avebury, forthcoming).

21. Wagstaff, A. and A. Maynard, *Economic Aspects of the Illicit Drug Market and Drug Enforcement Policies in the United Kingdom*, Home Office Research Studies, 95 (London: HMSO, 1988).

22. Berridge, V. 'Drugs and Social Policy', see note 8.

23. Lewis, R., R. Hartnoll, S. Bryer, E. Daviaud and M. Mitcheson, 'Scoring Smack: the Illicit Heroin Market in London, 1980–83', *British Journal of Addiction*, 80 (1985), pp. 281–90.

24. Ashton, M. 'Controlling Addiction: the Role of the Clinics', *Druglink*, 13 (1980), pp. 1–6.

25. DHSS, *Guidelines of Good Clinical Practice in the Treatment of Drug Misuse. Report of the Medical Working Group on Drug Dependence* (London: DHSS, 1984).

26. Edwards, G., A Arif and R. Hodgson, 'Nomenclasture and Classification of Drug and Alcohol Related Problems', Bulletin of World Health Organisation, 59 (1981), pp. 225–42.

27. DHSS, *Treatment and Rehabilitation. Report of the Advisory Council on the Misuse of Drug* (London: HMSO, 1982).

28. MacGregor, S., B. Ettorre and R. Coomber, *Summary of the First Phase of Research. An Assessment of the Central Funding Initiative on Services for the Treatment and Rehabilitation of Drug Misusers* (London: Birkbeck, 1987).

29. Department of Health civil servant, conference paper, June 1989.

30. Jordan, A. G. and J. J. Richardson, *British Politics and the Policy Process* (London: Allen & Unwin, 1987).

31. The membership of the ACMD is listed at the front of the reports on *Treatment and Rehabilitation* and *Prevention* (1984). Membership of the Working Group on AIDS and Drug Misuse is listed in the two ACMD AIDS reports, *AIDS and Drug Misuse, Parts 1 and 2* (London: HMSO, 1988 and 1989).

32. Strang, J. 'A Model Service: Turning the Generalist on to Drugs', pp. 143–69 in S. MacGregor (ed.), *Drugs and British Society*, see note 3.

33. Home Office, *Prevention. Report of the Advisory Council on the Misuse of Drugs* (London: HMSO, 1984).

34. Shapiro, H. 'Press Review July 1980–May 1981', *Druglink*, 16, pp. 6–8.

35. Dorn, N. 'Media Campaigns', *Druglink*, 1 (2) (1986), pp. 8–9.

36. Key figures were Dr John Strang, regional consultant in Manchester; Dr Dorothy Black, senior medical officer at the Department of Health; and Dr Philip Connell, chairman of the Advisory Council for the Misuse of Drugs.

37. Jaffe, J. 'Drug Addiction: The American Experience', Okey Memorial Lecture, Institute of Psychiatry, London, 1986.

38. Peutherer, J. F., E. Edmonds, P. Simmonds, J. D. Dickson, *et al.*, 'HTLV-III Antibody in Edinburgh Drug Addicts', *Lancet* 2 (1985), p. 1129; J. R. Robertson, A. B. V. Bucknall, P. D. Welsby *et al.*, 'Epidemic of AIDS Related Virus (HTLV-III/LAV) Infection among Intravenous Dru Abusers', *British Medical Journal*, 292 (1986), p. 527.

39. Berridge, V. and P. Strong, 'AIDS Policies in the UK', see note 5.

40. Scottish Home and Health Department, *HIV Infection in Scotland. Report of the Scottish Committee on HIV Infection and Intravenous Drug Misuse* (Edinburgh: SHHD, 1986).

41. Turner, D. 'AIDS and Injecting', *Druglink* 1, (3) (1986), pp. 8–9.

42. Newcombe, R. 'High Time for Harm Reduction', *Druglink* 2, (1) (1987), pp. 10–11.

43. Department of Health civil servant, observation to author, 1986.

44. Department of Health civil servant, conference paper, June 1989.

45. DHSS, *AIDS and Drug Misuse Part 1* (London: HMSO, 1988).

46. Stimson, G., L. Alldritt, K. Dolan, M. Donoghoe and R. Lart, *Injecting*

Equipment Exchange Schemes—Final Report (Goldsmith's College, Monitoring Research Group, 1988).

47. Stimson, G. 'AIDS and HIV: The Challenge for British Drug Services', see note 2.
48. Department of Health civil servant, conference paper, June 1989.
49. Stimson, G. 'AIDS and HIV', see note 2.
50. See speech by Chris Butler in House of Commons Debate on Drug Abuse, 9 June 1989, cols 470–4.
51. For example, an evaluation of Liverpool's 'prescribing' clinic found its actual practice little different from 'non-prescribing' Clinics. See C. Fazey, *An Evaluation of Liverpool Drug Dependency Clinic. The First Two years 1985 to 1987* (Liverpool: Research Evaluation and Data Analysis, 1988).
52. McRae, J. *AIDS, Agencies and Drug Abuse* (Norwich: Social Sork Monographs, 1989).
53. Interview, drug consultant, Jan. 1989.
54. Pimlott, B. paper on Thatcher: 'The First Ten Years' conference, LSE, 1989.
55. Interview, drug consultant, Jan. 1989.
56. Berridge, V. 'Drugs and Social Policy', see note 8. Alcohol and drug policy has long been an interesting example of the relationship between medicine and the state. See R. M. MacLeod, 'The Edge of Hope: Social Policy and Chronic Alcoholism, 1870–1900', *Journal of the History of Medicine and Allied Sciences*, 22, (1967), pp. 215–45.
57. Rathbone, T. 'A Problem of Co-operation' *Druglink*, 3, (6) (1988), p. 15.
58. For example, an innovation scheme in Southwark has begun to link police referrals from the courts to helping services, in particular the Maudsley Hospital's Community Drug Team.
59. 'HIV Top Priority, says Official Report', *Druglink* 3, (3) (1988), p. 6.
60. Berridge, V. and G. Edwards, *Opium and the People*, see note 6.
61. MacLeod, R. M. 'The edge of hope', see note 58.
62. Lewis, J. *What Price Community Medicine? The Philosophy, Practice and Politics of Public Health since 1919* (Brighton: Wheatsheaf, 1986).
63. For similar comments from a sociological perspective, see G. Stimson and R. Lart, 'HIV, Drugs and Public Health in England: New Words, Old Tunes' (forthcoming 1990).
64. Rose, M. 'The Success of Social Reform? The Central Control Board (Liquor Traffic) 1915–21', in M. R. D. Foot (ed.), *War and Society* (London: Joseph Elek, 1973).
65. Berridge, V. 'Drugs and Social Policy', see note 8.
66. Rolleston Report, *Report of the Departmental Committee on Morphine and Heroin Addiction* (London: HMSO, 1926).
67. In Scotland, the role of the pharmacist in the prevention of HIV spread has been important. There are parallels with the nineteenth-century role of the pharmacist in dispensing opiates and providing medical care to poor clients. See V. Berridge and G. Edwards, *Opium and the People*, note 6.

11 The Economics of Drug Policy

Richard Stevenson

If psychoactive substances were bought and sold like most other goods, drug addiction would still remain a social and medical problem. Drugs would interest economists as examples of demerit goods which can injure the health of users and impose costs on others. Health economists would have a role in helping to evaluate alternative therapies but general economic considerations would not loom large in discussions of drug issues. Economic (and political) matters have become central to drug issues and to the appraisal of public policy, mainly because the use and exchange of psychoactive substances is illegal. This paper reviews drug policy from an economic point of view. Most of the analysis is uncontroversial but no attempt is made to disguise the opinion that a large part of 'the evil of drug abuse' is the predictable consequence of legal prohibition.

THE UNEASY CASE FOR PROHIBITION

Addictive drugs do not differ obviously from other demerit goods such as alcohol and tobacco. Public policy usually attempts to influence consumers of demerit goods in the direction of restraint by fiscal and legal measures which fall short of prohibition. Thus, alcohol and tobacco are taxed. Availability is restricted and advertising is regulated. Governments also guard against the possibility that users are insufficiently aware of health risks by providing information and by requiring producers to issue health warnings. It is difficult, as Littlechild and Wiseman (1986) have shown, to find a generally acceptable intellectual framework within which to justify even these relatively minor restrictions on consumer choice. By comparison with other demerit goods, the legal prohibition of psychoactive substances stands out as an extreme and unusual policy which requires special justification.

If a case can be made for treating drugs differently, presumably it must depend on the pharmacological properties of the substances. It is therefore surprising to find that medical authorities such as Szasz (1974) find no basis in science for distinctions between psychoactive drugs and other substances which can be addictive and dangerous, but are freely bought and sold. Rightly or wrongly, many people regard drugs with special abhorrence, but policy seems to depend on no such special arguments. Instead official publications (for example, Home Office, 1988) lay stress on health risks to users and on external costs which spill over from users to the rest of society. These arguments apply at least as well to all demerit goods.

The external cost of drug abuse has never been quantified and its mere existence does not, by itself, justify government interference in the consumption decisions of users. Most would agree that drug consumption should be reduced but government intervention is costly. Thus it is possible that the cost of intervention could exceed the value of its benefits. An evaluation of drug policy requires benefits to be weighed against the costs of enforcing policy.

Difficulties and confusions arise in describing the costs which drug users impose on others because some of these costs are the consequences of drug use, and others are more properly attributed to public policy. It is helpful, therefore, to take a step back from the current situation, and to distinguish those external costs which would exist if drugs were freely available. They would consist of:

(a) pecuniary and non-pecuniary costs to users' friends and family;
(b) cost to the National Health Service and the social security system of caring for drug users;
(c) the value of production lost due to the morbidity and premature mortality of users;
(d) costs arising from the 'contagious' nature of drug use (Culyer, 1973).

Drug related crime is not included as an external cost of drug use because, in a free market, the prices of most drugs would fall (Michaels, 1987) so that few, if any, users would need to commit crime to fund their habit. It should also be noted that not all users impose costs on others. Some manage their habit and live reasonably normal lives. The external costs are generated by problem users, who constitute an unknown proportion of the total user population.

It is alleged that the external costs of drug use are substantial but so are the costs of attempting to reduce drug use by legal prohibition. These costs include:

(a) the value of resources used to enforce the law in police forces, Customs and Excise, the legal system and the prison and probation services;

(b) the public sector costs of that part of drug-related crime which can be attributed to drug policy;

(c) government contributions to international agencies and foreign governments in support of drug control programmes;

(d) the cost to the private sector of drug-related crime. This includes some part of the value of goods stolen; public health risks from prostitution; part of some insurance premiums and part of the cost of alarm systems;

(e) the cost associated with morbidity and mortality resulting from the hazards of using drugs in an illegal market. These arise mainly from the difficulties which users face in controlling drug quality;

(f) costs to the friends and family of those users who are convicted of drug law offences and drug-related crime. Some costs are private; others spill over to the social security system.

Prohibition surrenders the drug trade to criminals. Illegal trading imposes real economic costs because criminal firms are thought to be less efficient than legal firms (Rottenburg, 1968). However the distributional effects of the illegal trade is of greater public concern. Prohibition effects a transfer of income to the criminal sector which is used to corrupt legal and political systems and to finance other sorts of crime.

Estimates do not exist for the size of most of these cost categories, but they are large, and have to be set against the benefits which might be expected from any reduction in drug use which policy might achieve. Leaving aside the problem of attaching monetary values to benefits, and costs which include anxiety and loss of life, the logic of the cost-benefit approach is that drug use reduction policies should be pursued to the point where their marginal benefit equals their marginal cost.

This point is explained in Figure 11.1 in which costs and benefits are measured on the vertical axis, and are related to the total consumption of drugs, measured on the horizontal axis. The schedule E represents the cost of reducing consumption by one unit at each consumption level. It is drawn sloping up to the left on the assumption that it will be fairly cheap to reduce consumption when drug use is highly prevalent, but as zero is approached, it will become increasingly expensive to apprehend additional users and dealers.

The marginal cost (MC) schedule shows the external cost

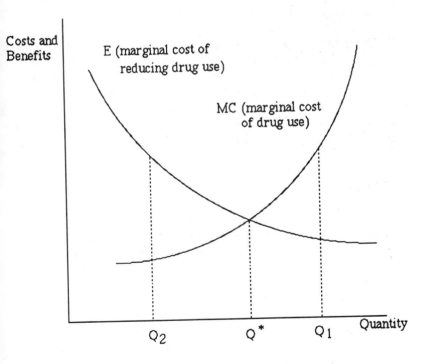

FIGURE 11.1 *Marginal cost of drug law enforcement (E) related to marginal cost imposed on society by drug users (MC) to show socially optimum level of drug consumtpion at p**

which one extra unit of drug use imposes on society. It is drawn sloping up to the right, to suggest that marginal costs might rise with consumption. The analysis is not affected if (as is quite possible), marginal costs are constant and MC is a horizontal line. Reading from right to left, the MC schedule can also be regarded as measuring the benefits (cost averted) by reducing drug use.

At any level of consumption greater than Q^*, such as Q_1, the cost of drug abuse (MC) is greater than the cost of law enforcement (E). It would therefore benefit society to reduce Q by enforcing the law more strictly. Conversely, at all consumption levels such as Q_2, which are less than Q^*, the cost of law enforcement exceeds the cost of drug abuse. It follows that a social saving could be made by relaxing law enforcement. At Q^*, the marginal cost of enforcement equals the marginal cost of drug abuse and Q^* can be regarded as a socially optimal level of drug consumption.

Provided that the E and MC schedules intersect on Figure 11.1, the analysis strongly suggests that, if prohibition can be interpreted as an attempt to reduce drug use to zero (or close to it), this policy is unlikely to be socially optimal. It is also possible that the current situation in the UK could be represented on Figure 11.1 by a point to the left of Q^*, so that the costs of policy exceed its benefits.

SPECIFIC POLICIES

Turning now to specifics, the government believes that drug problems should be tackled on a broad front by various means (Home Office, 1988). The individual strategies can be divided into two groups depending on whether they impact on the supply side or the demand side of the drug market.

One way of reducing drug use is to restrict supply at, or close to, the point of production. To this end, the UK government assists United Nations' agencies and foreign governments in coercive and persuasive initiatives directed at the producers and distributors of coca and opium. They involve police and military action against large growers and distributors, and crop eradication and crop substitution programmes.

Some local success has been reported for policies of this sort (Kaplan, 1983; Stewart-Clark, 1986) but they have made no global impact except perhaps in the short run. In countries where terrain is difficult and communcations poor, law enforcement is expensive. It is also likely to be ineffective where criminal firms are more powerful than elected governments.

Where coercion fails, governments could induce peasant growers to switch to other crops by offering a subsidy. The subsidy has to be close to the difference between the value of drugs and the value of the next best alternative crop. Since no substitute crop is nearly as valuable as drugs, the subsidy has to be large. Whynes (1989) has shown, for instance, that the cost of a subsidy for Latin American growers alone, would be about 300 times as much as the current annual budget of the International Narcotics Control Board, which supports programmes of this sort. Furthermore, subsidy schemes depend for their success on acreage control. Without acreage control, growers could take the subsidy and grow drugs on new land. As long as there is an abundant supply of land suitable for drug cultivation and it is difficult to police, acreage control is difficult to enforce.

A final reason for believing that crop control measures are unlikely to work is that, unless law enforcement is uniform internationally, action against producers in one country causes the trade to move across national borders. In the 1960s action against opium growers in Turkey was more than offset by increased output in Pakistan and Southeast Asia. Similarly, one might predict that if the current (1989) action in Colombia is successful, the principal beneficiaries will be competitors in other countries. As long as drugs remain so highly profitable, it seems unlikely that it will be possible to contain the drug trade at the production stage. Economists such as Holahan (1973) and Whynes (1989), who have conducted specific studies, conclude that present policies are both expensive and ineffective.

Domestic supply-side policies attempt to reduce the amount of drugs which reach the UK market by acting against dealers rather than users. Policies differ in their quantitative impact. Their cost effectiveness is also likely to be different according to whether legal interventions are made at the point of entry into the country or at the street level (Reuter and Kleiman, 1986; Wagstaff and Maynard, 1988). But, drug seizures, fines, imprisonment and the confiscation of assets all have the effect of increasing the cost of doing business in the illegal market.

The impact of supply-side policies is shown in Figure 11.2 which represents the market for a particular drug, of a specific purity, at a point in time. Street price is measured vertically and this is related to the quantity of the drug which is bought

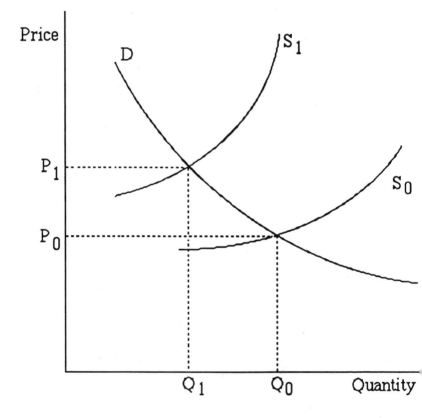

FIGURE 11.2   *The effect of intensified law enforcement against dealers on the market for a drug of specified purity*

and sold in the market. The demand schedule, D, shows the amount which users will buy at each price. D is drawn sloping downwards on the assumption that more will be purchased at lower prices. As price falls, some existing users will increase their consumption and some new users will be attracted into the market. It is important to note that this demand relationship holds only as long as all of the other factors which influence demand remain unchanged. If tastes or income or the price of substitute drugs change, the demand curve will shift.

The supply schedule, initially at S_0, indicates the amounts of the drug which firms will offer to the market at each price. S_0 slopes up to the right, to suggest that firms will have to be offered higher prices to induce them to increase the quantity supplied. The slope of S_0 depends on the ease with which extra drugs can be supplied. There is a plentiful supply of land: technology is simple; and, at current wage rates, criminal firms have little difficulty in recruiting labour. Thus S_0 is probably fairly flat.

The intersection between S_0 and D establishes an equilibrium price at P_0, and an equilibrium quantity at q_0, at which the willingness of users to buy is matched exactly by the willingness of firms to sell. If the price is set above or below P_0, there will be either excess supply or excess demand and competitive forces will tend to move the price back to P_0. Drugs will be traded at this price as long as demand and supply conditions remain unchanged.

Suppose now that the government intensifies action against dealers. Tighter law enforcement and increased penalties act like a probabilistically incurred tax on the trade. The cost of dealing increases and, in Figure 11.2, this is represented by a shift in the supply curve from S_0 to S_1. The effect is to increase price to p_1 and, at this higher price, users will purchase a reduced amount of the drug, q_1. In this way, supplyside policies achieve their objective. Drug use is reduced, but the amount of the reduction could be small or large: it depends on how sensitive demand is to changes in price.

If demand is responsive to price changes, demand is said to be price elastic, and a small increase in price will bring about a proportionately large reduction in the quantity demanded. In this case, supply-side policy will be effective. If, however, the

The Economics of Drug Policy

quantity demanded is proportionately unresponsive to price changes, demand is said to be price inelastic. When demand is price inelastic, supply-side policies will be less effective in reducing drug use. In the extreme case, where demand is perfectly price inelastic, supply-side policy will fail.

This extreme case of perfectly inelastic demand is shown in Figure 11.3, where the demand schedule is a vertical line so that the quantity demanded is independent of price. At the initial equilibrium p_0, the amount which users spend on drugs is represented by the area $p_0 q_0$. If law enforcement is now intensified, the supply curve shifts from S_0 to S_1, but there is

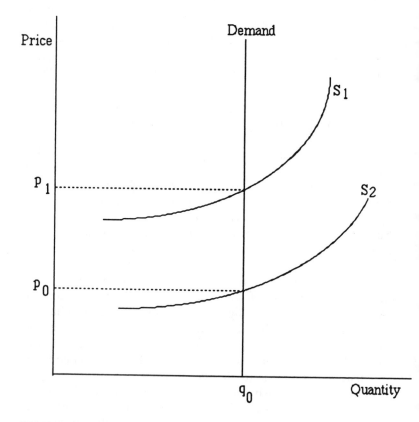

FIGURE 11.3 *The effect of intensified law enforcement against dealers on the market for a drug, when demand is perfectly price inelastic*

no reduction in the quantity demanded. The only effect of the policy is to increase the price so that, at the new equilibrium p_1, users will need to spend an amount shown in the area p_1q_1 to maintain their habits.

Some users will finance the increased cost of drugs out of legal income, but they will have less income left over for food, shelter and family support. Other users will be forced to seek additional income and, to the extent that they find it in theft and prostitution, the cost of policy will spill over to non-users. In this way, if demand is perfectly (or only fairly) inelastic, supply-side policy does not merely fail to reduce drug use, it also operates against the public interest.

In principle, the elasticity of demand for drugs can be measured and studies do exist (for example, Silverman and Spruill, 1977), but data on even the most basic dimensions of the illegal market are scarce and unreliable. This lack of hard data has left economists free to speculate in a literature which is surveyed by Wagstaff and Maynard (1988). Intuition suggests that the demand for an addictive substance is bound to be inelastic, or what other meaning can be attached to the notion of 'drug dependence'? Nevertheless, it is certain that demand is not perfectly inelastic (as in Figure 11.3) and possible that demand could be price elastic for some users, or for all users, at some prices.

Blair and Vogel (1973) suggest that demand might be inelastic for habitual users but elastic for casual users. This hypothesis is depicted in Figure 11.4, where supply-side policy which shifts S_0 to S_1 anywhere along the flat portion of the demand curve will reduce drug use by deterring casual users. When some price such as $\bar{p}$ is reached, only habitual users are left in the market, and further supply restrictions will only increase price (as in Figure 11.3).

Furthermore, White and Luksetich (1983) must be correct in supposing that at some very high price (but no one knows how high), demand will become elastic even for addicts. If law enforcement is pursued vigorously enough, a price must be reached at which addicts can no longer steal enough to maintain their habit, or they simply decide that the cost of continuing to use drugs exceeds the cost of giving up.

For these reasons it is not possible to say that supply-side policy will always perform badly. It is also likely that the

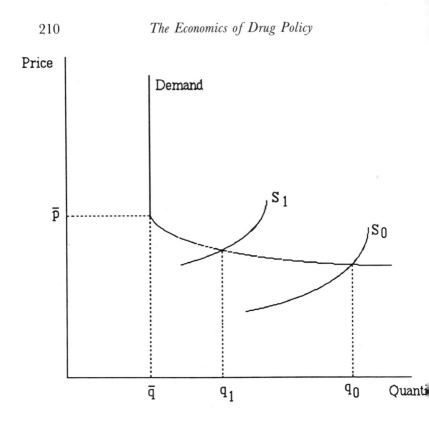

FIGURE 11.4 *Supply-side policy effective until price $\bar{p}$ is reached when casual users have been deterred and only addicts remain in the market*

demand for any single drug, such as heroin, is somewhat price elastic because some users will respond to a price increase by switching to another drug. This possibility is, however, much reduced when all psychoactive substances are considered as a group. There are far fewer substitutes for all psychoactive substances than for any individual drug, so the demand for all drugs is likely to be highly price inelastic. Unless law enforcement can be uniformly strict over all psychoactive substances (and there are many of them), supply-side strategies may reduce the consumption of a single drug, or several, but they will not reduce total drug use.

Unlike coercive supply-side policies examined above, controlled availability of drugs to registered users has much to recommend it. It is a form of price discrimination which makes use of the alleged difference between habitual and casual users in the elasticity of their demand schedules (Moore, 1972). Addicts, who generate most of the external cost of drug abuse, receive drugs free of charge, but the high price in the illegal market remains as a deterrent to new or casual users. In this way addicts come under medical supervision and are relieved of the need to commit crime to buy drugs.

This thinking was at the heart of the 'British System' to which Bing Spear contributed so much and which has been praised as a humane and cost-effective approach to drug abuse (Trebach, 1982). To be successful controlled availability schemes must attract a high proportion of the problem users by offering drugs which users want at a 'price' which they are willing to pay. Prescriptions are free, but the terms and conditions on which they are offered act as a price which deters some users. If the conditions are strict, more users will prefer to remain outside the system.

Judged by the proportion of users who receive prescription drugs, the British System as it now operates cannot be regarded as successful. Since the 1970s clinics have become reluctant to prescribe heroin and injectibles. Instead, most registered users receive the much less attractive oral methadone. In this and other ways, the system imposes constraints on users which makes it acceptable to no more than one fifth (and possibly only one tenth) of the drug using population.

The true heirs to the British System, as it was during most of Bing Spear's career, are those relatively few clinicians who make it their business to provide a service which users will accept. As an example, considerable success has been claimed for a policy in the Mersey Region which allows the prescription of injectible heroin in well-defined circumstances (Fazey, 1987). Users have been maintained in reasonable health and have avoided criminal acts and there was no evidence that prescribed drugs reached the illegal market.

Many advantages can be claimed for controlled availability schemes but, even if they were administered more liberally than at present, some drug problems would remain untouched. Criminals would still control the illegal market and controlled availability does nothing to deter new users. The removal of substantial numbers of habitual users from the illegal market may actually encourage new users by tending to reduce street prices. Nevertheless, controlled availability with terms and conditions reduced to the very minimum which the medical profession can tolerate, offers the most constructive single supply-side approach available to the government in the present state of the law.

Demand-side policies offer the best chance of reducing drug use without severe social consequences. The aim is to reduce drug use by policies which have the effect in Figure 11.5, of shifting the demand for drugs down to the left. In Figure 11.5,

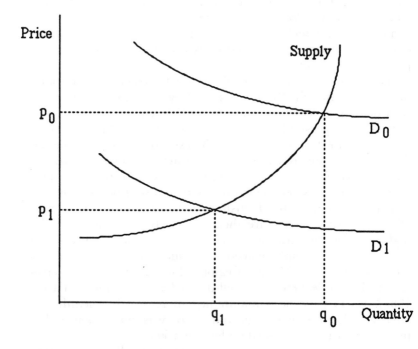

FIGURE 11.5   *The effect on the market for a drug of a policy which reduces demand from D_0 to D_1.*

a reduction in demand from D_0 to D_1 reduces both price and quantity from p_0 and q_0, to p_1 and q_1. The amounts by which price and quantity fall depend on the slope (elasticity) of the supply curve but, as was explained, the supply curve is likely to be quite flat (elastic), since extra supplies can be obtained at no great extra cost. If this is the case, a reduction in demand will reduce the quantity consumed by a greater proportion than the decrease in price.

The great advantage of demand-side over supply-side policies is that they reduce drug use without forcing up the price of a drug habit. Thus demand-side policy avoids spill-over effects from drug-related crime. This desirable objective can be approached by enforcing the law against users (rather than dealers) and through education programmes.

Law enforcement against users increases the cost of a drug habit. The cost of a habit is made up of the street price of drugs plus transaction costs. Transaction costs include the cost in time (and perhaps danger) of seeking out suppliers, and the risk of being caught in possession. Tighter enforcement and stiffer penalties increase these costs and reduce demand. Some have argued in favour of relaxing the law as it applies to users, but not to dealers. This is in accord with the popular notion that dealers are wicked, whereas users are merely weak. Any such relaxation of the law in the direction of the decriminalisation of users would reduce the cost of drug use. It would tend to shift the demand schedule in Figure 11.5 up to the right, and drug use as well as price would tend to increase. From the prohibitionist point of view, strenuous legal action against users probably offers the best chance of achieving government objectives at the least cost.

The other way of reducing demand is through education programmes which deter new users, and dissuade or frighten existing users. These programmes are in their infancy and have yet to be evaluated for effectiveness and cost-effectiveness. Nevertheless, demand reduction by education must be the best hope for the future although evidence from the campaign against smoking suggests that rapid results cannot be expected.

The suggestion that education programmes may be slow to produce results raises an issue which has not featured in the analysis so far, and is missing from most discussions of drug policy. Policies take effect over time and whether the benefits which are claimed for them accrue over six months, or 60 years, is a matter of the greatest importance. Timing is particularly important in drug policy since concern is continually expressed for children and for unborn generations.

Since it is believed that drug problems are urgent and tend to cumulate, policies which yield early benefits might be preferred to others which act more slowly. Thus it is possible that some alternatives to current policy (such as legislation), which most regard as worse than second best, could be superior to more generally acceptable policies which are slow to take effect.

CONCLUSIONS

It has been suggested that the case for prohibition is uneasy and that when the costs of drug law enforcement are taken into account, prohibition is almost certainly not an optimal policy. When specific policies are considered, those which act on the demand side of the market are preferable to others which attempt to suppress supply. Demand-side policies which involve coercion are likely to remain expensive but may be effective. Education programmes may, in principle, be superior but their effectiveness is uncertain.

It is difficult to detect merit in most supply-side measures. In producer countries local success is possible but the global impact of policies which try to reduce supply is likely to remain minimal at current levels of expenditure on law enforcement and crop substitution programmes. Supply-side policies in consumer countries are also likely to be ineffective and expensive (in social as well as economic terms) if, as seems likely, demand is price inelastic over a wide range of prices.

Controlled availability is the most attractive supply-side policy but its usefulness depends on the tightness of the controls. Substantial benefits might be expected from a more 'user friendly' system which would attract a high proportion of habitual users. At present the types of drugs on offer, and the conditions on which they are made available, depend to a degree which seems unreasonable on the discretion of individual clinicians. The decision whether to prescribe or not to prescribe psychoactive substances has a bearing on major social issues which reach far beyond the intimacy of the patient–doctor relationship. It might be fruitful therefore to enquire whether prescribing policy is too important to be left entirely to the medical profession.

Turning finally to opinion, but opinion based on the long history of government intervention in markets, it is doubtful whether a large and profitable market can be suppressed at any reasonable cost. All economics textbooks contain examples of ways in which government policy has produced results which were neither expected nor desired and may harm those whom the policies were designed to protect. Wartime rationing produced 'black markets'. Fair rent laws are subverted by side payments such as 'key money' and may actually increase the general level of rents by reducing the supply of accommodation. Agricultural subsidies can produce 'wine lakes' and 'butter mountains' and are notoriously susceptible to fraud. Countless other examples could be cited to demonstrate the endless ingenuity with which economic agents will flaunt the law in the pursuit of profit. Free markets may not be perfect but it does not follow that government can necessarily perform better. Governments can and do often make matters worse and there is reason to think that this may be the effect of current drug policies.

REFERENCES

Blair, R. D. and R. J. Vogel (1973) 'Heroin Addiction and Urban Crime', *Public Finance Quarterly*, 1(4), pp. 457–67.

Culyer, A. J. (1973) 'Should Social Policy Concern Itself with Drug Abuse?' *Public Finance Quarterly*, 1(4), pp. 449–56.

Fazey, C. S. J. (1987) 'The Evaluation of Liverpool Drug Dependency Clinic', *a Report to Mersey Regional Health Authority*.

Holahan, J. (1973) 'The Economics of Control of the Illegal Supply of Heroin', *Public Finance Quarterly*, 1(4), pp. 467–77.

Home Office (1988) *Tackling Drug Misuse: A Summary of the Government's Strategy* (3e) (London: HMSO).

Kaplan, J. (1983) *The Hardest Drug: Heroin and Public Policy* (Chicago University Press).

Littlechild, S. C. and J. Wiseman 'The Political Economy of Restriction of Choice', *Public Choice*, 51, pp. 161–72.

Michaels, R. J. (1987) 'The Market for Heroin before and after Legislation', in R, Hamowy (ed.), *Dealing with Drugs* (Lexington: D. C. Heath), pp. 289–326.

Moore, M. H. (1972) 'Policies to Achieve Discrimination on the Effective Price of Heroin', *American Economic Review*, 63(2), pp. 270–77.

Reuter, P. A. and M. A. R. Kleiman (1986) 'Risks and Prices: An Economic Analysis of Drug Enforcement', in M. Tonry and N. Morris (ed.), *Crime and Justice: An Annual Review of Research* no. 7.

Rottenburg, S. (1968) 'The Clandestine Distribution of Heroin, its Discovery and Suppression', *Journal of Political Economy*, 76(1), pp. 78–90.

Silverman, L. P. and N. L. Spruill (1977) 'Urban Crime and the Price of Heroin', *Journal of Urban Economics*, 4, pp. 80–103.

Stewart-Clark, J. (1986) (Rapporteur) *Report of the Committee of Inquiry into the Drugs Problem in the Member States of the Community*, European Parliament: Document A 2–114/86.

Szasz, T. S. (1974) *Ceremonial Chemistry: The Ritual Persecution of Drugs, Addicts and Pushers* (New York: Doubleday).

Trebach, A. (1982) *The Heroin Solution* (New Haven: Yale University Press).

Wagstaff, A. and A. Maynard (1988) *Economic Aspects of the Illicit Drug Market and Drug Enforcement Policies in the United Kingdom*, Home Office Research Study 95 (London: HMSO).

White, M. D. and W. A. Luksetich (1983) 'Heroin: Price Elasticity and Enforcement Strategies', *Economic Inquiry*, 21, pp. 557–64.

Whynes, D. K. (1989) 'Illicit Drug Production and Supply Side Policy in Asia and South America', in *An Examination of the Economic, Legal, Social, Medical and Ethical Factors of Drug Policy in the UK and The Netherlands*, pp. 24–35, Report to Commission of the European Communities (London: Drug Policy Advisory Group).

12 Drug Issues in Health Education: Demand Reduction or Public Panacea?

Jane Falk-Whynes

When health education developed from the basic medical model of intervention through inoculation and screening for disease, it brought with it a moral timbre which echoed with righteous determination to save our young people from, amongst other things, the dangers of drugs. Information was seen as the tool for this salvation. The model of health education that was originally used grew out the remarkable improvements in national health brought about by the public health movement of the 1930s. Using medical methods the reduction of the incidence of formally endemic diseases such as tuberculosis was drastically reduced so it was not surprising that such a tried and tested approach was also applied to other issues. However, as the century wore on medicine did not manage to provide all the solutions to health problems, as in the case of heart disease or cancer. The knife and the needle could not cure all, so other approaches were explored. The notion developed in preventative medicine that, instead of just trying to cure illness, perhaps people could be cured of doing things that were bad for them, and illness would thereby be replaced by health. This view, which relied on intervention through inoculation with knowledge, was the basis of early health education and, within this framework of health education, work on specific issues such as drugs was also developed.

Initially, drug-focused health education was based on the notion that if you tell young people how harmful drugs are then they will stop taking them, or better still, they will not even start. Unfortunately, this simplistic model, which still has not been entirely given up today in spite of its limitations, rests on erroneous presuppositions:

(a) that the drug takers *do not know* of the harmful effects of their behaviour;
(b) if they did know, they would not take the drugs;
(c) thus the receipt of information will change behaviour.

A simple illustration shows how misguided these ideas are. If knowledge was the deciding factor in drug use then professionals who know first hand the harmful consequences of, for example, the use of tobacco, would not by the logic given above find any smokers in their ranks. This is of course not the case. Some doctors and teachers are very heavy smokers (Lowry, 1989), yet people in these groups above all others surely know that smoking is a risky behaviour in terms of health? Perhaps knowledge, therefore, is not enough?

In the 1960s this conclusion was shared by such drug educators as the Central Council for Health Education, the forerunner to the Health Education Council and the Health Education Authority. In their publicity campaigns this group used slogans such as:

'Drugs? You don't need them!'
'. . . . The person who takes drugs unnecessarily or for kicks is often looked upon with suspicion by society because *normal people do not need drugs.*'
(Cited in Dorn and South, 1985, p. 209).

These and similar messages, embued with a persuasive air, offer a quite different perception of the drug taker. In campaigns like this the young person at risk was not perceived as ignorant or innocent, but rather as misguided, or even deliberately deviant.

This is an important difference and has to be set into perspective. In the 1960s and in the 1970s there was an atmosphere in the culture of young people that contained many positive images of drugs, hence a counter attack was deemed to be necessary; indeed it was seen as vital if the balance of view points was to be redressed. Therefore those concerned with drug issues in health education offered alternative images of drugs and their use which slowly became more and more drastic.

The above example of an anti-drugs slogan is mild compared

to some developed later which used fear tactics to get attention. Right up to recent years messages associated with drugs have often stressed the more grim effects of drug use. Degradation and self-torture have been included in presentations designed to deter the young. A case in point is the 'Gale is Dead' *Man Alive* film of the 1970s (first shown on BBC 2, 6 May 1970) made by the BBC and which was made into a film edition that was widely shown in schools. In this film the audience is offered the story of a young girl who comes from a background of children's home and remand school. As she grows up she becomes drawn into the world of drugs in spite of attempts by the authorities and caring agencies to help her. The film ends with a scene in the hospital showing Gale to be very seriously ill. As the film ends you are told that Gale dies shortly afterwards.

The film was made for many reasons. It certainly illustrated the point that drugs kill in horrible ways and perhaps it was hoped that young people would identify with the young person in the story and thus learn from the example that this is what happens to those who take drugs. It is a sordid tale, full of graphic descriptions of what happens to someone who sinks into the clutches of drug dependency yet, perhaps it and others like it, could also be likened to the Victorian practice of child discipline based on the myth of the 'bogey man'. Both images work just as long as the child believes in them. Unfortunately their credibility is limited. In the case of the 'Victorian' child the bogey man seldom appears. It is the same for the modern drug taker. The above mentioned film, similarly styled public service announcements and equally unpleasant examples given by local policemen in schools, all warn of danger but their impact is lost if a good friend says (not unjustifiably in the short term): 'I've tried it and I'm OK, there's nothing to be scared of, it's fun'.

Drug addicts frequently report that 'a friend' or 'someone I knew' was responsible for introducing them to drugs. In the face of this, media messages can only have limited credibility.

It can be argued that such fear tactics only inspire the rebellious to fortitude and offer them a means by which they can show positive contempt for adult concerns and warnings. As any parent knows it simply is not true that grown-ups always know best (or we would not teach our children to be wary of strangers). Parents also know that, with all the best will in the world, apparently heeded warnings and reasoning, couched in terms of an authoritarian 'Because I say so', are still easily forgotten in the heat of the moment.

Sadly this homespun wisdom is easily put aside, especially in recent years. It seems that when most adults think of drug issues in health education it is usually the more graphic, authoritarian, shocking, drug specific campaigns that they bring to mind such as the 'Heroin Screws You Up' poster, and the television campaign put out by the government in 1985, focusing on how boys lose control and girls lose their looks. This stereotype-confirming marketing exercise was carried out much to the dismay of and against the advice of health educators generally (Dorn, 1986: Power, 1989) since it relies on the 'bogey man' principle. According to the evaluators of the programme (Research Bureau Ltd 1986) there is no doubt that such campaigns do have an impact, especially as a motivator for parents and professionals who work with young people, but to my mind their contribution to effective drug education for young people is dubious. The stereotype images may have reinforced the convictions of those not involved with drugs but hold no credibility with those involved in the real world of the drug users. Because of this, as a demand reduction exercise it was not generally deemed to be a success (Hansen, 1985; Power, 1989).

Such fear tactics may give the impression that something is being done about the apparently huge problem of heroin use and it certainly puts the subject on the public opinion agenda. However, these sensational scare tactics may in fact stimulate an ethos of negative success amongst the young and thus inspire towards, rather than deter them from, risky behaviour. It is also possible, in the same vein, that this style of campaign may act as an advertisement or new trend-setter to behaviour that may well have not even occurred to people if it had not been shown on television.

Drug-specific campaigns focus attention on a particular substance in a way that emulates the media 'hype' of the fashion world and for this reason may attract young people to experiment. For this reason, the blanket coverage and drama-tic flavour of publicity campaigns are not popular with educationalists, health promotion officers and psychologists. They and others have all, at different times, shown a sceptical distrust of the heavy-handed approach to drug education, so they offer alternative strategies. As part of these it is considered important to understand the processes of learning and motivation, needs and influences that affect drug use and to develop new styles of dealing with drug issues, based on theories of health education which take extra factors into account. Education programmes may be far less sensational, but research so far argues that they are more effective and with a far greater deterrent impact especially when they focus not so much on the harmful effects of drug use but on the ability to say 'no' to involvement altogether.

> Drug Education as such is now widely discredited and teaching about drugs is increasingly seen as an integral part of health education, social education, political education and careers education which provide a teaching framework that differs from drug focused education.
>
> (ISDD, 1984, p. 1)

According to Tones (1987b) health can be promoted via one or more of four stereotypic forms: the medical model; voluntarism and the educational model; the radical model; the self-empowerment model. Very simply put the medical model is information-based, as described at the start of the chapter, whilst the voluntarism and educational model uses the development of decision-making skills. The radical model looks to social policy to change the environment of drug access and use, and the self-empowerment model looks at how individuals can be encouraged to build a positive self-concept that rules out the causes of self-abuse.

In my view no one method is effective in itself. It is the combined use of all the models that is required for success, but the strengths and weaknesses of each model needs to be understood so that the best attributes can be properly harnessed.

THE MEDICAL MODEL, VOLUNTARISM AND THE EDUCATIONAL MODEL

The characteristics of the medical model are that it views the body as a machine that can be repaired. With this emphasis it tends to neglect the relationship of the machine to the environment, concentrating instead on the inner workings. Prevention by intervention is its main role in the quest to avoid the onset of disease. In terms of health education generally it sees the school as part of the medical arena, as a place where knowledge is given. Indeed historically the school has always been a place where physicians have been active, through the definition of the balanced content of school meals, through health inspections, actual injections given and such activities as screening for headlice. However, in terms of education about health matters the medical approach has not been so welcome.

> . . . somewhat to the chagrin of those who view the school as a significant arm of preventative medicine, many teachers and educationalists have reservations and consider that the school is above all an educational establishment!
>
> (Tones, 1987b, p. 8)

In health education it is often said that the medium is the message. The delivery, and the style of delivery, affects the value of knowledge as a potent force on the audience, as every advertiser knows. Certain methods from the world of advertising have been used in some campaigns at the more acceptable end of the drug market. 'Smokebusters', a campaign started by the Health Education Authority in 1986, drew its images from a popular film, *Ghostbusters*, to persuade young children not to take up smoking and to argue against smokers. Behind the publicity, which was offered mainly through posters and which was delivered by footballers and other sports stars, was a youth club and school-based programme of activities. In its use of advertising this approach offered positive lifestyle messages delivered by credible people and it was backed up in extra activities which focused on the skills and knowledge required to refuse and avoid involvement in smoking. The programme also drew parents into the work.

As an educational strategy it was cognisant of the need to involve the participants. It was carefully targeted on younger children with a view to delaying the onset of smoking which, according to Perry (1986), is a factor which reduced prevalence in later years. This and other projects using a similar mixture of techniques have slowly made an impact on the social perception of smoking and its prevalence amongst parts of the community (Gillies and Wilcox, 1984). These types of strategy have come to be regarded as good practice in health education method and similar techniques have therefore been explored for other drug campaigns.

The use of cult figures and heroes in projects which are specifically directed towards the reduction of drug use was developed by the Institute for the Study of Drug Dependency (ISDD) and the national organisation TACADE who at the behest of the Department of Education and Science (DES) produced a video in 1986 called 'Double Take'. At the expense of the DES this video was offered *free* to every secondary school and college in England and Wales. Its production and distribution represents a considerable investment following in the wake of the 'Heroin Screws You Up' campaign of the previous year but it can be interpreted as a government response to the criticisms of the blanket approach since in this project the audience was so carefully targeted.

Of the two films on the video the first was by far the most popular. This was called 'A Little Bit of Give and Take', and it starred the characters from the Independent Television series 'Minder', George Cole and Denis Waterman. In the first film the story is told of a teenager who comes to London and, short of proper accommodation, ends up staying with the character played by Denis Waterman. It features familiar scenes such as a party, and conversations held sitting around at home. Problems such as relating to others and petty crime are explored along with messages against drugs, some of which are given by the television 'stars'. Some of the important points about heroin shown are that the 'junkie' is a very ordinary young person, and that his habit in the end causes him to steal from his friends and family. The film also illustrates that the invitation to try drugs can be given by friends.

Some have criticised the film's mixed messages concerning alcohol, and there is no doubt that its messages about drugs could have been made clearer. Even as it stands, however, it is entertaining and as professional as any television programme should be, which is an important part of its success since young audiences have come to expect a high standard of educational materials on video.

The second part of the video is bland by comparison with the messages skilfully hidden in the storyline of the entertainment in the first part of the package. To some extent this is just caused by an unfortunate juxtaposition because the second part of the video is of high quality although the format is quite different. It is a studio production of a youth project about drugs reverting to a more didactic style in spite of its pause for discussion. In my view the greatest educational virtue of such a production made by young people lies in the experience gained by the individuals who made it — not so much in the performance, but that is another issue — drug education through involvement in drama and role play, another excellent participative medium for learning about difficult issues.

In my experience teachers like the 'Minder Drug Video' in spite of its faults, because it is easy to use, it keeps the attention of the audience (which is always valuable in school) and because usually the class to whom it is shown do seem to become involved in the story and are thus usually able to debate about the subject matter. However, the real value of the product lies with its special message-givers, and therefore the educational value of this investment is still only as good as the use that is made of it. On its own it is still just an injection of information, albeit a much less painless inoculation. It is the quality of the teaching that surrounds it which moves its use in to the model of health promotion labelled Voluntarism or Educational, and it is the quality of the teaching that surrounds its use which determines whether or not it is an effective contribution to education about drugs and drug use.

Too often health education in schools falls down because the expert or the video is wheeled in and then wheeled out again whilst, all the time, the audience is passive. It may take more work, and it is more difficult to organise and to timetable active learning, but the consensus view is that for effective health education the audience needs to participate, preferably through the use of small group work and student centred activities. However, even in the case of the so called 'active' methods, there are many ways of approaching the task of reducing the likelihood of young people being involved with drugs and there are some who see this style of teaching as the thin edge of a difficult, or even worse, a dangerous wedge of activities.

The potential for control of health problems is deemed to exist in schooling, just as it is thought to be possible to inoculate good social values. Yet, 'schooling' is a world apart from 'education'. Some 'active' approaches apparently deal with choice but covertly they are often highly directive. A move may be made away from direct didactic methods but if these are being replaced by what some would suggest are social conditioning techniques, then some questions may have to be asked as to whether the ends do justify the means. The educational model is widely used and although it may be effective with some groups of pupils I would suggest that, where it is also overtly directive, it may also be a red rag to the rebellious making them even more determined to be different.

Whatever criticisms there may be of the methods of 'telling', it remains true that accurate knowledge and decision-making skills are important. Other examples of projects which produced materials specified for classroom use are the Schools Council (1976) *Health Education 11–18;* TACADE (1964) *Free to Choose;* Health Education Council/Heinemann Educational Books (1983); *My Body Project*, National Extension College; (1988) *Health Matters*. They are sold directly as printed materials to schools or colleges and they are sold to resource centres and health education units. Any teacher who can command the required resources can buy them or they can be borrowed from the health education units and teachers' centres. It is reasonably true to say that if a teacher decides to set up a classroom programme about drug use there is now a wealth of informative resources to choose from. Some are situation specific (for example, *Facts and Feelings about Drugs but Decisions about Situations*, ISDD, 1982), whilst other are more general including curriculum issues as well as classroom materials (for example, *Drugwise*, Health Education Council, 1986).

Materials quickly become dated so new programmes are being developed continually by such agents as the Health Education Authority, ISDD and TACADE. Different packs may be influenced by the different models of health promotion, but the greatest differences between them all lie in their attitudes towards delivery. In those which accord with the voluntarism and educational model the emphasis is on what can be put into the child's mind and since it is possible to condition the young — the Hitler youth were a prime example of this — it can be argued (see Reif and Massey, 1986) that this approach is in some measure effective in limiting drug use.

Criticism of this model is based on difficulties surrounding the notion of choice itself. Training for the anti-drug choice is a special form of social conditioning. If a child is asked to practice choosing in certain circumstances, after having been given information that might just be biased towards a desired outcome, then this education has to my mind a difficult ethical content, since it disposes of true freedom of choice. The required responses may be conditioned by utilitarian and paternalistic concern but individual or student-centred responsibility for learning has been removed. Unfortunately children able to make 'free' choices also might act in a way which was destructive to society. In the case of drug-related behaviour the state makes a firm statement about which 'good' choices are by law permitted and which are restricted. Because of this, the guided decision-making approach could be viewed as simply an attempt to make the pill of obedience easier to swallow. All this leaves aside understanding of the restrictions on choice experienced by a person who is addicted to a drug or by a person who suffers social, environmental or economic difficulties.

Thus in my view Drug Education based on the notion of training in decision-making skills is very limited in the long run. On top of all the external constraints it does not take into account the psychological factors that limit free choice such as low self-esteem or lack of self-confidence. It can be suggested that the prerequisite for assertive action is that the individual feels that they are worthwhile enough to have the right to exercise assertive choice. Consideration of these ideas leads to a completely different area of educational exploration fraught with problems and given these difficulties it is understandable that reversion to coercion is considered to be a viable alternative.

Within this frame of reference, which relies very heavily on the possibility that positive action may result from the exploration of information, the notion is that engaged and therefore heightened awareness will assist resistance to drugs.

This is well illustrated by another project that combined the use of personalities from a popular television series with an exploration of decision-making skills to meet the difficulty of resisting peer pressure. A television programme called 'Its not just Zammo' was put out by the BBC in 1986 (BBC 1, 1 April), based on the series 'Grange Hill' (a school-based soap opera). The series on which the programme was based received national coverage and it was much talked about by children in school even if they dislike it. In the programme about drug use the misfortunes of a character known as Zammo were discussed and the 'Just Say No' work done in the programme was used as a basis for a best-selling record made by the actors from the series. Later a book on the whole 'Drugwatch' campaign was also published (Caplin *et al.* 1986).

The reinforcement of the 'No' choice and the rehersal of a 'No Thanks' response in the face of peer pressure was an important feature of this project. The company of friends is recognised as an arena where choices are particularly hard to make and much work has been done to help young people confront the problems involved. It does not always involve the promotion of 'no' as the good choice. Some of the responses required to deflect peer pressure are directly influenced by noitions that are better described under the model of health promotion labelled self-empowerment but in both contexts practice of decision-making skills are required.

Although the 'Just Say No' campaign was eminently preferable to the spotty adverts which health educators abhorred, to my mind both these approaches fell down for another reason, namely, they were drug specific. They both focused on one drug, heroin, and with this narrow view they, like many other projects, neglected the general context of drug use in our society. Drug use and abuse are actually widespread and, in some cases, are not just socially acceptable, but considered to be a *vital* part of social life or a standard response to stress or illness. These responses are learned in the home. Given that parents are considered to be the prime health educators and that in some cases children learn substance abuse at home by understanding the accepted misuse of alcohol (Balding, 1989), then a wider brief for éducation about drugs needs to be considered and the specific drug-centred approach replaced with more general tactics.

For all the good results that may have been produced from the support offered to those who wished to say 'no', both to drugs and to their peers in the programmes described above, it could be argued that such campaigns also inadvertantly advertise extra ways of achieving negative success to those who crave it. This must be the perennial dilemma of education; in some cases ignorance is useful and knowledge is dangerous. I have a suspicion that this is particularly true of education about drugs. To quote a young girl interviewed on BBC television's 'Panorama' programme about crack cocaine, broadcast in October 1989:

> I think that you need publicity and you need information, but if someone keeps coming up to me every week, every hour talking about Crack, after a while I'm going to think, this must be good, perhaps I'll try it out.

'No' is not the preferred choice of the curious and carefree who believe that they are immortal and who achieve their self-esteem from risky behaviour. Thus this and other 'Say No' campaigns, for all their popular acclaim, are undermined by the fundamentally contrary nature of the young. To say 'No' is so negative, like going on a diet, and like going on a diet it is prone to failure. More emphasis is needed on exciting alternatives to substance abuse that give similar immediate pleasurable gratification and to which a satisfying 'yes' response can be given.

In all the debates as to the best way to help young people to 'say no' or to develop personal skills, the emphasis is on the responsibility of the individual to avoid drug abuse, which on top of all other shortcomings, has to be denigrated for its victim blaming. In this perspective the drug taker is viewed as someone who failed to say 'no' or who kept up with a bad lot of friends. It does not offer or even show any understanding of the problems behind these issues. The programmes which focus on individual responsibility may offer a cosy panacea to those who are worried about the 'problems of drug abuse' and who wish to feel that they are doing something useful, but they do not really attack the root causes of the problems. Unfortunately, because victims need saviours it can also mean that certain professional groups, such as teachers and parents, can be praised or blamed for their work. These two groups are the foundations of social conditioning so there will always be some who do absolve the child victims and who say that it is the parents' and the schools' job to ensure that students learn how to say 'No'. However, there has to be a case also for looking beyond the home or school that spawned the drug taker to some wider issues, such as to the appeal and excitement of the drug taker's life (including the economic rewards that can be gained by the adventurous who enjoy the criminal world) as compared to the law-abiding humdrum of poverty or unemployment.

This is of course very complicated. Choices are influenced by a subtle combination of personal beliefs, physical needs, cultural expectations and outside influences such as cost, availability and knowledge of supply and use (Tones, 1987a). Such are the concerns of both the radical and the self-empowered models of health promotion.

THE RADICAL AND THE SELF-EMPOWERMENT MODEL

The radical model of health promotion looks to stem the flow of problems 'upstream'. McKinlay (1979) argues for the refocusing of energy upstream to attend to the general causes and not just the results of ill health. This refocusing moves away from the traditional victim blaming stance that many take when confronted with individuals suffering from health problems and looks to change the environmental origins.

The process of examining general causes is often neglected in the consideration of drug abuse problems. Invariably these are perceived as the fault of the junkie or the delinquent child. In the radical model, however, action for health promotion is sought from those involved in the creation of national policy to facilitate changes in individual behaviour. Thus the 'blame' is shifted away from the individual to a sense of collective responsibility.

In the case of drugs and their use or abuse, national measures of control may be sought by restrictions on the legality of supply and in the possible fiscal policies that are required to support this. Control is also exerted by the extension of police involvement and in the development of criminal law. Policies concerning the provision of treatment and rehabilitation of offenders add to a generic picture as do policies concerning publicity, advertising and the media. Behind the policies that deal with drug abuse directly are measures which affect the background of people's lives. Political action to combat poverty, unemployment and environmental conditions all contribute to the tapestry of drug use and control. Since political or legal changes can have far-reaching effects, knowledge of such policies explored in political education, forever an emotive subject in schools, could be seen as part of education about drugs, as could general education for citizenship.

On this subject, recent developments towards a National Curriculum do in themselves represent a national intervention which will have far-reaching implications for the provision of education about drugs in school. The National Curriculum as part of the 1989 Education Reform Act influences changes in many things including what is said about drugs, when in the Health Career (Williams, 1985) of a child it is offered, by whom it is to be taught and to some extent even how. As the new Education Reform Act comes into force all these things will be, in some measure, prescibed by the law.

Unfortunately, in the original draft documents for the National Curriculum (DES 1988b), the main arena suggested for health education (and thereby education about drugs) was science education and, in particular, biology. The whole notion of health education was subjected to the exam-driven concerns of higher achievement. The subject, health education, which had until then been developing, suddenly all but evaporated from the required curriculum. Yet all this flies in the face of evidence such as that produced by Eiser *et al.* (1988) and Tones (1986b, 1986c) who argue not just that health education is an important subject in its own right but that health education is far more effective when it is presented and experienced from within the non-examination approach of the pastoral curriculum and delivered mainly within the context of personal and social education in schools.

This view was certainly supported in the recommendations made to the Minister for Education in the report presented by the working party set up in 1989 to consider personal and social education (PSE) matters (National Curriculum Council, 1989). Building upon the earlier report on science education (National Curriculum Council, 1988) the recommendations from this PSE group, and from Her Majesty's Inspectors of schools (DES, 1986 and 1988a), see that effective health education is that which is delivered in a student-centred style appropriate to the age and concerns of the child. Educationalists may interpret this to mean that cognisance of Bruner's (1985) notion of a spiral curriculum indicates that health education (and therefore education about drugs) should be delivered within a cross-curricular framework carefully co-ordinated by a high status member of staff. Such a cross-curricular approach would avoid unnecessary and unprofessional repeats of topics across the subjects. It would also allow the possible allocation of time in the curriculum for specialist and perhaps emotive subjects to be dealt with in more depth and in a sensitive way. The pastoral component of the timetable can emerge in particular lessons which, because of their non-examination orientation, can be structured to allow closer relationships to grow between teacher and pupil which foster the deeper trust and security required for open learning and discussion of personal issues.

A recent study of five different approaches to drug education in Nottinghamshire schools (Denman, 1989) illustrates clearly how the complexity of the different school organisms greatly influence the possible effectiveness of drug education. Blanket directives are interpreted in different ways, but they do ensure that action is initiated and attended to. However, in the end it falls back on the subtle combination of particular personalities in each school to put the policy into practice. This fact needs to be recognised for it has consequences for staff development and training and, in the end, affects the general ethos of the school (another important component that needs to be taken into account, see Rutter *et al.* 1979).

It is important that for the sake of ease teachers do not shepherd drug education into cosy information-centred examination slots. A multilateral multi-drug approach is what is required as part of the holistic development of the individual:

The message from health education research over the last decade indicates that for health education to be effective the individual needs to own the information, engage with the concepts, practise strategies, and affirm the desire to be healthy. (Falk, 1987, p. 8)

Educationalists argue long and hard over the exact details of projects about drugs and since the devolution of authority over some curriculum matters to the school governors has begun to gain momentum, fears such as those already described (that education itself will make experimentation with drugs more likely) are even more keenly felt. The changes in policy over school organisation also means that in each school even more people are involved in the process required by law, namely, that each school must develop its own policy on what to or not to tell the young about drugs.

Research from other highly-scrutinised subject areas such as sex education seems to show that knowledge does have an effect to both delay the onset of activity and reduce the risks incurred by involvement. Sex education supposedly ensures that sexual activity starts later and fewer girls become pregnant (Farrel, 1978). However, the aims of drug education are different; most are more concerned with total abstinence than with harm reduction. The acceptance that some experimentation with substance abuse is possible and that safety procedures might be useful is generally (although not totally) avoided.

To accept harm reduction approaches requires a different perspective on the nature of education and on the personalities of young people. Too often the educational model rests on a notion that knowledge is to be poured into an empty vessel. The self-empowerment model of health promotion espouses a rather different point of view. It cherishes an ideal based on enabling rather than directing the individuals and therefore it respects individual responsibility for learning. In my view it also sails very close to the victim-blaming stance of the educational model but it does have some important and subtle differences. The self-empowerment model recognises the complex blend of motivations for actions and it takes its rationale from an understanding of the psychological concept of self-esteem. According to Tones, (1987a) and Wright *et al.* (1989) this is a vital component influencing Health Action Choices which direct an individual whether or not to take drugs.

Self-esteem in itself is not a simple concept, being constructed from many components which for simplicity could be reduced to three important constituents, namely, belonging, uniqueness and influence.

Belonging can be taken to mean the sense of acceptance given by a group, it can mean the feeling of being welcomed and wanted by others. If these are not strong components in the experience of an individual then a strong sense of self-worth is hard to achieve. Similarly with the sense of uniqueness, if an individual does not have any belief in their special abilities, lack of self-confidence will inhibit their lifestyle. There is much literature on this subject especially with respect to the importance of self-esteem in education (Gammage, 1983) but to my mind the most important component of self-esteem is that of an individual's sense of influence or power in the world. This can be likened to Rotter's (1954) sense of 'Internal Focus of Control' without which an individual may be prey to a sense of impotence or even 'learned helplessness' (Seligmenan, 1975).

In theory, education designed to develop an individual's sense of internality or sense of influence in the world opens the possibility that responsible freedom will also be more likely. Education to enhance a sense of influence in the world involves far more than extending the ability to decide to say 'no', although such skills may be used. For individuals to behave in a positive life-enhancing way they must have high regard for themselves so the effort of education needs not just to be concerned directly with information about the actual substances but with the development of self-esteem in the users. In this country this style of education is often known as 'experiential' and is based on the philosophy of Human Relations in Education (Hall and Hall, 1989) or on the kind of 'Life Skills' training advocated by Hopson and Scally (1980). The focus of this type of approach is on the process of education rather than on the content, and according to those who have used this approach in the classroom, its impact is marked and lasting (Hall, Woodhouse and Wooster, 1984). Knowledge is seen as a tool which can facilitate values clarification, therefore decision-making skills are not learned conditioned responses but real, owned choices based on the concerns expressed by the people involved. The individual is necessarily viewed as part of a social matrix which both influences and is influenced by them. By enhancing self-worth, difficulties, such as dealing with stress, can be approached through a wider range of behaviour options, since interaction with others would become more assertive, successful and positive.

This approach has much in its favour but it seems almost too good to be true. In spite of the almost evangelical fervour with which health educationalists seem to embrace this model, there is still within it a great danger of covert manipulation and opportunity for social control, since the teachers' role in programmes based on this model demands an uncommonly high degree of impartiality which is difficult to achieve. Related criticisms are made by Kay (1987) and Howe (1987) who also cast doubt on the effectiveness of health education in schools. This all gives credence to the suspicion with which the self-empowerment model is viewed. It is also possible within this model to imagine someone with high self-esteem who, with confidence, uses the experience to justify an anti-social drug use in spite of the fact that our society does not permit such freedom. Although an empowered rebel is possibly the seed of a pressure for social change, our educational system may not wish to encourage such subversive behaviour, since education is usually viewed as a way to set standards not to challenge them. Therefore it is no small wonder that this model is not popular in traditional circles.

This becomes particularly apparent in some recent developments which have their origin in the self-empowerment model. As already mentioned some programmes concerned with demand reduction have focused on practising assertive responses to peers. This method also advocates influence in the opposite direction. Since peers are so influential, and since self-esteem is so dependant on acceptance by others, 'Peer Education', that is, using older or same age leaders to model behaviour and to influence others in positive ways is growing in acceptance. In some forms of this philosophy peers have also been encouraged to be counsellors, based on the notion that young people are more likely to talk to peers than adults about their problems. Whilst this has much to commend it, the risk exists that adults will project their responsibilities onto carefully selected young people in a way which focuses on adult-centred concerns. It is one matter for a friend to be elected to take the lead in an activity and quite another to have a 'mini-adult' placed in the group to persuade everyone to behave in a certain way. This field of health education and of drug education has gained in popularity in Britain since it has been widely used in North America in recent years (Falk 1990). In this country, for example, it has been used as the basis for popular classroom materials such as *Smoking and Me* (Gray, 1988) designed to encourage young children not to smoke. Building on the carefully evaluated success of these materials, plans are afoot in several camps to explore the same approach towards education about alcohol and drugs. The approach is deemed to have much potential but it is also a minefield of problems concerned with social control.

Looking beyond the basic classroom materials and strategies that drive them research has shown that the ethos of the school has a profound effect on the education received (Rutter *et al.*, 1979). Also, Williams (1985) has written extensively on the importance of the school as a health promoting arena which includes an understanding of the relationship of the school with the local community. The elements which affect the health promoting atmosphere of a school lie partly in the environment, the physical appearance of the school buildings and partly in the way that the staff relate to each other and in how they relate to the children through the schools pastoral system. Adams (1989) writes about how the development of a pastoral system can give rise to a philosophy which has a different bias in the strategies available for supporting health education (and thus education concerned with drugs) and which can in turn affect the whole ethos of the school. I am certain that new initiatives must share this concern and look to the development of a strong pastoral or personal and social education context in the school curriculum as *the* way forward.

RECENT INITIATIVES

One of the more significant contributions to the 'top down' change that has been made in the last few years has been a national scheme organised through the Department of Education and Science and funded centrally out of the Education

Support Grant. The scheme directed every local education authority in the country to appoint, on temporary contracts, Drug Education Coordinators whose job it would be to encourage every school in the country to develop a comprehensive drug education programme. In the first instance funding was only given for one year, but the work did receive further finance (Dunn, 1988) and has been running in one form or another since 1986 (DES, 1989). The scheme was ambitious and not without its difficulties.

The evaluation reports (Murphy, 1988; Turner *et al.*, 1989) were generally complementary about all the projects but comments were made about the way some counties had weakened the effectiveness of the work by exercising internal policies of secondment which appointed a new person each year instead of developing the expertise that one individual may have gained. Therefore some projects were felt to have achieved more than others. However, each county council went about the implementation of its project in its own way and, as a complete group, the achievements of the last few years were judged to be impressive. The activities carried out by the coordinators included support for curriculum development, enhancing the ethos of schools by encouraging team work, the dissemination of new teaching materials on drug-related matters — such as 'Skills for Adolescence' (TACADE, 1986) and the provision of in-service training.

At the same time as this concerted effort was being made the draft of the National Curriculum was published (DES, 1988b). This draft almost totally ignored the strength of these developments, leaving very little support for health education. This direct conflict of interests almost totally ignored the strength of the developments in the local education authorities and led many people to question whether the right hand of government knew what the left hand was doing when it came to drug education.

There is now some more evidence of consensus since in the meantime another arena of 'top down' initiative has been developing, in the area of teacher education. The Health Education Council, which became the Health Education Authority in 1987, has funded several initiatives to encourage Health Education training in teacher training. From these initiatives came the funding for the Health Education Academic

Lectures scheme, which placed temporary lecturers in several universities to carry out professional training in health education and included three posts which had teacher education as a special focus (see Falk, 1990).

This was the basis of the Nottingham initiative with which I was personally connected. The work at Nottingham offered teacher training focusing not only on the self-empowerment and self-esteem of the child in the classroom but also on the experience of the teacher. As in the philosophy put forward by De Charms (1976), it emphasised that, for teachers to feel able to create an open learning classroom environment, they must first experience these person-centred approaches; that is, for this to happen it is the teachers who require the experiential education and not just the pupils. If effective health education requires the provision of an informal learning environment that is student-centred, so that an atmosphere of mutual trust and cooperation can exist, then the health educator, the teacher, needs to be self-aware and able to understand his or her own hidden messages and value judgements. The teachers themselves need to participate in active learning to understand the experience by understanding their own attitudes so that they are likely to be more sensitive to group dynamics and to promote the opportunity for responsible freedom to occur (see also Rogers, 1983).

A similar philosophy is behind another recent initiative which concentrates on in-service training for teachers, known as Health Skills Training (Anderson, 1986). This work also uses Human Relations as its foundation and explores many of the issues behind staff management that contribute to the 'Health Promoting School' (Williams, 1985) such as the management of change and examination of teacher stress. Similar work has been carried out by the Health Education Authority Teaching Unit at Southampton University (Williams and Roberts, 1985) which has resulted in the development of teaching materials (Health Education Authority, 1990) to provide support for health education in teacher education.

Unfortunately, all these schemes are far from the public eye. They are not necessarily vote winners nor are they processes which comfort the worried parent with immediate action. All are long-term investments which will not show results until the teachers trained under them reach maturity in their careers. However, a small input in initial or in-service training to facilitate effective drug education will create a specially qualified teacher. That teacher may through his or her career have an effect for years on the 200 or so pupils whom he or she speaks to every day, and also affect the colleagues with whom he or she works. When this potential is compared to the hit or miss approach of the expensive media campaigns the latter pales in comparison. Advertisements may have an impact but this is quite different from a teacher's influence which remains for a long time. Such investments in human skills do not show immediate returns. Sadly, government and public alike are prone to opt for short-term results and avoid long-term commitments, in much the same way that the youngsters they are trying to protect also opt for the immediate gratification of drug use.

CONCLUSIONS

It is probably clear that I have strong views as to where effort and investment should be concentrated for the best results as far as education about drugs is concerned. I believe that it is very important to make known what options are available within this sphere, since it is a common cry that the hope for the reduction of drug use (and protection from AIDS) lies in this magical thing called 'Education'. Unfortunately the people who most often declare that 'Education' is the hope for the future are also those who have the least understanding of how 'Education' works. They might well miss the mark by flinging more money towards the development of classroom projects which soon fall out of fashion and date instead of sorting out the whole system. It is the living resources — the teachers — who will adapt and encourage real education about drugs throughout the 30 to 40 years of their careers. In daily use in a school a book or other printed resource has only a comparatively brief existence, during which it offers its contribution. Even then, to be effective, a book, or poster or video still depends on the skill of the teacher to make it really useful.

To my mind there is no question as to the preferable value

of 'top down' investment as the best form of national intervention and initative in the fight against drug abuse. Activities such as the Drug Education Coordinators programme, and the initiatives in professional training for teachers (which include health education offered in an experiential way at both initial and in-service level) have the most to offer. Even so, every approach has its part to play. What is needed is a comprehensive interdisciplinary view which combines the models of health education and, in particular, education about drugs, to provide the arena within which the following aims can be achieved:

(1) The provision of clear information.
(2) The provision of opportunities to explore personal values so that choices are considered choices.
(3) The provision of opportunities to explore and to practise personal strategies for effective communication, that is lifeskills training.
(4) The provision of opportunities to increase self-esteem as an individual and as part of a group.
(5) The provision of these opportunities early enough to delay the onset of drug use. (This may be joined with legal strategies.)
(6) The provision of opportunities to experience risk and competency, associated with the onset of adulthood, that can be substituted for drug use.
(7) The provision of opportunities to understand harm reduction strategies primarily based on separation of drug use from other dangerous activies such as driving, but in the last resort based on responsible use if it occurs.
(8) Control of availability.

(Adapted from Schankula, 1987)

Responsibility for meeting these objectives can be shared. Some of these are the responsibility of the individual, some of the objectives can be met within the family, opportunities for others can be provided at school. Some fall to the community and some to the government.

Education, of course, does not stop at the school gate. Much can be achieved through youth clubs and outward bound schemes, community action, neighbourhood and work-based projects. Continuing education for parenting, to build the most important influence on a young person's life, must not be forgotten. Teachers are not the only people who have a role in all this (Kay, 1987). If school becomes the first arena for demand reduction effort then the home/school exchange must be a close second. Parental involvement in activities is just as important to avoid a culture clash. Thus health education policy associated with schools merges with the policy concerned with community education programmes and the youth service. Action in these areas may offer the young person at risk of being 'screwed up by heroin' a chance if the schemes are attractive enough. Otherwise, to those who gain their identity from a drug culture 'the warnings' are no more than comic relief.

At the end of the day the final judgement has to be made on the basis of effect. Does education about drugs work? At present the evidence is very sparse. Data on prevalence give some notion of changes but these will only really give a clear picture of the effectiveness of drug education initiatives in the very long term. Success must surely be measured in terms of freedom from drug abuse. The effects of education given at 10 years old may not be acted upon until that child has left school. Research to measure effects would have to have an immensely long-term perspective and, since the projects themselves often fall by the wayside due to apparent lack of results, we remain very much in the dark.

Investment in long-term education about drugs is therefore very much an act of faith and it is not surprising that the more public presentations are most popular. Solving the upstream causes by systemic changes which require intricate fore-thought and planning is the Cinderella option since there is little glamour in teacher training, youth work, parent education and community centres.

The comparative costs are also hard to measure. An expensive advertisement campaign may cost several million pounds but it is just a one-off investment. In contrast, training initiatives require annual monies over a very long time for distant pay offs. However, I would argue that faith has got to be kept. The greatest waste of money occurs when long-term projects are scrapped before they have really become established (only to be replaced by another which is scrapped in turn). This and not the methods or the wording or the theory is *the* greatest weakness in the area of drug education. Unless this is resolved the finest efforts of the health educators will continue to evaporate and this nation will continue to encounter the drug problems it worries about. At the moment the whole system is crisis-driven rather than proactive. If education on these matters is just designed to keep our young people safe from corruption inside sanitised protective bubbles and inoculated against the world, where are the free adults who are able to face problems and overcome them?

In the summer of 1990 the 'spectre of Crack' hangs over Europe (Stutman, 1989). How are we now to face the new drug problem which has arisen? Whilst the public need to be informed of this danger, the risk exists that in the giving of information this will exacerbate the use of the substance. If another 'crisis' is perceived would it be tempting fate to repeat the 'media hype' strategy that was used over heroin? Education, it is announced in the media, is *the* weapon that is to be used, but it needs to offer a more positive answer than just saying 'no' today. We must be brave enough to ensure that our children receive an education based on long-term objectives which will help them to say 'no' or even completely avoid the difficulties of drug abuse in the future also.

REFERENCES

Adams, S. (1989) *A Guide to Creative Tutoring* (Kogan Page).

Anderson, J. (1986) 'Health Skills: the Power to Choose', *Health Education Journal*, vol. 45, no. 1 p. 19 ff.

Balding, J. (1989) *We Teach Them How to Drink* (HEA Schools Health Education Unit, Exeter University).

Beels, C. (1986) *Health Matters* (National Extension College/Health Education Council).

Bruner, J. (1985) *The Process of Education*, (Harvard University Press).

Caplin, S. and S. Woodward (1986) *Drugwatch — Just Say No* (Corgi).

de Charms, R. (1976) *Enhancing Motivation: Change in the Classroom* (New York: Halstead).

Denman, S (1989) *Drug Education in the Secondary School Curriculum: Five Case Studies* (Nottingham Iniversity/Nottingham County Council.

DES (1986) *Health Education from 5–15, Curriculum Matters 6* (London: HMSO)

DES (1988a) *The Curriculum from 5–16, The Response to Curriculum Matters 2* (London: DES)

DES (1988b) *National Curriculum, A Discussion Document* (London: HMSO)

DES (1989) 'LEAS Invited to Bid for 140 Million Programme of Education Support Grants', press release 192/89. 16 June 1989.

Dorn, N and N. South (1985) 'Return of the Topic Developments in Drug Education and Training', *Health Education Journal*, vol. 44, no. 4 pp. 208–12.

Dorn, N. (1986) 'Media Campaigns', *Druglink* (July–August) pp. 8–9.

Dunn, B. (1988) The Future of Drugs and Alcohol Education in the UK, speech notes for address to the National Drug Coordinators Conference in Nottingham, 12 July (London: DES Press Office).

Eiser, J. R., M. Morgan, and P. Gammage (1988) 'Social Education is Good for Health', *Educational Research*, vol. 30, no. I, p. 20–5.

Falk, J., S. Denman, M. Hoar (1989) 'The 6th Annual Conference on Drug Abuse: Action or Apathy? Addiction Research Foundation, Toronto Canada (November 1988), unpublished report, Health Education Authority.

Falk, J. (1987) *The Nottingham Initiative* (University of Nottingham.

Falk, J. (1990) *Health Education in Universities: Accounts of Recent Initiatives by Health Education Academic Lecturers* (London: Health Education Authority).

Farrel, C. (1978) *My Morther Said* (Routledge & Kegan, Paul).

Gammage, P. G. (1983) *Children and Schooling: Issues in Childhood Socialisation* (Unwin Educational).

Gilles, P. (1987) 'The Evaluation of the Health Education "My Body" Project', report to the health Education Authority, London.

Gillies, P. A. and B. Willcox, 'Prevalence of smoking among schoolchildren in Sheffield', Health Education Journal, 43, 57–60.

Gray, E. (1988) *Smoking and Me* (London: Health Education Authority).

Hall, E., D. A. Woodhouse, A. D. Wooster, (1984) 'An Evluation of In-service Courses in Human Relations', *British Journal of In-service Education*, vol. 11 no. 1, pp. 55–60.

Hansen, A. (1985) 'Will the Government's Mass Media Campaign Work?' *British Medical Journal*, no. 290, pp. 1054–55.

Health Education Council (1986) *Drugwise*, HEC/DES/Tacade/ISDD/Lifeskills Association).

Health Education Authority (1990) *Exploring Teaching Programmes No. 1*, (Leeds: Lifeskills Associates).

Hodgson, A. and D. Streatfield (1986) 'What are the LEAs doing about Drugs?' *Education* p. 59, results of survey by NFER for DES.

Home Office (1984) *Prevention: Report of the Advisory Council on the Misuse of Drugs* (London: HMSO).

Home Office (1985) *'Tackling Drug Misuse: A Summary of the Government's Strategy'* (London: HMSO).

Hopson, B and M. Scally (1980) *Lifeskills Teaching Programmes No. 1*, (Leeds: Lifeskills Associates).

Howe, B. (1987) 'Approaches to Prevention from Grass-roots to Campaigns', paper 30 in Heller *et al.* (eds.), *Drug Use and Misuse: A Reader* (Open University/John Wiley).

ISDD (1984) *Drugs in Health Education: Trends and Issues* (USDD).

ISDD (1982) *'Facts and Feelings about Drugs but Decisions about Situations' (ISDD)*.

Kay, L. (1987) *'Preventing Drug Problems', paper 29 in T. Heller, M. Gott, C. Jeffrey (eds.) (1987) Drug Use and Misuse: A Reader* (Open University/John Wiley).

Lowry, S. (1989) 'Teaching by Example', *British Medical Journal*, vol. 299, 14 Oct, 1989, p. 936.

Murphy, R., T. Williams and G. Turner. (1988) *The ESG funded Drug Education Co-Ordinators Initiative — A National Evaluation* (interim report) (University of Southampton).

McKinlay, J. B. (1979) 'Patients, Physicians and Illness, a Case for Refocusing Upstream. The Political Economy of Illness,' in E. G. Jaco (ed.), *Patients, Physicians and Illness*, 3rd edition (London: Collier Macmillan).

National Extension College (1988) *Health Matters*.

National Curriculum Council (1988) *Consultation Report: Science* (York NCC).

National Curriculum Council (1989) *Personal and Social Education*, Interim report.

Perry, C. (1986) 'Drug Abuse Prevention', Journal of School Health, vol. 56, no. 9.

Power, R. (1989) 'Drugs and the Media: Prevention Campaigns and Television' in S. MacGregor (ed.) (1989) *Drugs and British Society: Responses to a Social Problem in the 1980s* (London: Routlege).

Reid, D. and D. E. Massey (1986) 'Can School Health Education be More Effective?' *Health Education Journal*, vol. 45, no. 1, pp. 7–14.

Research Bureau Ltyd (1986) *Heroin Misusers Campaign Evaluation. Report of Findings — Stages I–III.*

Rogers, C. R. (1983) *Freedom to Learn for the Eighties* (Merril).

Rotter, J. B. (1954) *Social Learning Theory and Clinical Psychology*, (New York: Prentice Hall).

Rutter, M, B. Maughan, and J. Ousten (1979) *Fifteen Thousand Hours, Secondary Schools and Their Effects on Children* (London: Open Books).

Schankula, H. (1987) 'Preventing Alcohol Misuse Amongst the Young', paper presented at Institute of Alcohol Studies Conference, 25 Feb. 1987.

Seligman, M. E. P. (1975), *Helplessness? on depression, development and death* (San Francisco: Freeman).

Stutman, R. (1989) 'Crack Stories from the States' *Druglink*, Sept.–Oct., p. 6–7 (ISDD).

Tacade (1984) *Free to Choose* (Tacade/Health Education Council).

Tacade (1986) *Skills for Adolescence* (Manchester: Tacade/Quest International).

Tacade (1986) 'Double Take' (video) CSL Vision.

Tones, B. K. (1986a) 'Health Education and the Ideology of Health Promotion: a Review of Alternative Approaches', *Health Education Research: Theory and Practice* 1 (1), p. 3–12.

Tones, B. K. (1986b) 'Promoting the Health of Young People — the Role of Personal and Social Education' *Health Education Journal*, vol. 45, no. 1, pp. 14–19.

Tones, K. (1986c) 'Preventing Drug Misuse: the Case for Breadth, Balance and Coherence'. *Health Education Journal*, vol. 45, no. 4, pp. 223–230.

Tones, K. (1987a) 'Devising Strategies for Preventing Drug Misuse: The Role of the Health Action Model', *Health Education Research, Theory and Practice*, vol. 2, no. 4, p. 305–17.

Tones, K. (1987b) 'Health Promotion, Affective Education and the Personal–social Development of Young People', in David K. and T. Williams (1987)

Health Education in Schools (London: Harper Rowe).

Turner, C., r. Murphy and T. Williams (1979) *Education and the Misuse of Drugs, A National Evaluation of the Drug Education Co-ordinators Initiative*, a report to LEAs (University of Southampton).

Williams T. (1985) 'Health Education and the School–Community Interface: Towards a Model of School Community Interaction', in Campbell (1985) *New Directions in Health Education* (London: Falmer Press).

Williams, T. and J. Roberts (1985) *Health Education in Schools and Teacher Training Establishments* (HEC Health Education Unit, Dept. of Education, University of Southampton).

Wright, L., T. Tones, and B. Howe (1989) 'Understanding Drug Misuse — Linking Theory with Practice', *Health Education Journal*, vol. 48, no. 2.

13 Criminalisation and Control

Gordon Graham

In almost all modern societies, the use of drugs is highly regulated, and the use of at least some addictive drugs[1] (nicotine is a notable exception) is against the law. Anyone who anxiously draws the attention of politicians to the increasing quantities being used, traded, grown or transported, or greets the news of drug seizures by government officials with enthusiasm, assumes that this should be so, that such drugs should indeed be outlawed, and, since almost everyone who addresses the so-called drug 'problem' speaks in this way and hence makes this assumption, the question 'should it be so?' is scarcely ever addressed.

When it is, and when the legislation of drugs *is* contemplated, this is usually from a libertarian point of view, that is, the relatively extreme view that what the individual does is a matter for that individual alone and state intervention is always wrong. This view is often propounded in the face of objections about the social harm that drugs cause, and in particular the damage that is to be found in the lower echelons of society. Consequently, the debate very easily comes to look like a dispute between those interested in the liberties of the relatively rich and mature on the one hand, what we might call the champions of the leisured classes, and on the other hand, the champions of the underprivileged, the young and relatively poor.

But in this essay I hope to show this conception of the debate to be quite mistaken. Whether we approach the matter from the point of view of liberty or harm there is good reason to think that drugs ought not to be criminalised.

I

Why should the use of drugs of any kind be against the law? One simple answer, which I shall consider in more detail later, is that widespread drug-taking has bad results for society as a whole. That harmful consequences do indeed follow from

245

widespread drug-taking is an assumption of almost all discussions of the drug 'problem', but of course if the argument from harm to illegality is to be a good one, this empirical claim about effects must not be assumed, but confirmed by substantial social investigation, investigation which, as a matter of fact hardly ever takes place.

There is another assumption at work too, however. Not only do we need reason to think that widespread drug-taking would lead to widespread harm of one kind or another, we also need reason to think that a change in the law which made it permissible to take drugs would, in all probability, lead to their being widely taken, that legislation of marijuana and cocaine, for instance, would lead to much more widespread use. Since both drugs are already widely used in the United States where they are illegal, the truth of this further assumption may be doubted, but the chief point is that without this assumption about illegality and the consumption of drugs, the conclusion about harmful consequences for society as a whole does not follow. It is only if large numbers of people take to drugs that such dire consequences as drug-taking is said to have, could reach those proportions which would allow us to describe the result as widespread social harm, and it is only if legislation would lead to widespread use that there is reason to favour outlawing them on these grounds.

But if this were indeed the case (though such evidence as we have suggests that this is unlikely), if, that is to say, we could demonstrate that incipient drug takers abound, we should, in that very fact, have encountered another problem. If large numbers of people, given freedom to decide matters for themselves would choose to take drugs, to make them illegal is to thwart the freedom of choice of individual citizens on a large scale. And this reveals a third assumption at work in the common defence of outlawing drugs, the assumption that the freedom of the individual may justifiably be overridden by law in order to prevent undesirable outcomes.

It hardly needs to be said that not all political theories share this assumption. Those of a broadly liberal kind are to be characterised by precisely the opposite — that considerations of social welfare cannot in general override the freedom of the individual, even though there may have to be exceptions for special cases. Moreover, since much (though not all) of the damage that widespread drug-taking is expected to have, is direct, that is, damage to the welfare and prospects of addicts themselves, the bald assertion that drug-taking should be illegal because of its consequences falls foul of anti-paternalist restrictions on how the law may be used, restrictions characteristic of many of the best known political theories.

In short, even if facts about drug-taking turn out to be as this common argument supposes, we have an argument for the prescription of drugs *only* if we are prepared to accept the essentially Platonic conception of society in which the freedom of individual citizens may be restricted whenever it seems likely that they will misuse it. If, in common with liberal political theory, we reject this conception of society, we are left with a problem — why *should* drugs be outlawed?

II

Those who are liberals at heart but anxious about the use of addictive drugs have at least one important line of argument available to them. It is one which questions the accuracy of describing drug-users as freely choosing to take drugs. Doesn't calling them *addictive* drugs point to the fact that even though addicts express a strong desire for drugs, they cannot be said to be freely choosing them? If so, a government which uses the law to thwart their desires, discourage their dependency and prevent the habit forming among others, cannot be said to be acting contrary to the free choice of its citizens, and may be said to be promoting individual autonomy, the value, presumably, upon which the importance of anti-paternalism is built.

This sort of argument is important for liberal political theory, because it employs the idea that the desires of individual citizens may be over-ridden by the law, not merely without any infringement of, but actually *in the name of* liberty properly so-called, and does so in a connection that most people find plausible. But it, too, has a questionable assumption built into it, an assumption about the nature of free choice. We are to deny the title 'free choice' to the express desires and deliberative actions of heroin addicts because they arise from addiction, and this, presumably, is because the desires are caused by the drug itself.

This, however, invokes a highly contentious account of

freedom. According to one very familiar strand of political (and liberal) thought, to say that citizens are free to do something is to say nothing more than that they are not prevented by the coercive will of another. This is the so-called 'negative' conception of freedom, and it is a conception of freedom which carries the implication that the cause of an action is irrelevant to its being free or unfree. Consequently, the physical basis of the addict's desire cannot, on this account, be a reason to discount his choice as that of a self-determining agent. It follows that the liberal's proscription of addictive drugs will have to call upon some other conception of freedom. In itself this is not a great weakness, because the 'absence of constraint' conception of freedom is not the only one there is, nor, perhaps, is it very widely accepted. But the point is that any attempt to square liberal political learnings with the desire to make drugs illegal must *presuppose* its inadequacy, because if it is indeed an adequate conception of freedom, the line of argument we have been considering fails.

What appears to be needed, then, is some consideration of the grounds upon which this elementary conception of civil liberty might be rejected, but in fact it is not altogether easy to see how the argument should go at this point. Often, objections to the conception of negative freedom take the form of counter-examples. We are given intuitively different cases which come out the same on this conception — the carefully considered conduct of the hygenically-minded surgeon is compared with the compulsive hand-washing of the neurotic. Whatever such a strategy may on occasions accomplish, it is plainly useless in the present context, however. We cannot establish the unfreedom of the drug-addict by comparing deliberative and compulsive choice, because what is at issue is whether compulsive choice, such as the addict's, may nevertheless be described as free.

An alternative strategy would be to offer another account of freedom, and show it to be superior. This is what John Stuart Mill does. In the *System of Logic* he presents a conception of freedom which is, I think, intended to remedy the defects of his father's purely negative conception. Mill begins by agreeing that the human agent as much as anything else is subject to the universal laws of causation. But this, he maintains, does not mean that human agents are not free in every important sense, because any individual may still have the power to alter his character and actions. As Mill says:

> [a man's character] being, in the ultimate resort, formed for him, is not inconsistent with its being, in part, formed by him as one of the intermediate agents. . . . Indeed, if we examine closely, we shall find that [the] feeling, of our being able to modify our character if we wish, is itself the feeling of moral freedom which we are conscious of.[2]

Freedom on this view is more than the simple absence of constraint. It is a consciousness on our part of being able to modify our own characters. And this, it might be supposed, shows that the desires of the addict and the deliberative reasoner cannot be equated, for if we distinguish between those actions whose causes include the deliberate choices of the agents whose actions they are, and those actions whose causes are to be found among external factors or wholly unreflective desires, it is only the former which may properly be described as free.

This account of freedom has its own problems, but whatever its merits, and despite first appearances, it cannot be used to discount the desires of the addict. There is in principle no reason why someone's craving for heroin should not in part be the result of a decision to become an addict. Nor is this so unlikely as it may sound. Taking illegal drugs is a well recognised way of demonstrating one's rejection of the established values of a society. As such it may be highly objectionable, but if so, it is objectionable on moral or religious grounds, and to object to it in this way is precisely to recognise it as the decision of a morally free agent. Indeed there is a lot to be said in favour of the view that heroin taking is a relatively straightforward pursuit of a hedonistic style of life, just the sort of 'experiment in living' which Mill himself insisted people must be free to engage in, however offensive to the moral majority. In short, there is nothing in Mill's 'self-realisation' account of freedom which counts decisively against the actions of the heroin addict, such that they cannot be regarded as free and hence denied the respect which liberalism requires the law to give to the freely chosen actions of others.

Both the simple account of negative freedom and Mill's amendment of it are varieties of 'compatibilism'. That is to say both accept the compatibility of causality and freedom, which is to say, the view that there is nothing contradictory in describing a given action as both caused and free. But neither can offer us a distinction between the desires and actions of the addict and those of the deliberative reasoner, such that the latter can be graced with, and the former denied, the status of free actions. Some people will think that this result is un- surprising since it is an inevitable result of their compatibilism.

There is indeed some reason to share this view. It is precisely because we know, or think we know, that the addict's craving for heroin has a physical basis that we find ourselves inclined to deny that the actions which flow from it can properly be described as free. And this may tempt us to explore the common, if philosophically somewhat unfashion- able idea, that free actions have no causes at all, but arise from an uncaused 'act of will'.

This view raises many familiar difficulties, but the most important point to be observed here is that, even if true, it does not serve in the present case. From the fact, if it is one, that free actions cannot spring directly from felt desires, it does not follow that desires cannot enter into practical deliberation. Indeed it would be very odd if they could not, because hunger could not then count as a reason for searching for food. But if one physiological desire can enter our practical deliberations, why not another? Heroin addicts need and desire heroin in exactly the way that very hungry people need and desire food. The strength of either desire can thus become an important factor in practical deliberation.

To many minds, of course, there is an important difference — heroin addicts, unlike the very hungry, cannot do other- wise. They are not free to refuse heroin, in the way that even someone very hungry can refuse food. And since the truth of the counterfactual 'He could have done otherwise' is essential to the ascription of freedom, freedom of choice cannot properly be ascribed to the desires and actions of the addict.

It is essential to observe here that this sort of argument makes an appeal to matters of fact. Is it true that heroin addicts cannot stop themselves? One point of clarification is needed. Heroin addicts cannot stop themselves *desiring* heroin, but neither can very hungry people stop themselves feeling hungry. The only question, then, is whether they can stop themselves *taking* it. At this point there is a strong tendency to offer a pseudo-conceptual answer — 'of course they cannot stop themselves, that is what we mean by saying they are "addicted"'.

It is interesting here to observe the great difficulty encountered by legislation and health organisations in arriving at a satisfactory definition of 'addiction'. Some definitions, on the strength of which regulations and health education campaigns have been devised, are astonishingly sloppy and ill-considered (those of the World Health Organisation are perhaps the best examples). In point of fact 'addiction' is something we know so little about, that it is questionable whether there is any one thing that can be referred to in this way. The most useful definitions are generally those which have to do with physical dependence and the effects of withdrawal and make virtually no reference to behaviour, and this is reflected in the fact that, despite its continued and extensive use on television and in the press, medical discussions of drug use and abuse have increasingly dropped the term 'addiction' in favour of 'dependence'.[3]

But even if it were the case that there is a useful concept of addiction which can properly be applied to many of those who abuse drugs such as heroin and cocaine, it is beyond reasonable doubt that those so described can stop taking the drug to which they are addicted, otherwise there would be no former addicts. In reality, of course, many heavy users do give up, and there seems good reason to think that physical addiction and an exercise of the will are intimately connected. In a recent British survey it was found that 70 per cent of former drug users gave up voluntarily and without any form of treatment.[4] (Of course, to say that they gave up voluntarily, is not to imply that they did so easily). Furthermore, almost everyone with experience of drug abuse, including users themselves, agree that without a self-generated decision to give up drugs no form of 'treatment' is of any avail, and indeed the very idea of 'addiction' may itself have hindered those who would otherwise have been able to give up.[5]

Since no one supposes that merely being subject to strong desires is incompatible with free action, it seems that drug addicts freely choose to take drugs. That is to say, it is no less true of addicts that they could stop taking drugs if they so wished, than it is of anyone under the influence of strong desires. Construing free action along commonplace lines, therefore, still gives us no reason to suppose that the actions of heroin addicts are not those of free agents.

The three conceptions of freedom we have briefly explored, it may be argued, exhaust the possibilities. At any rate, they are the conceptions of freedom most closely associated with liberalism, and on none have we found reason to suppose that the actions of drug addicts are any less entitled to the protection which liberalism traditionally says must be given to the freely chosen actions of individual citizens, however foolish or objectionable those actions might be from a moral or religious point of view. It follows that liberal theory cannot defend the practice of making heroin and similar drugs illegal.

So much the worse for liberal theory, it might be thought. This is an important thought. The argument so far could be turned on its head and used as a *reductio ad absurdum*: the use of addictive drugs is obviously a serious problem which society must control; if liberal theory cannot justify such control, this merely demonstrates its inadequacy as a normative social theory.

Such a head-on attack amounts in fact to the rehearsal of a familiar anti-liberal theme, the claim that unbridled liberty can have socially detrimental effects. It is a commonplace of both conservative and socialist critiques of liberalism that individuals acting freely may cause social harm which all of us, as individuals, may have reason to regret and good cause to prevent. But the raising of this criticism means that our attention must now turn from freedom to harm.

III

It is widely believed that the use of drugs such as heroin and cocaine is harmful, not just to those who use them, but to the user's family and to society at large. As a result of drug-taking, marriages and other family relationships collapse, babies are born addicts so that their first experience of life is the agony of withdrawal, crime increases, the addict's health declines and the additional costs involved in the loss of production and increased burdens on health care facilities must be borne by the community at large. If this is true, there seems reason, under the harm condition, to outlaw their use and the penalise those who use them, and more especially those who trade in them — the 'pushers'.

Rather obviously this conclusions follows only if: (a) the prevention of social harm does indeed legitimise restrictions on individual liberty; and (b) if drug-taking really does cause harm.[6] Consider the first point. It has often been argued that what we may call the harm condition is questionable because of uncertainty about what exactly is to count as 'harm'. But even if we take an uncontentious sort of harm — bodily injury — there are obvious differences between instances of causing this sort of harm which the law ought to take into account, for example, the difference between boxing and common assault. A boxer may cause just the same degree of injury as a chance assailant, but his action differs significantly from a moral and legal point of view, because he has the consent of the other boxer. Or again, a fine and a theft may constitute the same degree of financial harm to those who suffer them, but it would be absurd to suppose that they do not differ from a legal point of view, and that both ought or ought not to be against the law. This sort of example can be multiplied almost indefinitely and this shows that the causing of harm cannot be a sufficient condition of making something against the law. If so, the harmfulness of drug-taking and selling is not, by itself, enough to show that it should be illegal. It follows that any attempt to rescue laws against addictive drugs in the name of liberalism by appealing to the harm condition fails.

To some minds, those of a more robustly utilitarian cast perhaps, all this is mere quibbling. Whatever may be true of harm in the context of a general abstract principle, it is evident that where there is a real risk of widespread physical and psychological harm any government has a clear duty, and right, to take steps to prevent it.[7] This is precisely, of course, what liberalism, in the name of individual autonomy, denies, but its position on this point is usually seen by its opponents as an objectionable accommodation with evil. Their view is a good one, of course, even on its own terms, only if what is accommodated is evil and, in the present case this means 'causes widespread physical and psychological harm'. And so we are brought, by another route, to the second of the questions which headed this section: do drugs, such as cocaine and heroin, cause harm?

The first point to be made here is one about evidence gathering. Drug-taking is often supposed to be accompanied by crime, and often it is quite easy to find statistics which show that, as drug-taking increases, so does the number of criminal convictions. But such statistics, on their own, are quite worthless, because if drug taking and trafficking are themselves crimes, it is inevitable that with an increase in the use of drugs, there will be an increase in crime. The increase, however, does not show any independently significant social *harm* arising from drug-taking, as is demonstrated by the fact that the 'problem' could be solved simply by repealing the laws against drugs; if there are no laws against it, there will be no criminal breaking of them.

Of course, those who believe that drugs lead to increases in crimes are generally alive to this point. The increases in crime they have in mind are increases in break-ins, burglaries, muggings, racketeering and so on, and here too, it is fairly easy to gather statistical evidence. But though these crimes are not crimes in virtue of the anti-drug laws themselves, it does not follow that those laws cannot be their *cause*. The fact that drugs are illegal makes them expensive, and hence worth trading in. This means both that those who want drugs are more likely to have to steal to obtain money to buy them, and that the rewards of trading in them on a grand enough scale[8] will entice those who are not adverse to the tactics of the bully and bandit. If heroin were not illegal the price would drop dramatically, and most of those who steal and cheat in order to pay for it would not have to do so, and some of the worst racketeers in the world would go out of business. Such, at any rate, is a plausible scenario, and its plausibility shows that the illegality of drugs may be a major factor in their causing harm.

Pursuing the same line of thought suggests further that a major cause of the physical harmfulness of drug-taking to the addicts themselves may also lie with the fact that they are illegal. It is now fairly well established that the most serious disease of which drug-users run a high risk do not result from the use of drugs, so much as the way in which they are taken.[9] Hepatitis and AIDS, to name the two most serious, are transmitted by shared and dirty needles. But the necessity of sharing needles arises chiefly from the fact that drug-taking, being against the law, is an underground activity. If it were widely accepted, in the way that opium taking was until the beginning of this century, it is certain that virtually *none* of these problems would arise.

To see which harms can properly be attributed to drugs we have to imagine a world in which heroin, opium, cocaine and so on are available in the way in which alcohol and nicotine currently are in the Western world, that is, widely available under licensing restrictions. If so, I have been arguing, we would be imagining a world in which many of the harms associated with drugs were ameliorated. But, proponents of the anti-drug laws will argue, we would also be seeing a world in which drug-addiction was widespread. What may be true is that the incidental harms of illegal drug-taking would be eliminated, but only at the cost which making drugs against the law is intended to prevent — large numbers of addicts.

What is this cost, exactly? Just how widespread addiction would be if heroin, cocaine and so on were widely available is a very speculative matter. We know that only a minority of those who take alcohol become alcoholics, and though there is some reason to suppose that the rate of serious addiction would be higher among heroin users, there is no reason to think that it would come to 100 per cent or anything near it. Research on this score with respect to heroin has been undertaken in both the USA and the UK, and though there are the usual difficulties in interpreting evidence correctly, it suggests that most heroin users start taking the drug between the ages of 17 and 24, but in the majority of cases heroin use is periodic and decreases as time goes by. Most users reach an age where they stop altogether.[10] Moreover, though evidence gathering about illegal activities is difficult, it seems that there are many heroin users who do not become ill, do not come into conflict with the law or need social services and who regularly use such small quantities of the drug that they are not technically dependent still less addicted. However much popular opinion is against this idea, controlled use of illegal drugs appears to be as common as controlled use of alcohol. If so the threat of widespread 'addiction' has more charm than reality.

But more important perhaps is a dissimilarity between alcohol and opiates; while the former is known to cause organic damage to those who use it to excess, there is much less evidence that heroin or opium *in themselves* cause any long-term medical ailments. Heroin for instance:

> when used in controlled doses under sterile conditions is a relatively non-toxic drug and there are many well documented cases of people using heroin, either intravenously or by inhalation for many years with no evident ill effects.[11]

Moreover, while drunks cease to function properly as a result of their intake of alcohol, it is possible for users of other drugs to function effectively over periods of many years, to the benefit of themselves and those around them. In other words, regular heroin, cocain and opium users, unlike heavy drinkers, can be as good employees, parents and citizens as those who never take drugs. It follows, not only that widespread addiction cannot be predicted as the result of legalising drugs with any confidence, but that the basis upon which such a result is to be feared is obscure and probably has more to do with folk lore than with any realistic assessment of evidence.

IV

The conclusion must be that neither on grounds of protecting the autonomy of the individual, nor preventing harm to the community is there good enough reason to make drug-taking illegal. The basis upon which this conclusion is reached is fairly straightforward — drug addicts choose to take drugs as freely as most people choose to do many things, and in doing so they are choosing an activity which, in itself, is relatively harmless.[12]

This liberating conclusion is invariably greeted with doubt rather than enthusiasm. The grounds of this doubt are twofold, I think. First it leaves us with a puzzle. If we accept that drugs are relatively harmless, the almost universal belief in the 'drug problem' is a cultural delusion of immense proportions. Moreover, we must accommodate the views of addicts themselves. Very few are recorded as being in favour of legalisation, and most, whatever their reluctance to give up or even try to give up, advise others not to start and hope that their children will avoid addiction. If this view derives from their experience of addiction, can there really be nothing wrong with it? Secondly, doubt about the conclusion of my argument also arises from the belief that in legalising drugs we are entering uncharted waters; that whatever arguments are brought to show their relative harmlessness, these are all *a priori* and to legalise them would be to run a very great risk. In other words, the argument in favour of legalisation may be the sort that enjoys theoretical merit but produces practical disaster.

To consider these two aspects of the question properly requires more space than is available here, so that a few remarks will have to suffice for each in turn.

Why should it not be the case that a widespread and firmly held belief is nonetheless mistaken? This is certainly a logical possibility, and neither in general or in this case is it so unlikely. First, it is a fact that social attitudes to drugs have undergone a great change in the last 100 years or so (witness nineteenth-century attitudes to opium), and that here as elsewhere, exploring changes in attitude over the years can lead to a better appreciation that what we generally take to be obvious may not be obvious at all. And even addicts may share conventional assumptions.[13] Furthermore, the same contrast over time is to be found in geography. Contemporary Western attitudes to drugs are a mystery to many in the Third World, not least peasants whose saleable crops are destroyed at the instigation of Western governments.

Secondly, history is instructive in another way here. If we study the genesis of drug regulations we can see a discrepancy between the reasons given for the introduction of controls and those commonly given for their maintenance. In the UK for instance, substances were added to the list of dangerous drugs more because of the social and political values of those who were likely to take them, than because of any addictive or otherwise harmful character which the drugs themselves were alleged to have. This is especially striking in the case of cannabis.[14] The evidence in favour of the hypothesis that cannabis is addictive and causes harm to both individuals and society has always been weak. What motivated those who strove to make it illegal was the popular association between cannabis taking and the political and social radicalism of those who, generally, were found to be taking it. We do not need to lend credence to the many absurd and ephemeral views of enthusiasts for flower-power and the like to see that any objection to their social beliefs is not in itself a good reason to outlaw their social habits. From the fact, if it were one, that those who smoke cannabis generally hold views that would lead to the destruction of social life as we know it, we cannot conclude that cannabis is itself socially destructive.

Nor has this been held for long. Rather, the original actions against cannabis having been motivated by a fear of the beliefs of its users, an alternative, altogether baseless, fear of cannabis itself, relating it vaguely to health and sickness has arisen. The result in this and indeed in several other instances is a divorce between the effective rationale behind the laws against 'dangerous drugs' (UK terminology) or 'controlled substances' (US) on the one hand and their official rationale on the other, and this, to my mind, is as clear a case of ideological belief on the Marxist model as one is likely to find.

The second source of doubt — that the legalisation of drugs, however good the abstract arguments, takes us into dangerous waters — is, if anything, more easily dispelled because its force rests upon the supposition that legalisation and criminalisation exhaust the possibilities. But this is obviously false. In considering the conflicting treatment which law and social policy metes out to different types of drugs, it is often overlooked that nicotine and alcohol are almost everywhere controlled substances. But the form of control is not criminalisation but *licence*. This useful social device means that we need not contemplate as the only alternatives a wholesale ban on use or availability to all and sundry. Licences may be used to secure quality control, responsible sellers and restricted consumer groups, such as restriction of the production and sale of alcohol and nicotine seek to secure. All these controls have things to commend them. In the case of drugs that are currently illegal, however, they have this more to recommend them. Not only are they more likely to minimise and mitigate such attendant harms as all drug-taking may produce than outright criminalisation is likely to do, they would make both more plausible and more enforceable a total ban on those drugs (crack and LSD may well be cases) which *are* extremely ?? harmful.

The licence, in short, is a social device specially suited to accommodate the claims of individual liberty on the one hand and social protection on the other. And if the general tenor of this argument is sound, such a device is just what the use of drugs needs.

All these considerations lend weight to the suggestion that as a culture Western society *is* self-deceived in the matter of drugs and their control. Nonetheless people are not easily dissuaded of the idea that heroin, opium, crack, cocaine and all so-called 'hard' drugs are best avoided. But it is no implication of the argument I have been advancing that they need be. What we need to abandon is the assumption that the only objection to drug-taking is the harm, individual or social, that it causes. In fact the most marked feature of the true addict's life is the importance he or she gives to the sort of experience a drug can supply. It comes to occupy a place which excludes so much that it can properly be regarded as impoverished and degrading. This is so in the sort of case much loved of the press and television, in which a young girl is persuaded to sell her body under the direction of a vicious pimp and at the risk of fatal diseases, all for the sake of 'feeding the dragon', that is, ensuring a continuous supply of drug induced pleasure. Such cases are, I am certain, atypical, but such a girl, if she were philosophically inclined, might resort to a Utilitarian-style defence of the rationality of her conduct, and insist that the pleasure outweighs the risk of serious harm. From this it follows that any objection we continue to press against her lifestyle had better have some other basis than straightforward harm.

What is wrong with her attitude, in fact, is the absurd importance it lends to pleasure of a mundane sort. One way of characterising this is to say that the addict's heart, whether fixed on drugs or fruit machines, is fixed where true joys are *not* to be found. This express appeal to religious language[15] suggests, rightly in my view, that the real objection to drug addiction is to a way of spending a human life. That such an objection may be made to stick I do not doubt, but this is quite consistent with the conclusion of the paper, since any decent legal system must allow the individual moral and religious freedom, and this includes the freedom for moral and religious error.

NOTES

1. Though I shall speak indiscriminately of 'drugs' from time to time throughout this paper, and mean by that pretty much what this term means in the press, on television, in the mouths of government agencies and so on, there is in fact no feature that all illegal drugs have in common. Indeed there seems very good reason to draw a distinction between cannabis (whose illegality is hard to reconcile with the legality of tobacco) and the so-called 'hard' drugs. For this reason I shall use heroin, opium and cocaine as my examples.

2. J. S. Mill, *System of Logic*, book VI, chap. 2, sect. 3.

3. On this see Roy Robertson, *Heroin, Aids and Society* (London: 1987) chap. 1.

4. Sarah Caplin and Shaun Woodward, *Drugwatch — Just Say No* (London: 1986) p. 59. This is important to note that this survey was based on a self-selected sample. It may mean that the real percentage of those who give up drugs without treatment is lower (few chronic addicts are likely to write in), but it may also mean that it is much higher since people who tried hard drugs a few times without any move to regular use are also unlikely to write in.

5. Ibid., p. 74. See also Tam Stewart *The Heroin Users* (London: 1987) chap. 7.

6. In this section there is no room for a sustained examination of empirical evidence and I am obliged to make brief generalisations in response to various lines of argument. These brief generalisations seem to me to be fairly well borne out by the evidence, but of course the facts are more complicated than this way of employing them suggests.

7. This is the sort of line taken by one of Mill's most celebrated contemporary critics, J. F. Stephen, see *Liberty, Fraternity, Equality*.

8. Although popular opinion feels happier about condemning 'pushers' than it does about condemning 'users', most pushers *are* users, and only a very small proportion of those dealing in drugs are the wealthy traffickers of fiction, press and television.

9. See, for instance, Robertson, op. cit., chap. 5 and J. C. Ball and J. C. Urbaitis 'Absence of Major Medical Complications among Chronic Opiate Addicts', *British Journal of Addiction*, 65, no. 2 (1970).

10. See for instance C. Winick, 'Maturing out of Narcotic Addiction', *Bulletin of Narcotics*, 14 (1962).

11. Robertson, op. cit., p. 64. Robertson thinks this a 'curious conundrum', but it is curious only taken in connection with prevailing beliefs and attitudes.

12. Ibid.

13. This is the topic of several essays in Stanley Einstein (ed.), *The Community's Response to Drug Use* (Oxford: 1979).

14. See Philip Bean, *The Social Control of Drugs* (London: 1973).

15. From the *Book of Common Prayer*.

14 Rethinking American Policy: A Bundle of Peaceful Compromises
Arnold Trebach

We are witnessing a continuing national tragedy. For seven decades, the United States has pursued a harmful drug policy. During the Reagan–Bush era, that policy has been pushed to its most destructive extremes. After eight years of a multi-billion dollar drug war, our prisons are filled to record levels, violent drug traffickers pollute our cities, and drug abuse is rampant. Despite the most aggressive drug war campaign in history, so much cocaine has been imported since 1981 that the price has dropped to a fraction of its former level. While some of our children now find it more difficult to buy marijuana, many find it much easier to buy crack and cocaine.

Yet, the Bush–Bennett National Drug Control Strategy, unveiled as required by law on 5 September 1989, promises only to continue and expand this disaster. The congressional Democrats have criticised the $7.9 billion plan only to say that it does not go far enough and does not spend enough money. It is likely that the final federal drug package passed into law will reach a record $10 billion. The states will spend many billions more. Four more years of the current drug war promise more illegal drugs on our streets, more crime, more Americans in prison, and more youth enticed into drug dealing and drug abuse.

There will soon come a time when we all will look back on the excesses of the current anti-drug campaigns with shame. They will join the roster of national embarrassments that include alcohol Prohibition in the 1930s, internment of Japanese-Americans in the 1940s, McCarthyism in the 1950s, and the Viet Nam War in the 1960s and 1970s.

Now is the time, before any more damage is done, before our leaders further embarrass the American people in the eyes of the world and history, for the healing process to begin in the harsh anti-drug war. We Americans are at our worst when we get a moralistic, patriotic, crusading fire in our bellies and go roaring off wide-eyed after a convenient enemy. We are at our best when we sit down with the supposed enemies and work out compromises in the middle ground between the extremes. It is often forgotten that in the 1780s, after the victory of the revolution, the new American nation was on the verge of civil war. During a long hot summer, cooler heads prevailed at that secret convention in Philadelphia and produced the American Constitution, which has been called a bundle of peaceful compromises. We should follow that example now as the drug civil war tears at the vitals of this democracy.

In summary form, my proposals for reform are, first, that this nation recognise the futility of the very concept of a war on drugs. Instead we should be fashioning peaceful methods — those not involving the criminal law or the military — for curbing drug abuse while preserving constitutional freedoms. Second, we should medicalise the use of marijuana and heroin to ease the suffering of those millions of our citizens afflicted with such diseases as cancer, glaucoma, and multiple sclerosis. Third, we should experiment with various forms of decriminalisation or legalisation of currently outlawed recreational drugs during the remainder of this century. This could include experiments that involve state laws providing full legalisation of virtually all illegal drugs for adults. If the experiments work well, we can move on to more widespread use of legalisation; if not, we should again invoke the full weight of the criminal law. Fourth, we should invest billions now in treatment methods and invite the best brains in the nation to participate in attempts to help rather than harm our neighbours who are addicts and abusers.

The leaders of American government and society have played a major role in creating the underlying conditions for the illegal drug markets, for the crime and violence, and for the drug abuse that harms our citizens. They act as if they had no responsibility for these horrors, always preferring to place the blame elsewhere — on the 1960s generation, on foreign dictators, or even on terrorists. Yet, a significant share of the blame for these conditions lies at the feet of draconian drug laws and enforcement policies.

The destructive impact of those policies is now just beginning to be understood by most ordinary Americans and by the citizens of other countries, who are starting to reconsider their slavish imitations of the American drug war. As I travel about the United States and other countries, I find that revulsion appears more and more on the faces of my audiences as I recite the basic facts about the Reagan–Bush–Bennett holy war.

Revulsion greets my recitation, for example, of official federal data showing how the United States is leading the democracies to become prison states. Between the beginning of January 1981 (the month Mr Reagan assumed office) and the end of June 1989, the US prison population expanded a record 104 per cent, from 329 821 to 673 565. These figures cover only inmates serving long sentences, those of at least a year or more. The rate of increase during the first six months of 1989 was a shocking 14.3 per cent. If that rate continues, the American prison population will be 2.8 million at the beginning of the next century. If the Bush–Bennett policy continues in related areas, it is reasonable to project that there could be another 2.8 million Americans institutionalised in jails, juvenile facilities, so-called boot camps for first offenders and casual users, and psychiatric institutions for the recalcitrant cases. A significant percentage of the 5.6 million inmates of the new American gulag will have been imprisoned as a result of the drug war.

DRUG REFORMERS WANT THE SAME OBJECTIVES AS DRUG WAR SUPPORTERS

Most drug policy reformers and most drug war supporters want similar goals. Certainly, we law reformers want to see our children grow up drug free in a healthy, democratic and safe society. We want all Americans to be able to walk the streets without worrying about harm from violent crime. We want the freedom and privacy of all Americans to be preserved and protected by the government. We want the twin scourges of AIDS and drug abuse to be controlled and its victims treated effectively and compassionately by medical authorities and society. We want uncorrupted police institutions capable of providing the intelligent assistance that a democratic people expect of their law enforcement agencies.

We oppose the drug war because it does not bring us these

important goals which are vital to a free society with an expanding economy. Indeed, the drug war creates conditions that prevent proper controls on drug abuse, on crime, on corruption, and on invasions of privacy.

Drug war hysteria creates an Orwellian mind-set in which perverse Big Brother tactics are made to appear as patriotic measures to save the soul of America. My upbringing and my old-fashioned New England schooling would lead me to believe it is undignified, un-American, and downright perverse for government officials to order female Navy personnel to disrobe and then to observe them eye-to-eye sitting on toilets urinating. Yet, the country is told by its leaders that such perversions — and a thousand permutations — are not perversions or in violation of American traditions at all.

Many of us old-fashioned Americans no longer believe our leaders in the White House or here on Capitol Hill when they tell us that they see light at the end of the drug-war tunnel — and that if only we stay the course in the war, if we have courage to gut it out and commit more troops and treasure, violate just a few more insignificant rights, we can achieve victory. We have heard that line not too long ago in regard to another emotional conflict. And as in Viet Nam, the cause was noble and shared by most decent citizens. Then we fought communism, now drug abuse.

By 1968, however, massive numbers of Americans who opposed communism became opponents of the View Nam war as well because they came to believe that it was an ineffective way to save our people from communism. Now, 22 years later, a similar popular revulsion is developing. It is smaller than that against the Asian war but it is large enough and powerful enough to be heard throughout the land, in all major newspapers and on all national media networks, and in the halls of legislatures around the world. We at the Drug Policy Foundation now receive so many requests for information that we find it difficult to respond within a reasonable time. During the past year or so, I have personally testified before major drug policy hearings of the US House of Representatives in Washington, the Bundestag in Bonn, and the New York State Senate in Manhattan.

As was the case during Viet Nam, proponents of continuing the war paint the peace movement as being in league with the enemy or even sponsored by them. However, the Viet Nam peace movement came to span such a wide spectrum of respectable political opinion that this gambit was eventually dismissed as a desperate joke. Today, however, fear of being seen as soft on drugs continues to be a vibrant political reality.

The staid *New York Times* was moved to headline a major story on 11 September 1988, 'Tougher Than Thou'. Commenting on a series of harsh drug-war measures passed by overwhelming majorities that week, the *Times* observed that when it comes to illegal drugs, most members of the House of Representatives 'want no enemies to the right of them.' The same might have been said at the time of the two major presidential candidates, Messrs Bush and Dukakis. It could be repeated today as the Bush–Bennet plan is being pushed through Congress with overwhelming support. No enemies to the right.

Yet, the movement for drug reform continues in the face of this new form of McCarthyism. We reformers oppose drug abuse. Therefore, we oppose the drug war. We propose fundamental changes in American drug policy.

Experiment with Full Legalisation in some States

My perception of what is a reasonable compromise in the drug war has changed in recent months. For years, I have been accused by government officials and other critics of wanting to legalise all the drugs. For years, I have denied that charge. Now, I plead guilty, but with mitigating circumstances.

This is a recent change of heart brought on by the realisation, really an epiphany, that full legislation of drugs would create order out of chaos, not vice versa as drug war advocates believe. Tim, a caller to a Seattle radio talk show in which I was participating long distance, put it best recently: 'Prohibition is deregulation'. In other words, the real effect of the criminal drug laws is exactly the opposite of the intended result. Anarchy now rules the distribution and sale of drugs. No government authority checks into the backgrounds and ages of sellers. No agency sets rules on the conditions of sale or the age of buyers. No distributor fills in a tax return form and sends in a tax check to the government office on even one dollar of the 100 to 200 billion dollars in sales that take place each year in the American illegal drug market — or in the rich illegal drug markets that pervert and undermine the very foundations of many other democratic nations.

Prohibition has created a jungle. When turf and territory are invaded, the only law that controls is the law of the jungle, the tooth and the claw. Or, in America now, the Uzi and the Mac-10.

Such thoughts led me to testify in support of the Galiber Bill on 16 June 1989. This proposed law, S. 1918, Senate of the State of New York, 'would legalise drugs for adults and also would provide for regulation by a Controlled Substances Authority'. The position of the sponsor, Senator Joseph L. Galiber of the Bronx, is that currently illegal drugs should be controlled and sold like alcohol. The CSA would grant licences to qualified sellers and set conditions for sale. Initially, only doctors and pharmacists could apply for sales licences. No prescriptions would be necessary but purchasers would have to prove that they were 21 years of age. Places of sale could not be near schools or religious establishments. Sales to minors or near schools would be criminal acts.

I have made a number of criticisms and suggestions for improvement regarding the Galiber Bill. The same is true of other such legalisation bills that have been drafted in recent years, some of which appear in publications of the Drug Policy Foundation. Indeed, the only debate worth having is one that deals with the practicalities of reforms that assume prohibition is dead, those that deal with practical alternatives to the war on drugs.

These bills and reform plans propose to replace the law of the jungle with the rule of civilised law. Even though a part of my own mind and emotions recoils at the very though of the legal sale of heroin and crack, the idea that the rule of law might soon prevail makes a lot of sense to me.

Accordingly, I now see experiments with state legislation laws as part of the middle ground between the extremes. Such bills might well allow for the gradual implementation of their provisions. For example, they might provide that at first marijuana and hashish would be made available to adults. If that worked, coca leaves and oral methadone. Then powdered cocaine and injectable methadone. And so on.

I realise that it is unlikely that even one such bill will pass a state legislature in the near future. Accordingly, other less far-reaching compromises must also be considered.

Tolerance, Compassion, and Help for Users and Abusers

We must develop means of opposing some of the destructive ideology that lies at the heart of the drug war. One of the worst examples is that which treats users and abusers of illegal drugs as the enemy. Mrs Reagan, when she was First Lady, labelled casual users of drugs as 'accomplices to murder'. Drug Czar William Bennett has made casual users of illegal drugs the principal targets in his drug war strategy. He has proposed that severe penalties be imposed on those who are found to be 'using or possessing even small amounts of drugs'.

Few people, even in America, seem to understand the full scope of the penalties that now exist or will soon be enacted. Casual users or those found possessing tiny amounts of drugs, such as a few marijuana cigarettes, could lose their cars and homes, be fired from their jobs, have their driver's licences suspended for one to five years, and be prohibited from obtaining student loans and grants. Such casual users might also be imprisioned for months in boot camps or hospitalised against their will through civil commitment procedures in psychiatric institutions. Under some drug-free workplace regulations, employees may loose their jobs if they refuse to take a urine test when ordered. When a supervisor claims to see an appearance of impairment, employees may also be fired if the test shows signs of any drug *including alcohol.*

We should use every strategy at our command to oppose such policies, starting with opposition to appointments of extremists to official leadership positions in the drug arena. In addition, we should encourage tolerance and compassion for users and abusers — at the same time that we try to educate them to the dangers of drugs. When the government mounts attacks on users or suspected users, we should encourage legal action to prevent these attacks from invading rights.

National Leadership and Funds for Treatment

We should constantly point out to the public that users and abusers are members of our family (a kindly phrase I learned from Dutch officials) and that we want to help, not punish, them. We should encourage leading police organisations and thinkers to join with reformers to mutually support a vast increase in treatment facilities for legal and illegal drug abuse.

Treatment is the one area in which positive drug legislation is possible during the current session of Congress. There are many hopeful treatment provisions being put forward, but none, to my knowledge, goes far enough. I think it might be politically acceptable to recommend that the federal government take a leadership role in demanding experiments with new treatment models supervised by ADAMHA and NIDA and fuelled by a vast infusion of funds, perhaps working up to $3 billion per year by the early 1990s. The Reagan Administration has cut treatment funds and put the pittance remaining into state block grants. Many congressmen across the political spectrum oppose this penurious approach.

These experiments should allow for a wide array of models, including drug-free detoxification, drug maintenance, and needle exchange features. They should emphasise not just charitable treatment but also those paid for in whole or in part by the patients. Thus, all economic classes would benefit and all classes might support this legislation.

Treatment on demand for every drug abuser in need — that would be a great compromise victory in the best spirit of America. We can accomplish that wonderful goal by the early 1990s.

Treatment on demand should replace the war on drugs. To lead this dominant effort we need a new kind of drug czar, a competent health professional who is respected across the political and ideological spectrum. If Mr Bush were serious about dealing with drugs, he would retire Mr Bennett and bring back the former Surgeon General, the best appointment President Reagan ever made. Dr C. Everett Koop, a conservative actually loved by liberals, should be given the funds and the mandate to turn America's best minds to the task of helping rather than destroying the addicts and users among us.

The same approach should be taken by every nation seriously concerned with coping realistically with their drug problems.

AIDS Treatment: a Special Priority

AIDS is a greater threat to our survival than all of the drugs combined. The major engine for the transmission of AIDS is the heterosexual injecting addict. Every nation should stand solidly behind any proposal that promises to provide better treatment for AIDS sufferers and that might curb the spread of the disease. Properly designed drug maintenance (even those providing for medical heroin and other feared drugs) and needle-exchange programmes should be advocated as essential elements in all AIDS-control strategies and bills. While it is sad to say, the AIDS threat makes for a much more compelling argument for decent treatment of addicts than a simple appeal to human compassion.

Adopt 'Harm Reduction' as a Unifying Theme

A combination of moral and medical philosophy lies at the core of national strategies for dealing with drugs. The best unifying strategy theme may well be that known as harm reduction, a concept that seems to have its most viable roots in Amsterdam, Holland and in Liverpool, England. However, it has hidden roots in many countries over decades of emotional experience in dealing with addicts.

Indeed, one of the most ignored aspects of the American experience has been the use of narcotic drugs in the maintenance treatment of addicts. Between 1919 and 1923 there were at least 40 maintenance clinics in the United States. Clinic doctors dispensed a number of powerful injectable drugs, including morphine and heroin, to thousands of addicts. While often criticised by American experts, on the whole those early clinics were very helpful to many addicts. They were closed as a result of irrational actions by police and leaders of the medical profession.

The modern era of American narcotic maintenance commenced in January 1964 when Dr Vincent Dole and Dr Marie Nyswander commenced a series of experiments in New York City with methadone, a drug developed, as was heroin, for the relief of pain by German experts. Methadone maintenance is the most successful innovation in American drug control in modern history. While it cured no person of addiction, it helped tens of thousands of addicts to lead legal, useful lives. For some, this led eventually to abstinence. The drug, in oral form only, is still available through specially licenced doctors and clinics as one treatment option. I know personally of some addicts now living productive lives who receive regular prescriptions of methadone from private clinics. Unfortunately, there is great ambivalence about methadone maintenance among the leadership of American drug control. Yet, the modality continues to function, legally and quietly behind the scenes.

The leadership in the United Kingdom talk loudly about fighting shoulder-to-shoulder with their American friends in the war on drugs while quietly pouring millions of pounds into humane experiments that run counter to much of the harsh American ideology. Some of the most ambitious of these experiments have taken place in the Liverpool–Mersey region. Health and education experts, working with the enthusiastic cooperation of the police, have developed a series of related projects that are as effective as any in the world.

These experts conceptualise control and treatment programmes as a series of safety nets. The most important safety net is abstinence. The best result of an intervention programme would be to help an addict get off drugs entirely. However, these English experts know that the zealous and sole pursuit of abstinence could and does result in harm to many addicts. And, as one Liverpudlian observed to me, 'It is very difficult to rehabilitate a dead addict'. As a result, they have developed other safety nets or programme components: the dispensation of regular maintenance prescriptions of oral and injectable drugs, including heroin in a few cases; free needle exchange and instruction in the proper use of needles; detoxification and abstinence counselling; free condoms and advice on safe sex; general health care; and mental health counselling.

While the Mersey region has many problems of crime and addiction, these harm reduction efforts seem to have had a good impact. The police continue to support them because of humanitarian concerns and also because they have become convinced that these programmes reduce crime. Health authorities are pleased that addicts seem healthier, with some coming off drugs entirely while others are taking better care of themselves even though they are still on drugs. Of stunning significance to the world, moreover, is the fact that AIDS is virtually unknown among addicts who have presented themselves for treatment to Liverpool clinics. Recent tests on approximately 3000 injecting addicts showed few positive for AIDS or the HIV virus. In the entire Mersey Health region, comprising 2.5 million people, authorities are aware of only five addicts with AIDS and nine HIV positive.

Medicine for Sufferers of More Traditional Diseases

Making feared drugs, such as heroin and marijuana, available as medicines for our sick people would seem to be a centrist proposal on which all sensible people could agree. Because of irrational fears of encouraging recreational use by our youth and others, even this most compassionate of proposed legislation may fail in Congress within the near future. If so, then Congress could pass legislation upholding most of the existing control scheme but demanding that the Food and Drug Administration and the Drug Enforcement Administration, working together, see to it that heroin and marijuana were made available through doctors to those afflicted with cancer, glaucoma, multiple sclerosis, and other diseases who might be helped by these drugs. This availability could be part of a massive series of experiments in the control of pain and anxiety among our millions of sick people. An element in those experiments could be the more aggressive use of existing analgesics with less interference from the police.

Experimental use of any prohibited drug is allowed in medicine now, but federal officials set up impossible conditions for these experiments. Many innocent patients have died in agony from cancer or gone blind from glaucoma while waiting in vain for experimental protocols to be approved by DEA or FDA.

Powerful support for fundamental revisions in our attitudes and policies towards marijuana was contained in a historic decision on 6 September 1988 by Francis L. Young, the chief administrative law judge of the Drug Enforcement Administration. For the first time in history, to my knowledge, there has been a full review of the evidence about marijuana in medicine before an impartial judicial tribunal. The federal government and reform organisations, including the Drug Policy Foundation, presented documents and expert witnesses on all sides of the issue over a period of many months. There was vigorous cross examination and the submission of extensive briefs. After presiding over this exhaustive inquiry, the DEA official recommended that marijuana be rescheduled so that it could be used by doctors in medicine.

In reaching that decision, Judge Young reviewed the massive body of evidence and came to conclusions that, while focused on the issue of medical use, destroy many of the funadmental ideas at the base of the drug war. Examples:

'There is no record in the extensive medical literature describing a proven, documented cannabis-induced fatality.'

'. . . the record on marijuana encompasses 5000 years of human experience. . . . Yet, despite this long history of use and the extraordinarily high number of social smokers, there are no credible medical reports to suggest that consuming marijuana has caused a single death.'

'In strict medical terms marijuana is far safer than many foods we commonly consume'.

'Marijuana, in its natural form, is one of the safest therapeutically active substances known to man'.

'The evidence in this record clearly shows that marijuana has been accepted as capable of relieving the distress of great numbers of very ill people, and doing so with safety under medical supervision. It would be unreasonable, arbitrary and capricious for DEA to continue to stand between those sufferers and the benefits of this substance in light of the evidence . . . '

'There are those who, in all sincerity, argue that the transfer of marijuana to Schedule II will 'send a signal' that marijuana is 'OK' generally for recreational use. This argument is specious.'

The top officials of the Drug Enforcement Administration seem stunned by Judge Young's rational decision. If they refuse to endorse it, Congress could pass legislation to implement it and simply place marijuana in Schedule II of the Federal Controlled Substances Act. It will also be necessary to force compassionate action from Food and Drug Administration so that the drug may be prescribed by American doctors when they deem it medically advisable. If Congress does not act, then what signal does that send about the level of humanity of this great nation as it enters its third century?

Experiments with Decriminalisation or Limited Legalisation

Full legalisation, as I have said, should be considered one option for experimentation in some states. Other options could include variations on that theme.

Working with police and prosecution leaders, Congress should encourage carefully researched experiments in decriminalisation or *de facto* legalisation of possession and small sales of all drugs. This is a major part of the Dutch approach and is controlled by an extensive set of written guidelines prepared by the prosecutors and police with the support of the judges. In essence, all drugs remain illegal; but peaceful users and small sellers are left alone; blatant sellers and those who are violent or connected with organised crime are arrested. The results here could be a reversal of the swamping of the criminal justice system, jails, and prisons with drug offenders, a reduction in street violence and police corruption, and greater overall efficiency for the police and the criminal justice system.

Carefully guided experiments might also take place with other models of limited legalisation. The Alaskan approach might be more acceptable in some areas than the Dutch; namely, allow legalisation, not decriminalisation, of growth and possession of marijuana for personal use based upon a state supreme court decision. We might also consider variations of the new law being proposed by the Oregon Marijuana Initiative: upon the payment of a $50 annual tax, adults would be given a certificate by the county which would allow them to grow and possess a small amount of marijuana for personal use. Again, all other drugs would remain fully criminal under this model.

Experiments also should be considered that would explore the industrial and commercial uses of the marijuana plant. Hemp has a vast commercial potential as a fibre for rope and clothing, among other uses. It is possible that experiments will produce strains of marijuana that have a high fibre value and a low intoxication potential. In the current martial climate, research on such developments is not possible.

Remember the Legal Drugs

We must continue to support enlightened action that places greater legal and cultural controls on alcohol, tobacco and caffeine. Positive steps are taking place in this arena — perhaps more in the United States than any other country — and we drug policy reformers support them. We also must emphasise that the greatest need for treatment remains in providing affordable help for legal drug abusers.

Create Reliable International Data Centres

In the course of writing this statement, I have cited comparative data on crime, violence and drug abuse. Yet, I have serious reservations as to just how reliable those statistics are. Existing international bodies, including agencies of the United Nations, have not proven equal to the task of producing usable comparative data. It is time that the western democracies combined to create a non-political scholarly centre or centres that produced reliable, objective studies on the basic comparative facts about crime and drugs in each country.

HOW MUCH DO YOU GIVE AN ADDICT?

As I have made clear, I am a strong advocate of drug maintenance as one among many optional treatments that should be available to addicts. In addition, I support the provision of injectable narcotic drugs and clean needles by doctors. Thus, I will deal briefly with questions about addict maintenance which trouble many good people.

For many years, I researched questions that, as it happened, were raised by Congressman Charles Rangel, Chairman of the

House of Representatives Select Committee on Narcotics Abuse and Control, in a popular magazine article just before the congressional hearings on legalisation in September 1988. In the article, Mr Rangel wrote: 'And how much will you give an addict? A maintenance dose? They don't want to be maintained. They need to get high'. Both the questions and the statements are misleading and reveal the basic misunderstandings at the highest levels of power that prevent rational consideration of new drug policies, ones that might work.

Some addicts need to get high. Some do not. Some do not want drugs at all but simply need a strong, sympathetic hand and close supervision while being detoxified. On the same day that the misleading article appeared, I had the joy of attending the wedding of a recovering heroin addict. He claims I saved his life because when he came to me one day in London in 1983 (where we both were visiting) and told me he was in trouble with heroin, I asked him what he wanted to do. He replied that he was totally out of control and that he needed to be 'locked up'. I immediately made arrangements and took him by the hand, as it were, and deposited him at a good psychiatric hospital. While in the locked ward, he was detoxified.

Had I suggested heroin to him, I would have been irresponsible. It is unfair therefore, to paint all heroin addicts with the same criminal, irresponsible brush. They are no more alike than cigarette addicts or alcoholics – or members of congress or university professors. When heroin addicts harm other people, I believe that they should be treated as criminals and punished. When heroin addicts reach that point in their lives that finds them seeking to come in from the criminal streets, society should treat them with compassion and care. That care should be inexpensive and readily available, virtually on demand, time and time again, since relapse is part of the process of cure.

The care should cover the full range of possibilities: locked psychiatric wards, drug-free detoxification, religious counselling, group therapy, out-patient psychiatric therapy, drug maintenance, and clean needles, among others. We must include drugs and needles because we do not now have, and never will have, a method for pushing addicts off drugs immediately, even when the addict desperately wants to be rid of them. Maintenance is not surrender but recognition of realities. It is an essential part of harm reduction in many cases. Properly operated maintenance programmes do not kill addicts — because none of the opiates are toxic in proper doses — and allow many addicts to live fairly normal lives. When an addict is 'ready' to come off drugs, experienced doctors tell me that it is fairly easy to gradually accomplish that feat. But not before the patient, rather than the doctor or the police, is ready. Compassionate maintenance programmes keep many addicts functioning, working, and paying taxes for years until that great day when they are ready to quit. For too many, that day never comes, but society and the patient are still better off because drug maintenance was available.

It is extremely difficult for doctors to determine the proper dosage of narcotics for any condition, including cancer pain. This is not a new issue for medicine. It is no surprise, therefore, that it is difficult to determine the proper dosage during maintenance and also to determine when an addict is actually ready to be properly weaned from powerful narcotic drugs. These questions should become some of the most important elements in the new wave of treatment experiments that democratic governments should launch under the leadership of health experts. The questions should be dealt with by doctors in consultation with their addict-patients, nurses, and other doctors — not by legislators and criminologists.

One of the great mistakes of American drug policy has been that politicians and police made it their business to tell the doctors how to prescribe drugs. Any nation that wishes to make progress must pull the government and the criminal law back from addiction treatment and let the healers debate issues of health policy.

British doctors have openly debated maintenance issues for decades. In 1924 their Minister of Health put some of the central questions to a group of leading doctors: 'to consider and advise as to the circumstances, if any, in which the supply of morphine and heroin . . . to persons suffering from addiction to those drugs may be regarded as medically advisable'. In 1926 the Rolleston Committee issued its historic report which described two types of patients for whom long-term maintenance on these powerful narcotics was considered proper and helpful. First, 'those in whom a complete withdrawal of morphine or heroin produces serious symptoms which cannot be treated satisfactorily under the ordinary conditions of private practice'. Second, 'those who are capable of leading a fairly normal and useful life so long as they take a certain quantity, usually small, of their drug of addiction, but not otherwise'.

In other words, the Rolleston Committee saw the prescription of powerful narcotic drugs not as a means of destroying normal life or of killing a worthless addict off, but rather of making it possible for an addict to survive and to lead a fairly normal life outside a hospital. This medical advice is both compassionate and ageless. It is the original intellectual basis for modern harm reduction.

Applied today, it would mean that doctors would never provide drugs to patients not addicted and they would never provide such a high dosage to addict-patients that they became stuporous and unable to work or to be good family members. By implication, then, good maintenance programmes should involve a social contract: we in society will see to it that you receive your drugs of addiction and clean needles legally through doctors; you, the addict-patient, must in return see to it that you function as a good citizen, employee and family member.

Does this mean that we would allow addicts on maintenance to work as pilots on aeroplanes and captains of nuclear submarines? Of course not. At the same time, we must realise that the greatest chemical threats to our air pilots and sea captains are found in alcohol abuse, a problem that the current war on drugs almost totally ignores. Even if all drugs were legal, alcohol would still be a greater threat to transportation safety than all of the currently illegal drugs combined.

USE AND ABUSE: WILL THEY RISE DESTRUCTIVELY?

We all should be concerned about the possibility of a great rise in use and abuse should the criminal drug laws be relaxed. I certainly worry about that, as should all sensible reformers. If I believed that law reform would bring a destructive explosion of use, I would rethink my position. However, my review of the evidence leads me to more comforting conclusions.

Some of my greatest comfort is found in a review of the historical record on the reports of impartial study commissions and authorities over the years. Many of them have recommended a relaxation of harsh criminal prohibition laws and experimentation with various compromise provisions allowing for greater freedom in the use of some drugs. Thus, we reformers have a good deal of scholarly history on our side.

This is particularly true of the record of marijuana reports. There have been at least seven major studies by impartial bodies of experts over the years in various countries. One of the most notable was *The Indian Hemp Drugs Commission Report* (1894) which was undertaken by British and Indian experts, who secured testimony from 1193 witnesses from throughout the Indian subcontinent. In addition, there has been *The Panama Canal Zone Military Investigations* (1916–29); *The La Guardia Committee Report* (1939–44) on conditions in New York City; *The Baroness Wootten Report* (1968) on the United Kingdom; *The Interim Report of the Canadian Government's Le Dain Commission* (1970); the National Commission on Marijuana and Drug Abuse, *Drug Use in American: Problem in Perspective* (1973); and the National Research Council of the National Academy of Sciences, *An Analysis of Marijuana Policy* (1982).

The congruence in basic findings of these studies spanning nearly a century is truly remarkable. None found marijuana to be harmless. All found marijuana to present some dangers to some people but concluded that the actual level of harm was consistently exaggerated and that control measures were frequently too harsh. Several of the studies stated flatly that rigid criminal prohibition laws were harmful.

The last two reports were issued by Americans and happen to be the only two major national studies performed by impartial groups of experts in our history. The report of the National Commission on Marijuana and Drug Abuse was mandated by Congress during the Nixon war on drugs and was carried out by a generally conservative commission appointed by the Republican President. After a massive series of studies of the entire illicit drugs situation in the United States, the first recommendations of the commission were, to the dismay of President Nixon and many supporters of harsh drug laws, as follows:

(1) Possession of marijuana for personal use would no longer be an offense, but marijuana possessed in public would remain contraband subject to summary seizure and forfeiture.

(2) Casual distribution of small amounts of marijuana for no remuneration, or insignificant remuneration not involving profit, would no longer be an offense.

These proposals for moderate compromises have been treated with disdain by the American Congress and ignored by drug abuse experts around the world — but not by the prestigious National Academy of Sciences, a quasi-governmental body, in the latest comprehensive American report in 1982. The Academy reiterated its support for the recommendations of the Nixon commission a decade earlier but then went dramatically further. It recommended that carefully prepared and researched experiments be considered that would involve removal of federal criminal penalties for cultivation and distribution of marijuana. Under this thoughtful plan, states would be encouraged to devise individual methods of control as they now do with alcohol. Thus, some states might have systems that provided for regulated sale and taxation of legal marijuana. This is consistent with the first compromise proposal that I made.

In making those recommendations the National Academy of Sciences carefully reviewed all of the available evidence on the relationship between the proposed changes in the criminal law and the possibility of an increase in use and abuse. Some of the most important evidence was found in the 11 American states that decriminalised possession during the 1970s. The Academy saw that these relaxed criminal laws had no significant impact on use but that the new laws had helped curb massive criminal justice expenditures and injustices to many people. The council projected the estimate that even the more far-reaching legal distribution and sale were not likely to produce significant changes in use — if governments, opinion leaders, and families employed sensible, non-criminal control methods.

The National Academy of Sciences placed great emphasis on building up public education and informal social controls, which often have a greater impact on personal behaviour than the criminal law. The NAS also had these comforting thoughts for those who would expect to see disaster for our young in a change so radical as to allow regulated marijuana sales such as with alcohol:

> . . . there is reason to believe that widespread uncontrolled use would not occur under regulation. Indeed, regulation might facilitate patterns of controlled use by diminishing the 'forbidden fruit' aspect of the drug and perhaps increasing the likelihood that an adolescent would be introduced to the drug through families and friends, who practice moderate use, rather than through their heaviest-using, most drug-involved peers.

ALLEGED HEALTH SUCCESS OF ALCOHOL PROHIBITION

However, whenever such arguments are made, even by authorities as respected as the NAS, someone (recently, it was Drug Czar Bennett) always points out the alleged lesson of alcohol prohibition. The standard argument goes that while alcohol Prohibition was an overall failure in America, especially because of the crime and corruption it engendered, it was a resounding success in terms of public health. Support is found in such statistics as those on alcohol consumption: during the period 1916–19, per capita consumption of absolute alcohol for the drinking age population in the United States was 1.96 gallons; during Prohibition, it dropped by more than half to 0.90 gallons; after Repeal, during 1936–41, it went up again to 1.54. By 1986, it had reached 2.58.

This argument about the health-success of alcohol Prohibition during the 1920s ignores a number of salient facts, starting with the observation that the low figures during the 1920s are suspect because at that time people hid their use. Moreover, the highest periods of known mass alcohol consumption were during our earliest years as a nation when popular culture and private predilections made us a nation of hard drinkers. The high point was 1830 when Americans consumed 7.10 gallons of absolute alcohol per capita! By

1871–80, it had dropped to 1.72. All of these changes took place within an atmosphere of legality. Culture is often more powerful than the law.

Today, Americans are benefiting from a health culture. As a result, per capita tobacco use has been dropping dramatically recently. The percentage of smokers in the general population dropped from 41.7 per cent in 1965 to 32.6 per cent in 1983. And all the time, tobacco was fully legal.

On the other side of the coin, during the past 20 years we have had periodic explosions in use and abuse of, successively, marijuana, heroin, cocaine, PCP and crack. In regard to most of these drugs, explosions in use were followed by periodic downswings. And all the time, each had been illegal. Culture and mass popular tastes again were more powerful than the law.

If, then, we implement reforms in laws or enforcement practices, we must also continue and enlarge programmes of school and parental involvement in drug control. Teachers and parents have more impact on curbing drug abuse than police and jailers. Similar positive thoughts apply to ministers and treaters, especially if we invest in the recommended new array of treatment facilities.

Were the current system working so as to curb drug abuse and AIDS, I would hesitate to recommend changes. It is not working. On balance, the possibility of an overall gain in control of crime and of drug abuse from all types of drugs and alcohol outweighs the risk of an explosion in abuse of the illegal drugs.

CONCLUSION

Drug policy is more akin to religion than science. The truths about it lie more in the heart than the head. Yet, the head helps to count the gains and losses from alternate practical theologies. My argument is that drug policy reform is needed not so much because current policy is totally wrong as that its excesses cause a great deal of harm and injustice. As the extent of harm becomes obvious and painful to the masses, more politicians will be willing to take the risk in voting for radical new experiments.

REFERENCES

American Bar Association, *Drug Addiction: Crime or Disease?*, Interim and Final Reports of the Joint Committee of the American Bar Association and the American Medical Association on Narcotic Drugs (Bloomington: Indiana University Press, 1961).

Bakalar, James B. and Lester Grinspoon, *Drug Control in a Free Society* (Cambridge University Press, 1984).

Brecher Edward M., and the editors of consumer reports, *Licit and Illicit Drugs* (Boston and Toronto: Little, Brown, 1972).

Drug Abuse Council, *The Facts about Drug Abuse* (New York: Free Press, 1980).

Drug Policy Foundation, 'The Reform of Basic Drug Control and Treatment Policies — Beginning Proposals', First set of resolutions of the Drug Policy Foundation, revised draft B (Washington DC: December 1987).

Hamowy Ronald (ed.), *Dealing with Drugs* (New York: Free Press, 1980).

Hamowy, Ronald (ed.), *Dealing with Drugs* (Lexington Books, 1987).

King, Rufus. *The Drug Hang-Up, America's Fifty-Year Folly* (Springfield: Charles C. Thomas, 1972).

Lindesmith, Alfred R., *The Addict and The Law* (New York: Vintage, 1965).

Nadelmann, Ethan A., 'Drug Prohibition in the United States: Costs, Consequences, and Alternatives', *Science*, vol. 245, 1 September 1989).

Trebach, Arnold S., *The Heroin Solution* (New Haven and London: Yale University Press, 1982).

Trebach, Arnold S., *The Great Drug War* (New York: Macmillan, 1987).

Weil, Andrew. and Winifred Rosen, *Chocolate to Morphine, Understanding Mind-Active Drugs* (Boston: Houghton Mifflin, 1983).

Zinberg, Norman E., *Drugs, Set, and Setting, The Basis for Controlled Intoxicant Use* (New Haven and London: Yale University Press, 1984).